MW01000646

Problem Solving
with Algorithms
and Data Structures
Using Python

Bradley N. Miller
Luther College

David L. Ranum
Luther College

Franklin, Beedle & Associates, Inc. + 8536 SW St. Helens Drive, Suite D
Wilsonville, Oregon 97070 + 503/682-7668 + www.fbeedle.com

President and Publisher	Jim Leisy (jimleisy@fbeedle.com)
Manuscript Editor	Stephanie Welch
Production	Tom Sumner
Proofreader	Brenda Jones

Printed in the U.S.A.

Names of all products herein are used for identification purposes only and are trademarks and/or registered trademarks of their respective owners. Franklin, Beedle & Associates, Inc., makes no claim of ownership or corporate association with the products or companies that own them.

©2006 Franklin, Beedle & Associates Incorporated. No part of this book may be reproduced, stored in a retrieval system, transmitted, or transcribed, in any form or by any means—electronic, mechanical, telepathic, photocopying, recording, or otherwise—without prior written permission of the publisher. Requests for permission should be addressed as follows:

Rights and Permissions
Franklin, Beedle & Associates, Incorporated
8536 SW St. Helens Drive, Suite D
Wilsonville, Oregon 97070

Library of Congress Cataloging-in-Publication Data

Miller, Bradley N.
  Problem solving with algorithms and data structures using Python / Bradley N. Miller, David L. Ranum.
    p. cm.
  Includes index.
  ISBN 1-59028-053-9
  1. Python (Computer program language) 2. Computer algorithms. 3. Data structures. I.
Ranum, David L. II. Title.
  QA76.73.P98M54 2005
  005.13'3--dc22
                          2005023180

Contents

Chapter 3   Recursion   99

Chapter 4   Algorithm Analysis 129

Chapter 5   Trees 183

Chapter 6   Graphs   237

Chapter 7   Advanced Topics   281

Preface

To the Student

Since you have started to read this book, we can only assume that you have an interest in computer science. You may also be interested in the programming language Python and have likely done some programming, either in an earlier computer science course or perhaps on your own. In any case, you are hoping to learn more.

This textbook is about computer science. It is also about Python. However, there is much more. The study of algorithms and data structures is central to understanding what computer science is all about.

Learning computer science is not unlike learning any other type of difficult subject matter. The only way to be successful is through deliberate and incremental exposure to the fundamental ideas. A beginning computer scientist needs practice so that there is a thorough understanding before continuing on to the more complex parts of the curriculum. In addition, a beginner needs to be given the opportunity to be successful and gain confidence.

This textbook is designed to serve as a text for a first course on data structures and algorithms, typically taught as the second course in the computer science curriculum. Even though the second course is considered more advanced than the first course, we still assume that you are beginners at this level. You may still be struggling with some of the basic ideas and skills from your first computer science course and yet you are ready to further explore the discipline and continue to practice problem solving.

As we said earlier, this book is about computer science. It is about abstract data types and data structures. It is also about writing algorithms and solving problems. In the following chapters, we will look at a number of data structures and solve classic problems that arise. The tools and techniques that you learn in these chapters will be applied over and over as you continue your study of computer science.

To the Instructor

Many students discover at this point that there is much more to computer science than just writing programs. Data structures and algorithms can be studied and understood at a level that is independent of writing code.

We assume that students have had a traditional first course in computer science, preferably although not necessarily in Python. They understand basic programming constructs such as selection, iteration, and function definition. They have been exposed to object-oriented programming in that they can construct and use simple classes. Students also understand the basic Python data structures such as sequences (lists and strings) and dictionaries.

This textbook has two key features:

• A strong focus on problem solving introduces students to the fundamental data structures and algorithms by providing a very readable text without introducing an overwhelming amount of new language syntax.

• Python is used to facilitate the success of beginning students in using and mastering data structures and algorithms.

We begin our study of data structures by considering the linear structures; in particular, stacks, queues, and deques. Python lists are used for implementation. We then transition to the nonlinear structures related to trees and introduce a number of techniques including linked node and reference architectures (linked lists). We conclude with graphs, using linked structures, lists, and Python dictionaries for implementation. In each case, we have strived to show a variety of implementation techniques while also taking advantage of the built-in collections that Python provides. This mix exposes the students to all of the major implementation approaches while focusing on the ease of use with Python.

Python is a compelling language for algorithm education. It has a clean, simple syntax and an intuitive user environment. The basic collections are very powerful and yet easy to use. The interactive nature of the language creates an obvious place to test data structure components without the need for additional coding of driver functions. Finally, Python provides a textbook-like notation for representing algorithms, alleviating the need for an additional layer of pseudocode. This allows the illustration of many relevant, modern, and interesting problems that make use of the algorithm and data structure ideas.

We believe that it is advantageous for beginning students to spend time learning the rudimentary ideas relating to algorithms and data structures. We also believe that Python is an exceptional language for teaching beginning computer science students, in both the first course and the second. Many languages require that students jump right into more advanced programming concepts, clouding the basic understanding that these students need. This sets them up for possible failure, not because of the computer science but because of the language vehicle being used. Our goal is to provide a textbook that is tailored to the material these students need to understand, written in a way that is within their ability, and that creates and fosters an environment where success can happen.

Organization

We have designed this textbook around problem solving using classic data structures and techniques. This organizational chart depicts possible ways to use the material:

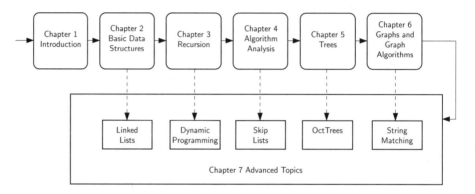

Chapter 1 is intended to provide background material with a review of computer science, problem solving, object-oriented programming, and Python. It is very possible that well-prepared students can skim this chapter and quickly move to Chapter 2. However, we find that a bit of review is never a waste of time.

Chapters 2 through 6 provide a thorough mix of algorithms and data structures, often presented in context of a classic computer science problem. Although there is some latitude in terms of order, many of the topics have a sequential dependency and should be completed in the order provided. For example, in Chapter 2, we introduce stacks. We use stacks to explain recursion in Chapter 3 and then use recursion to implement binary search in Chapter 4.

Chapter 7, "Advanced Topics," is an optional chapter consisting of individual sections, each of which is linked back to a previous chapter. As noted in the organization chart, it is possible to take these topics together after completing Chapter 6. The individual sections can also be linked to their specific chapters. For example, instructors wishing to introduce linked lists early can move to Section 7.2 immediately after Chapter 2 and use linked structures to implement stacks and queues.

Acknowledgments

There are many people who have helped us to complete this book. Thanks to our computer science colleagues Kent Lee, Steve Hubbard, and Walt Will. We are grateful to Amanda Payne and the rest of our students in CS151 who used early drafts of this book. Their willingness to provide feedback was invaluable. Thanks to the staff at Franklin, Beedle, and Associates, especially Jim Leisy and Tom Sumner. They were great to work with. And finally, special thanks goes to our spouses, Jane Miller and Brenda Ranum. Their love and support made this book a reality.

—Bradley N. Miller
David L. Ranum

Chapter 1   Introduction

1.1   Objectives

- To review the ideas of computer science, programming, and problem-solving.

- To understand abstraction and the role it plays in the problem-solving process.

- To understand and implement the notion of an abstract data type.

- To review the Python programming language.

1.2   Getting Started

The way we think about programming has undergone many changes in the years since the first electronic computers required patch cables and switches to convey instructions from human to machine. As is the case with many aspects of society, changes in computing technology provide computer scientists with a growing number of tools and platforms on which to practice their craft. Advances such as faster processors, high-speed networks, and large memory capacities have created a spiral of complexity around which computer scientists must navigate. Throughout all of this rapid evolution, a number of basic principles have remained constant. The science of computing is concerned with using computers to solve problems.

You have no doubt spent considerable time learning the basics of problem-solving and hopefully feel confident in your ability to take a problem statement and develop a solution. You have also learned that writing computer

1

programs is often hard. The complexity of large problems and the corresponding complexity of the solutions can tend to overshadow the fundamental ideas related to the problem-solving process.

This chapter emphasizes two important areas for the rest of the text. First, it reviews the framework within which computer science and the study of algorithms and data structures must fit, in particular, the reasons why we need to study these topics and how understanding these topics helps us to become better problem solvers. Second, we review the Python programming language. Although we cannot provide a detailed, exhaustive reference, we will give examples and explanations for the basic constructs and ideas that will occur throughout the remaining chapters.

1.3 What Is Computer Science?

Computer science is often difficult to define. This is probably due to the unfortunate use of the word "computer" in the name. As you are perhaps aware, computer science is not simply the study of computers. Although computers play an important supporting role as a tool in the discipline, they are just that, tools.

Computer science is the study of problems, problem-solving, and the solutions that come out of the problem-solving process. Given a problem, a computer scientist's goal is to develop an **algorithm**, a step-by-step list of instructions for solving any instance of the problem that might arise. Algorithms are finite processes that if followed will solve the problem. Algorithms are solutions.

Computer science can be thought of as the study of algorithms. However, we must be careful to include the fact that some problems may not have a solution. Although proving this statement is beyond the scope of this text, the fact that some problems cannot be solved is important for those who study computer science. We can fully define computer science then by including both types of problems and stating that computer science is the study of solutions to problems as well as the study of problems with no solutions.

It is also very common to include the word **computable** when describing problems and solutions. We say that a problem is computable if an algorithm exists for solving it. An alternative definition for computer science then is to say that computer science is the study of problems that are and that are not computable, the study of the existence and the nonexistence of algorithms. In any case, you will note that the word "computer" did not come up at all. Solutions are considered independent from the machine.

Computer science, as it pertains to the problem-solving process itself, is also the study of **abstraction**. Abstraction allows us to view the problem and solution in such a way as to separate the so-called logical and physical perspectives. The basic idea is familiar to us in a common example.

Consider the automobile that you may have driven to school or work today. As a driver, a user of the car, you have certain interactions that take place in order to utilize the car for its intended purpose. You get in, insert the key, start the car, shift, brake, accelerate, and steer in order to drive. From an abstraction point of view, we can say that you are seeing the logical perspective of the automobile. You are using the functions provided by the car designers for the purpose of transporting you from one location to another. These functions are sometimes also referred to as the **interface**.

On the other hand, the mechanic who must repair your automobile takes a very different point of view. She not only knows how to drive but must know all of the details necessary to carry out all the functions that we take for granted. She needs to understand how the engine works, how the transmission shifts gears, how temperature is controlled, and so on. This is known as the physical perspective, the details that take place "under the hood."

The same thing happens when we use computers. Most people use computers to write documents, send and receive email, surf the web, play music, store images, and play games without any knowledge of the details that take place to allow those types of applications to work. They view computers from a logical or user perspective. Computer scientists, programmers, technology support staff, and system administrators take a very different view of the computer. They must know the details of how operating systems work, how network protocols are configured, and how to code various scripts that control function. They must be able to control the low-level details that a user simply assumes.

The common point for both of these examples is that the user of the abstraction, sometimes also called the client, does not need to know the details as long as the user is aware of the way the interface works. This interface is the way we as users communicate with the underlying complexities of the implementation. As another example of abstraction, consider the Python `math` module. Once we import the module, we can perform computations such as

```
>>> import math
>>> math.sqrt(16)
4.0
>>>
```

This is an example of **procedural abstraction**. We do not necessarily know how the square root is being calculated, but we know what the function is called and how to use it. If we perform the import correctly, we can assume that the function will provide us with the correct results. We know that someone implemented a solution to the square root problem but we only need to know how to use it. This is sometimes referred to as a "black box" view of a process. We simply describe the interface, what is needed, and what will be returned, and the details are hidden inside (Figure 1.1).

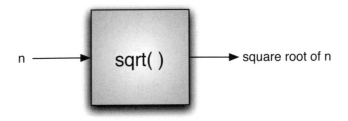

Figure 1.1: Procedural Abstraction

1.3.1   What Is Programming?

Programming is the process of taking an algorithm and encoding it into a notation, a programming language, so that it can be executed by a computer. Although many programming languages and many different types of computers exist, the important first step is the need to have the solution. Without an algorithm there can be no program.

Computer science is not the study of programming. Programming, however, is an important part of what a computer scientist does. Programming is often the way that we create a representation for our solutions. Therefore, this language representation and the process of creating it becomes a fundamental part of the discipline.

Algorithms describe the solution to a problem in terms of the data needed to represent the problem instance and the set of steps necessary to produce the intended result. Programming languages must provide a notational way to represent both the process and the data. To this end, languages provide control constructs and data types.

Control constructs allow algorithmic steps to be represented in a convenient yet unambiguous way. At a minimum, algorithms require constructs that perform sequential processing, selection for decision-making, and iteration for repetitive control. As long as the language provides these basic statements, it can be used for algorithm representation.

All data items in the computer are represented as strings of binary digits. In order to give these strings meaning, we need to have **data types**. Data types provide an interpretation for this binary data so that we can think about the data in terms that make sense with respect to the problem being solved. These low-level, built-in data types (sometimes called the primitive data types) provide the building blocks for algorithm development.

For example, most programming languages provide a data type for integers. Strings of binary digits in the computer's memory can be interpreted as integers and given the typical meanings that we commonly associate with integers (e.g. 23, 654, and -19). In addition, a data type also provides a description of the operations that the data items can participate in. With integers, operations such as addition, subtraction, and multiplication are common. We have come to expect that numeric types of data can participate in these arithmetic operations.

The difficulty that often arises for us is the fact that problems and their solutions are very complex. These simple, language-provided constructs and data types, although certainly sufficient to represent complex solutions, are typically at a disadvantage as we work through the problem-solving process. We need ways to control this complexity and assist with the creation of solutions.

1.3.2 Why Study Data Structures and Abstract Data Types?

To manage the complexity of problems and the problem-solving process, computer scientists use abstractions to allow them to focus on the "big picture" without getting lost in the details. By creating models of the problem domain, we are able to utilize a better and more efficient problem-solving process. These models allow us to describe the data that our algorithms will manipulate in a much more consistent way with respect to the problem itself.

Earlier, we referred to procedural abstraction as a process that hides the details of a particular function to allow the user or client to view it at a very high level. We now turn our attention to a similar idea, that of **data abstraction**. An **abstract data type**, sometimes abbreviated **ADT**, is a logical description of the domain and operations for a piece of data without regard to how it will be implemented. This means that we are concerned only with what the data is representing and not with how it will eventually be constructed. By providing this level of abstraction, we are creating an **encapsulation** around the data. The idea is that by encapsulating the details of the implementation, we are hiding them from the user's view. This is called **information hiding**.

Figure 1.2 shows a picture of what an abstract data type is and how it operates. The user interacts with the interface, using the operations that have been specified by the abstract data type. The abstract data type is the shell that the user interacts with. The implementation is hidden one level deeper. The user is not concerned with the details of the implementation.

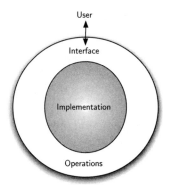

Figure 1.2: Abstract Data Type

The implementation of an abstract data type, often referred to as a **data structure**, will require that we provide a physical view of the data using some collection of programming constructs and primitive data types. As we discussed earlier, the separation of these two perspectives will allow us to define the complex data models for our problems without giving any indication as to the details of how the model will actually be built. This provides an **implementation-independent** view of the data. Since there will usually be many different ways to implement an abstract data type, this implementation independence allows the programmer to switch the details of the implementation without changing the way the user of the data interacts with it. The user can remain focused on the problem-solving process.

1.3.3 Why Study Algorithms?

Computer scientists learn by experience. We learn by seeing others solve problems and by solving problems by ourselves. Being exposed to different problem-solving techniques and seeing how different algorithms are designed helps us to take on the next challenging problem that we are given. By considering a number of different algorithms, we can begin to develop pattern recognition so that the next time a similar problem arises, we are better able to solve it.

Algorithms are often quite different from one another. Consider the example of `sqrt` seen earlier. It is entirely possible that there are many different ways to implement the details to compute the square root function. One algorithm may use many fewer resources than another. One algorithm might take 10 times as long to return the result as the other. We would like to have some way to compare these two solutions. Even though they both work, one is perhaps "better" than the other. We might suggest that one is more efficient or that one simply works faster or uses less memory. As we study algorithms, we can learn analysis techniques that allow us to compare and contrast solutions based solely on their own characteristics, not the characteristics of the program or computer used to implement them.

In the worst case scenario, we may have a problem that is intractable, meaning that there is no algorithm that can solve the problem in a realistic amount of time. It is important to be able to distinguish between those problems that have solutions, those that do not, and those where solutions exist but require too much time or other resources to work reasonably.

There will often be trade-offs that we will need to identify and decide upon. As computer scientists, in addition to our ability to solve problems, we will also need to know and understand solution evaluation techniques. In the end, there are often many ways to solve a problem. Finding a solution and then deciding whether it is a good one are tasks that we will do over and over again.

1.4 Review of Basic Python

In this section, we will review the programming language Python and also provide some more detailed examples of the ideas from the previous section. If you are new to Python or find that you need more information about any of the topics presented, we recommend that you consult the resources listed at the end of this book. Our goal here is to reacquaint you with the language and also reinforce some of the concepts that will be central to later chapters.

Python is a modern, easy-to-learn, object-oriented programming language. It has a powerful set of built-in data types and easy-to-use control constructs. Since Python is an interpreted language, it is most easily reviewed by simply looking at and describing interactive sessions. You should recall that the interpreter displays the familiar >>> prompt and then evaluates the Python construct that you provide. For example,

```
>>> print "Algorithms and Data Structures"
Algorithms and Data Structures
>>>
```

shows the prompt, the `print` statement, the result, and the next prompt.

1.4.1   Getting Started with Data

We stated above that Python supports the object-oriented programming paradigm. This means that Python considers data to be the focal point of the problem-solving process. In Python, as well as in any other object-oriented programming language, we define a **class** to be a description of what the data look like and what the data can do. Sometimes this is referred to as the state and the behavior of data. Data items are called **objects** in the object-oriented paradigm. An object is an instance of a class.

1.4.1.1   Primitive Classes

We will begin our review by considering the primitive classes. Python has three built-in numeric classes: integer, long integer, and floating point. The standard arithmetic operations, +, -, *, /, and ** (exponentiation), can be used with parentheses forcing the order of operations away from normal operator precedence. Another very useful operation is the remainder operator, %. Operations such as these are commonly referred to as **methods** in the object-oriented paradigm. Note that when two integers are divided, the result is an integer. At least one floating point operand must be present to cause a floating point result. In addition, Python provides a long integer class (shown below with the L character) that can represent any size integer limited only by the memory of your computer.

```
>>> 2+3*4
14
>>> (2+3)*4
20
>>> 2**10
1024
>>> 6/3
2
>>> 7/3
2
>>> 7.0/3
```

```
2.3333333333333335
>>> 7%3
1
>>> 3/6
0
>>> 3.0/6
0.5
>>> 2**100
1267650600228229401496703205376L
>>>
```

The boolean class will be quite useful for representing truth values. The possible state values for a boolean object are **True** and **False** with the standard boolean operators, **and**, **or**, and **not**.

```
>>> True
True
>>> False
False
>>> False or True
True
>>> not (False or True)
False
>>> True and True
True
```

Boolean data objects are also used as results for comparison operators such as equality (==) and greater than (>).

```
>>> 5==10
False
>>> 10 > 5
True
>>>
```

Identifiers are used in programming languages as names. In Python, identifiers start with a letter or an underscore (_), are case sensitive, and can be of any length. Remember that it is always a good idea to use names that convey meaning so that your program code is easier to read and understand.

Python variables are created when they are used for the first time on the left-hand side of an assignment statement. Assignment statements provide a way to associate a name with a value. The variable will hold a reference to a piece of data and not the data itself. Consider the following session:

```
>>> sum = 0
>>> sum
0
>>> sum = sum + 1
>>> sum
1
>>> sum = True
>>> sum
True
>>>
```

The assignment statement `sum = 0` creates a variable called `sum` and places a reference to the data object `0` inside the variable (see Figure 1.3). In general, the right-hand side of the assignment statement is evaluated and a reference to the resulting data object is "assigned" to the variable. At this point in our example, the type of the variable is integer as that is the type of the data currently being referred to by `sum`. If the type of the data changes (see Figure 1.4), as shown above with the boolean value `True`, so does the type of the variable (`sum` is now of the type boolean). The assignment statement changes the reference being held by the variable. This is a dynamic characteristic of Python. The same variable can refer to many different types of data.

Figure 1.3: Variables Hold References to Data Objects

1.4.1.2   Built-in Collections

In addition to the primitive numeric and boolean classes, Python has a number of very powerful built-in collection classes. Lists, strings, and tuples are sequential collections that are very similar in general structure but have specific differences that must be understood for them to be used properly.

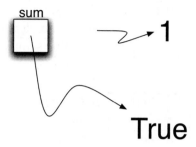

Figure 1.4: Assignment Changes the Reference

A list is an ordered collection of zero or more Python data objects. Lists are written as comma-delimited values enclosed in square brackets. The empty list is simply [ ]. Lists are heterogeneous, meaning that the data objects need not all be from the same class and the collection can be assigned to a variable as below. The following fragment shows a variety of Python data objects in a list.

```
>>> [1,3,True,6.5]
[1, 3, True, 6.5]
>>> mylist = [1,3,True,6.5]
>>> mylist
[1, 3, True, 6.5]
>>>
```

Note that when Python evaluates a list, the list itself is returned. However, in order to remember the list for later processing, its reference needs to be assigned to a variable.

Since lists are considered to be sequential, they support a number of operations that can be applied to any Python sequence. Table 1.1 reviews these operations and the following session gives examples of their use.

```
>>> mylist
[1, 3, True, 6.5]
>>> mylist[2]
True
>>> mylist + mylist
[1, 3, True, 6.5, 1, 3, True, 6.5]
>>> False in mylist
False
```

Operation Name	Operator	Explanation
Indexing	[ ]	Access an element of a sequence
Concatenation	+	Combine sequences together
Repetition	*	Concatenate a repeated number of times
Membership	in	Ask whether an item is in a sequence
Length	len	Ask the number of items in the sequence
Slicing	[:]	Extract a part of a sequence

Table 1.1: Operations on Any Sequence in Python

```
>>> mylist * 3
[1, 3, True, 6.5, 1, 3, True, 6.5, 1, 3, True, 6.5]
>>> mylist[1:3]
[3, True]
>>> len(mylist)
4
>>> len(mylist*4)
16
>>>
```

Note that the indices for lists (sequences) start counting with 0. The slice operation, mylist[1:3], returns a list of items starting with the item indexed by 1 up to but not including the item indexed by 3.

One very important aside relating to the repetition operator is that the result is a repetition of references to the data objects in the sequence. This can best be seen by considering the following session:

```
>>> mylist = [1,2,3,4]
>>> A = [mylist]*3
>>> A
[[1, 2, 3, 4], [1, 2, 3, 4], [1, 2, 3, 4]]
>>> mylist[2]=45
>>> A
[[1, 2, 45, 4], [1, 2, 45, 4], [1, 2, 45, 4]]
>>>
```

The variable A holds a collection of three references to the original list called mylist. Note that a change to one element of **mylist** shows up in all three occurrences in A.

A useful function for creating lists of integers is the **range** function shown below.

```
>>> range(10)
[0, 1, 2, 3, 4, 5, 6, 7, 8, 9]
>>> range(1,10)
[1, 2, 3, 4, 5, 6, 7, 8, 9]
>>> range(1,10,3)
[1, 4, 7]
>>>
```

range will return a list of integers starting with 0 or, if you provide more parameters, it will start and end at particular points and even skip items. In our example, **range(1,10)** starts at 1 and goes up to but not including 10. **range(1,10,3)** performs similarly but skips by threes (10 is not included).

Another way that a list can be initialized is with repetition. For example,

```
>>> mylist = [23] * 6
>>> mylist
[23, 23, 23, 23, 23, 23]
>>>
```

Lists support a number of methods that will be used to build data structures. Table 1.2 provides a summary. Examples of their use follow.

```
>>> mylist
[1024, 3, True, 6.5]
>>> mylist.append(False)
>>> mylist
[1024, 3, True, 6.5, False]
>>> mylist.insert(2,4.5)
>>> mylist
[1024, 3, 4.5, True, 6.5, False]
>>> mylist.pop()
False
>>> mylist
[1024, 3, 4.5, True, 6.5]
>>> mylist.pop(1)
3
>>> mylist
[1024, 4.5, True, 6.5]
```

Method Name	Use	Explanation
append	`alist.append(item)`	Adds a new item to the end of a list
insert	`alist.insert(i,item)`	Inserts an item at the ith position in a list
pop	`alist.pop()`	Removes and returns the last item in a list
pop	`alist.pop(i)`	Removes and returns the ith item in a list
sort	`alist.sort()`	Modifies a list to be sorted
reverse	`alist.reverse()`	Modifies a list to be in reverse order
del	`del alist[i]`	Deletes the item in the ith position
index	`alist.index(item)`	Returns the index of the first occurrence of `item`
count	`alist.count(item)`	Returns the number of occurrences of `item`
remove	`alist.remove(item)`	Removes the first occurrence of `item`

Table 1.2: Methods Provided by Lists in Python

```
>>> mylist.pop(2)
True
>>> mylist
[1024, 4.5, 6.5]
>>> mylist.sort()
>>> mylist
[4.5, 6.5, 1024]
>>> mylist.reverse()
>>> mylist
[1024, 6.5, 4.5]
>>> mylist.count(6.5)
1
>>> mylist.index(4.5)
2
>>> mylist.remove(6.5)
>>> mylist
```

```
[1024, 4.5]
>>> del mylist[0]
>>> mylist
[4.5]
>>>
```

You can see that some of the methods, such as pop, return a value and also modify the list. Others, such as reverse, simply modify the list with no return value. pop will default to the end of the list but can also remove and return a specific item. The index range starting from 0 is again used for these methods. You should also notice the familiar "dot" notation for asking an object to invoke a method. mylist.append(False) can be read as "ask the object mylist to perform its append method and send it the value False." Even simple data objects such as integers can invoke methods in this way.

```
>>> (54).__add__(21)
75
>>>
```

In this fragment we are asking the integer object 54 to execute its add method (called __add__ in Python) and passing it 21 as the value to add. The result is the sum, 75. Of course, we usually write this as 54+21. We will say much more about these methods later in this section.

Strings are sequential collections (lists) of characters only. Literal string values are differentiated from identifiers by using quotation marks (either single or double). A character is treated as a string of length 1.

```
>>> "David"
'David'
>>> myname = "David"
>>> myname[3]
'i'
>>> myname*2
'DavidDavid'
>>> len(myname)
5
>>>
```

Since strings are sequences, all of the sequence operations described above work as you would expect. In addition, the string module can be

imported to provide many more functions. A number of these functions,
some of which are shown in Table 1.3, can also be invoked directly by a
string object. For example,

```
>>> myname
'David'
>>> myname.upper()
'DAVID'
>>> myname.center(10)
'  David   '
>>> myname.find('v')
2
>>> myname.split('v')
['Da', 'id']
```

Of these, split will be very useful for processing data. split will take
a string and return a list of strings using the split character as a division
point. In the example, v is the division point. If no division is specified, the
split method looks for blank spaces.

Method Name	Use	Explanation
center	astring.center(w)	Returns a string centered in a field of size w
count	astring.count(item)	Returns the number of occurrences of item in the string
ljust	astring.ljust(w)	Returns a string left-justified in a field of size w
lower	astring.lower()	Returns a string in all lowercase
rjust	astring.rjust(w)	Returns a string right-justified in a field of size w
find	astring.find(item)	Returns the index of the first occurrence of item
split	astring.split(schar)	Splits a string into substrings at schar

Table 1.3: Methods Provided by Strings in Python

A major difference between lists and strings is that lists can be modified while strings cannot. This is referred to as **mutability**. Lists are mutable; strings are immutable. For example, you can change an item in a list by using indexing and assignment. With a string that change is not allowed.

```
>>> mylist
[1, 3, True, 6.5]
>>> mylist[0]=2**10
>>> mylist
[1024, 3, True, 6.5]
>>>
>>> myname
'David'
>>> myname[0]='X'

Traceback (most recent call last):
  File "<pyshell#84>", line 1, in -toplevel-
    myname[0]='X'
TypeError: object doesn't support item assignment
>>>
```

Tuples are very similar to lists in that they are heterogeneous sequences of data. The difference is that a tuple is immutable, like a string. A tuple cannot be changed. Tuples are written as comma-delimited values enclosed in parentheses. As sequences, they can use any operation described above. For example,

```
>>> mytuple = (2,True,4.96)
>>> mytuple
(2, True, 4.96)
>>> len(mytuple)
3
>>> mytuple[0]
2
>>> mytuple * 3
(2, True, 4.96, 2, True, 4.96, 2, True, 4.96)
>>> mytuple[0:2]
(2, True)
>>>
```

However, if you try to change an item in a tuple, you will get an error. Note that the error message provides location and reason for the problem.

```
>>> mytuple[1]=False

Traceback (most recent call last):
  File "<pyshell#137>", line 1, in -toplevel-
    mytuple[1]=False
TypeError: object doesn't support item assignment
>>>
```

Our final Python collection is an unordered structure called a **dictionary**. Dictionaries are collections of associated pairs of items where each pair consists of a key and a value. This key-value pair is typically written as key:value. Dictionaries are written as comma-delimited key:value pairs enclosed in curly braces. For example,

```
>>> capitals = {'Iowa':'DesMoines','Wisconsin':'Madison'}
>>> capitals
{'Wisconsin': 'Madison', 'Iowa': 'DesMoines'}
>>>
```

We can manipulate a dictionary by accessing a value via its key or by adding another key-value pair. The syntax for access looks much like a sequence access except that instead of using the index of the item we use the key value. To add a new value is similar.

```
>>> capitals['Iowa']
'DesMoines'
>>> capitals['Utah']='SaltLakeCity'
>>> capitals
{'Utah': 'SaltLakeCity', 'Wisconsin': 'Madison',
        'Iowa': 'DesMoines'}
>>> capitals['California']='Sacramento'
>>> capitals
{'Utah': 'SaltLakeCity', 'Wisconsin': 'Madison',
        'Iowa': 'DesMoines', 'California': 'Sacramento'}
>>> len(capitals)
4
>>>
```

It is important to note that the dictionary is maintained in no particular order with respect to the keys. The first pair added (`'Utah'`: `'SaltLakeCity'`) was placed first in the dictionary and the second pair added (`'California'`: `'Sacramento'`) was placed last. The placement of a key is dependent on the idea of "hashing" which will be explained in more detail in Chapter 4. We also show the length function performing the same role as with previous collections.

Dictionaries have a set of common methods. Table 1.4 describes them and the following session shows them in action. You will see that there are two variations on the `get` method. If the key is not present in the dictionary, `get` will return `None`. However, a second, optional parameter can specify a return value instead.

```
>>> phoneext={'david':1410,'brad':1137}
>>> phoneext
{'brad': 1137, 'david': 1410}
>>> phoneext.keys()
['brad', 'david']
>>> phoneext.values()
[1137,1410]
>>> phoneext.items()
[('brad', 1137), ('david', 1410]
>>> phoneext.get('brad')
1137
>>> phoneext.get('kent')
>>> phoneext.get('kent','NO ENTRY')
'NO ENTRY'
>>>
```

1.4.2 Control Structures

As we noted earlier, algorithms require two important control structures, iteration and selection. Both of these are supported by Python in various forms. The programmer can choose the statement that is most useful for the given circumstance.

For iteration, Python provides a standard **while** statement and a very powerful **for** statement. The while statement repeats a body of code as long as a condition is true. For example,

Method Name	Use	Explanation
keys	adict.keys()	Returns a list of keys in the dictionary
values	adict.values()	Returns a list of values in the dictionary
items	adict.items()	Returns a list of key-value tuples
get	adict.get(k)	Returns the value associated with k, None otherwise
get	adict.get(k,alt)	Returns the value associated with k, alt otherwise
in	key in adict	Returns True if key is in the dictionary, False otherwise
has_key	adict.has_key(key)	Returns True if key is in the dictionary, False otherwise
del	del adict[key]	Removes the entry from the dictionary

Table 1.4: Methods Provided by Dictionaries in Python

```
>>> counter = 1
>>> while counter <= 5:
...      print "Hello, world"
...      counter = counter + 1


Hello, world
Hello, world
Hello, world
Hello, world
Hello, world
```

prints out the phrase "Hello, world" five times. The condition on the while statement is evaluated at the start of each repetition. If the condition is True, the body of the statement will execute. It is easy to see the structure of a Python while statement due to the mandatory indentation pattern that the language enforces.

The while statement is a very general purpose iterative structure that we will use in a number of different algorithms. In many cases, a compound condition will control the iteration. A fragment such as

```
while counter <= 10 and not done:
...
```

would cause the body of the statement to be executed only in the case where both parts of the condition are satisfied. The value of the variable `counter` would need to be less than or equal to 10 and the value of the variable `done` would need to be `False` (`not False` is `True`) so that `True and True` results in `True`.

Even though this type of construct is very useful in a wide variety of situations, another iterative structure, the `for` statement, can be used in conjunction with many of the Python collections. The `for` statement can be used to iterate over the members of a collection, so long as the collection is a sequence. So, for example,

```
>>> for item in [1,3,6,2,5]:
...     print item
...
1
3
6
2
5
```

assigns the variable `item` to be each successive value in the list [1,3,6,2,5]. The body of the iteration is then executed. This works for any collection that is a sequence (lists, tuples, and strings).

A common use of the `for` statement is to implement definite iteration over a range of values. The statement

```
>>> for item in range(5):
...     print item**2
...
0
1
4
9
16
>>>
```

will perform the `print` statement five times. The `range` function will return the list [0,1,2,3,4] and each value will be assigned to the variable `item`. This value is then squared and printed.

The other very useful version of this iteration structure is used to process each character of a string. The following code fragment iterates over a list of strings and for each string processes each character by appending it to a list. The result is a list of all the letters in all of the words.

```
>>> wordlist = ['cat','dog','rabbit']
>>> letterlist = [ ]
>>> for aword in wordlist:
...     for aletter in aword:
...         letterlist.append(aletter)
...
>>> letterlist
['c', 'a', 't', 'd', 'o', 'g', 'r', 'a', 'b', 'b', 'i', 't']
>>>
```

Selection statements allow programmers to ask questions and then, based on the result, perform different actions. Most programming languages provide two versions of this useful construct: the `ifelse` and the `if`. A simple example of a binary selection uses the `ifelse` statement.

```
if n<0:
    print "Sorry, value is negative"
else:
    print math.sqrt(n)
```

In this example, the object referred to by **n** is checked to see if it is less than zero. If it is, a message is printed stating that it is negative. If it is not, the statement performs the **else** clause and computes the square root.

Selection constructs, as with any control construct, can be nested so that the result of one question helps decide whether to ask the next. For example, assume that **score** is a variable holding a reference to a score for a computer science test.

```
if score >= 90:
    print 'A'
else:
    if score >=80:
        print 'B'
    else
        if score >= 70:
            print 'C'
```

```
else:
    if score >= 60:
        print 'D'
    else:
        print 'F'
```

This fragment will classify a value called **score** by printing the letter grade earned. If the score is greater than or equal to 90, the statement will print A. If it is not (**else**), the next question is asked. If the score is greater than or equal to 80 then it must be between 80 and 89 since the answer to the first question was false. In this case print B is printed. You can see that the Python indentation pattern helps to make sense of the association between **if** and **else** without requiring any additional syntactic elements.

An alternative syntax for this type of nested selection uses the **elif** keyword. The **else** and the next **if** are combined so as to eliminate the need for additional nesting levels. Note that the final **else** is still necessary to provide the default case if all other conditions fail.

```
if score >= 90:
    print 'A'
elif score >=80:
    print 'B'
elif score >= 70:
    print 'C'
elif score >= 60:
    print 'D'
else:
    print 'F'
```

Python also has a single way selection construct, the **if** statement. With this statement, if the condition is true, an action is performed. In the case where the condition is false, processing simply continues on to the next statement after the **if**. For example, the following fragment will first check to see if the value of a variable n is negative. If it is, then it is modified by the absolute value function. Regardless, the next action is to compute the square root.

```
if n<0:
    n = abs(n)
print math.sqrt(n)
```

Returning to lists, there is an alternative method for creating a list that uses iteration and selection constructs. The technique is known as **list comprehensions**. List comprehensions allow you to easily create one list from another based on some processing or selection criteria. For example, if we would like to create a list of the first 10 perfect squares, we could use a `for` statement:

```
>>> sqlist=[]
>>> for x in range(1,11):
        sqlist.append(x*x)

>>> sqlist
[1, 4, 9, 16, 25, 36, 49, 64, 81, 100]
>>>
```

Using list comprehension, we can do this in one step as

```
>>> sqlist=[x*x for x in range(1,11)]
>>> sqlist
[1, 4, 9, 16, 25, 36, 49, 64, 81, 100]
>>>
```

The variable `x` takes on the values 1 through 10 as specified by the `for` construct. The value of `x*x` is then computed and added to the list that is being constructed. The general syntax for a list comprehension also allows a selection criteria to be added so that only certain items get added. For example,

```
>>> sqlist=[x*x for x in range(1,11) if x%2 != 0]
>>> sqlist
[1, 9, 25, 49, 81]
>>>
```

This list comprehension constructed a list that only contained the squares of the odd numbers in the range from 1 to 10. Any sequence that supports iteration can be used within a list comprehension to construct a new list.

```
>>>[ch.upper() for ch in 'comprehensions' if ch not in 'aeiou']
['C', 'M', 'P', 'R', 'H', 'N', 'S', 'N', 'S']
>>>
```

1.4.3   Defining Functions

The earlier example of procedural abstraction called upon a Python function
called `sqrt` from the math module to compute the square root. In general,
we can hide the details of any computation by defining a function. A function
definition requires a name, a group of parameters, and a body. It may also
explicitly return a value. For example, the simple function defined below
returns the square of the value you pass into it.

```
>>> def square(n):
...     return n**2
...
>>> square(3)
9
>>> square(square(3))
81
>>>
```

The syntax for this function definition includes the name, `square`, and
a parenthesized list of formal parameters. For this function, `n` is the only
formal parameter, which suggests that `square` needs only one piece of data
to do its work. The details, hidden "inside the box," simply compute the
result of `n**2` and return it. We can invoke or call the `square` function by
asking the Python environment to evaluate it, passing an actual parameter
value, in this case, `3`. Note that the call to `square` returns an integer that
can in turn be passed to another invocation.

We could implement our own square root function by using a well-known
technique called "Newton's Method." Newton's Method for approximating
square roots performs an iterative computation that converges on the correct
value. The equation $newguess = \frac{1}{2}*(oldguess+\frac{n}{oldguess})$ takes a value n and
repeatedly guesses the square root by making each $newguess$ the $oldguess$ in
the subsequent iteration. The initial guess used here is $\frac{n}{2}$. Listing 1.1 shows
a function definition that accepts a value n and returns the square root of n
after making 20 guesses. Again, the details of Newton's Method are hidden
inside the function definition and the user does not have to know anything
about the implementation to use the function for its intended purpose.

```
>>>squareroot(9)
3.0
>>>squareroot(4563)
67.549981495186216
>>>
```

```
1  def squareroot(n):
2      root = n/2
3      for k in range(20):
4          root = (1.0/2)*(root + (n / root))
5
6      return root
```

Listing 1.1: Function to Compute a Square Root Using Newton's Method

1.4.4   Object-Oriented Programming in Python: Defining Classes

We stated earlier that Python is an object-oriented programming language. So far, we have used a number of built-in classes to show examples of data and control structures. One of the most powerful features in an object-oriented programming language is the ability to allow a programmer (problem solver) to create new classes that model data that is needed to solve the problem.

Remember that we use abstract data types to provide the logical description of what a data object looks like (its state) and what it can do (its methods). By building a class that implements an abstract data type, a programmer can take advantage of the abstraction process and at the same time provide the details necessary to actually use the abstraction in a program. Whenever we want to implement an abstract data type, we will do so with a new class.

1.4.4.1   A Fraction Class

A very common example to show the details of implementing a user-defined class is to construct a class to represent the abstract data type Fraction. We have already seen that Python provides a number of numeric classes for our use. There are times, however, that it would be most appropriate to be able to create data objects that "look like" fractions. Fractions are also referred to as rational numbers.

A fraction such as $\frac{3}{5}$ consists of two parts. The top value, known as the numerator, can be any integer. The bottom value, called the denominator, can be any integer greater than 0 (negative fractions have a negative numerator). Although it is possible to create a floating point approximation for any fraction, in this case we would like to represent the fraction as an exact value.

The operations for the Fraction type will allow a Fraction data object to behave like any other numeric value. We need to be able to add, subtract, multiply, and divide fractions. We also want to be able to show fractions using the standard "slash" form, for example 3/5. In addition, all fraction methods should return results in their lowest terms so that no matter what computation is performed, we always end up with the most common form.

In Python, we define a new class by providing a name and a set of method definitions that are syntactically similar to function definitions. For this example,

```
class Fraction:

    #the methods go here
```

provides the framework for us to define the methods. The first method that all classes should provide is the constructor. The constructor defines the way in which data objects are created. To create a **Fraction** object, we will need to provide two pieces of data, the numerator and the denominator. In Python, the constructor method is always called __init__ (two underscores before and after **init**) and is shown in Listing 1.2.

```
1  class Fraction:
2
3      def __init__(self,top,bottom):
4
5          self.num = top
6          self.den = bottom
```

Listing 1.2: Fraction Class with the Constructor

Notice that the formal parameter list contains three items (**self**, **top**, **bottom**). **self** is a special parameter that will always be used as a reference back to the object itself. It must always be the first formal parameter; however, it will never be given an actual parameter value upon invocation. As described earlier, fractions require two pieces of state data, the numerator and the denominator. The notation **self.num** in the constructor defines the **fraction** object to have an internal data object called **num** as part of its state. Likewise, **self.den** creates the denominator. The values of the two formal parameters are initially assigned to the state, allowing the new **fraction** object to know its starting value.

To create an instance of the **Fraction** class, we must invoke the constructor. This happens by using the name of the class and passing actual values for the necessary state (note that we never directly `invoke` `__init__`). For example,

```
myfraction = Fraction(3,5)
```

creates an object called `myfraction` representing the fraction $\frac{3}{5}$ (three-fifths). Figure 1.5 shows this object as it is now implemented.

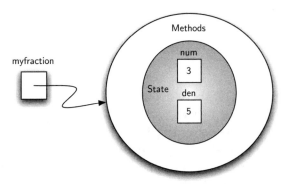

Figure 1.5: An Instance of the Fraction Class

The next thing we need to do is implement the behavior that the abstract data type requires. To begin, consider what happens when we try to print a `Fraction` object.

```
>>> myf = Fraction(3,5)
>>> print myf
<__main__.Fraction instance at 0x409b1acc>
>>>
```

The `fraction` object, `myf`, does not know how to respond to this request to print. The `print` statement requires that the object convert itself into a string so that the string can be written to the output. The only choice `myf` has is to show the actual reference that is stored in the variable (the address itself). This is not what we want.

There are two ways we can solve this problem. One is to define a method called `show` that will allow the `Fraction` object to print itself as a string. We can implement this method as shown in Listing 1.3. If we create a `Fraction` object as before, we can ask it to show itself, in other words, print itself in the proper format. Unfortunately, this does not work in general. In order to make printing work properly, we need to tell the `Fraction` class how to convert itself into a string. This is what the `print` statement needs in order to do its job.

```
1    def show(self):
2        print self.num,"/",self.den
```

Listing 1.3: show Method for Fractions

```
>>> myf = Fraction(3,5)
>>> myf.show()
3 / 5
>>> print myf
<__main__.Fraction instance at 0x40bce9ac>
>>>
```

In Python, all classes have a set of standard methods that are provided but may not work properly. One of these, `__str__`, is the method to convert an object into a string. The default implementation for this method is to return the instance address string as we have already seen. What we need to do is provide a "better" implementation for this method. We will say that this implementation **overrides** the previous one, or that it redefines the method's behavior.

To do this, we simply define a method with the name `__str__` and give it a new implementation as shown in Listing 1.4. This definition does not need any other information except the special parameter `self`. In turn, the method will build a string representation by converting each piece of internal state data to a string and then placing a / character in between the strings using string concatenation. The resulting string will be returned any time a `Fraction` object is asked to convert itself to a string. Notice the various ways that this function is used.

```
1    def __str__(self):
2        return str(self.num)+"/"+str(self.den)
```

Listing 1.4: __str__ Method for Fractions

```
>>> myf = Fraction(3,5)
>>> print myf
```

```
3/5
>>> print "I ate", myf, "of the pizza"
I ate 3/5 of the pizza
>>> myf.__str__()
'3/5'
>>> str(myf)
'3/5'
>>>
```

We can override many other methods for our new **Fraction** class. The most important of these are the basic arithmetic operations. We would like to be able to create two **Fraction** objects and then add them together using the standard "+" notation. At this point, if we try to add two fractions, we get the following:

```
>>> f1 = Fraction(1,4)
>>> f2 = Fraction(1,2)
>>> f1+f2

Traceback (most recent call last):
  File "<pyshell#173>", line 1, in -toplevel-
    f1+f2
TypeError: unsupported operand type(s) for +:
          'instance' and 'instance'
>>>
```

If you look closely at the error, you see that the problem is that the "+" operator does not understand the **Fraction** operands.

We can fix this by providing the **Fraction** class with a method that overrides the addition method. In Python, this method is called __add__ and it requires two parameters. The first, **self**, is always needed, and the second represents the other operand in the expression. For example,

```
f1.__add__(f2)
```

would ask the **Fraction** object **f1** to add the **Fraction** object **f2** to itself. This can be written in the standard notation, **f1+f2**.

Two fractions must have the same denominator to be added. The easiest way to make sure they have the same denominator is to simply use the product of the two denominators as a common denominator so that $\frac{a}{b} +$ $\frac{c}{d} = \frac{ad}{bd} + \frac{cb}{bd} = \frac{ad+cb}{bd}$. The implementation is shown in Listing 1.5. The addition function returns a new **Fraction** object with the numerator and denominator of the sum. We can use this method by writing a standard arithmetic expression involving fractions, assigning the result of the addition, and then printing our result.

```
def __add__(self,otherfraction):

    newnum = self.num*otherfraction.den + \
                self.den*otherfraction.num
    newden = self.den * otherfraction.den

    return Fraction(newnum,newden)
```

Listing 1.5: __add__ Method for Fractions

```
>>> f1=Fraction(1,4)
>>> f2=Fraction(1,2)
>>> f3=f1+f2
>>> print f3
6/8
>>>
```

The addition method works as we desire, but one thing could be better. Note that 6/8 is the correct result ($\frac{1}{4} + \frac{1}{2}$) but that it is not in the "lowest terms" representation. The best representation would be 3/4. In order to be sure that our results are always in the lowest terms, we need a helper function that knows how to reduce fractions. This function will need to look for the greatest common divisor, or GCD. We can then divide the numerator and the denominator by the GCD and the result will be reduced to lowest terms.

The best-known algorithm for finding a greatest common divisor is Euclid's Algorithm which will be discussed in detail in Chapter 3. Euclid's Algorithm states that the greatest common divisor of two integers m and n is n if n divides m evenly. However, if n does not divide m evenly, then the answer is the greatest common divisor of n and the remainder of m divided by n. We will simply provide an iterative implementation here (see Listing 1.6) and wait until Chapter 3 to explore it further.

Now we can use this function to help reduce any fraction. To put a fraction in lowest terms, we will divide the numerator and the denominator by their greatest common divisor. So, for the fraction 6/8, the greatest

```
1   #Assume that m and n are greater than zero
2   def gcd(m,n):
3       while m%n != 0:
4           oldm = m
5           oldn = n
6
7           m = oldn
8           n = oldm%oldn
9
10      return n
```

Listing 1.6: Greatest Common Divisor Function

common divisor is 2. Dividing the top and the bottom by 2 creates a new
fraction, 3/4.

```
>>> f1=Fraction(1,4)
>>> f2=Fraction(1,2)
>>> f3=f1+f2
>>> print f3
3/4
>>>
```

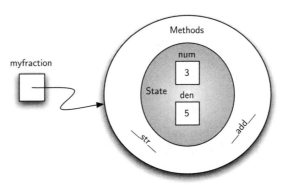

Figure 1.6: An Instance of the Fraction Class with Two Methods

Our Fraction object now has two very useful methods and looks like Figure 1.6. One final method that we need to include in our example Fraction
class will allow two fractions to compare themselves to one another. Assume
we have two Fraction objects, f1 and f2. f1==f2 will only be True if they

are references to the same object. Two different objects with the same numerators and denominators would not be equal under this implementation. This is called **shallow equality** (see Figure 1.7).

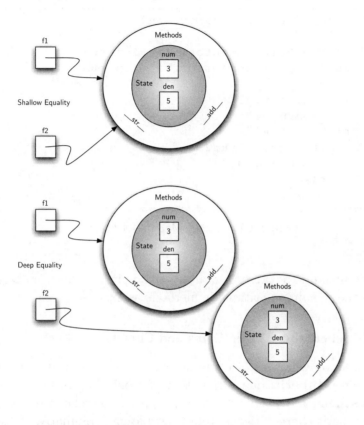

Figure 1.7: Shallow Equality Versus Deep Equality

We can create **deep equality** (see Figure 1.7)–equality by the same value, not the same reference–by overriding the __cmp__ method. The __cmp__ method is another standard method available in any class. The __cmp__ method compares two objects and returns a value less than zero if the first is less than the second, returns zero if they are equal, and returns a value greater than zero if the first is greater than the second. It is common to return the values -1, 0, and 1 for these three cases.

In the Fraction class, we can implement the __cmp__ method by again putting the two fractions in common terms and then comparing the numerators (see Listing 1.7). It is important to notice that the relationship operators all work once we override __cmp__ since their default behavior is to use __cmp__ if it exists. It is possible to override the individual operators, such as __lt__ (for less than) as well, but __cmp__ takes care of things in one method.

```
 1   def __cmp__(self,otherfraction):
 2
 3       num1 = self.num*otherfraction.den
 4       num2 = self.den*otherfraction.num
 5
 6       if num1 < num2:
 7           return -1
 8       else:
 9           if num1 == num2:
10               return 0
11           else
12               return 1
```

Listing 1.7: __cmp__ Method for Fractions

The complete `Fraction` class, up to this point, is shown in Listing 1.8. We leave the remaining arithmetic methods as exercises.

1.4.4.2 Inheritance: Logic Gates and Circuits

Our final section will introduce another important aspect of object-oriented programming. **Inheritance** is the ability for one class to be related to another class in much the same way that people can be related to one another. Children inherit characteristics from their parents. Similarly, Python child classes can inherit characteristic data and behavior from a parent class. These classes are often referred to as **subclasses** and **superclasses**.

We have already seen an example of how these relationships can be structured with Python collections. Figure 1.8 shows the built-in collections and their relationships to one another. This is called an **inheritance hierarchy**. We say that the list **IS-A** sequential collection, the list is a child of the sequential collection, because lists inherit important characteristics from the notion of sequences, namely the ordering of the underlying data and operations such as concatenation, repetition, and indexing. In this case, we call the list the child and the sequence the parent (or subclass list, superclass sequence).

Lists, tuples, and strings are all types of sequential collections. They all inherit common data organization and operations. However, each of

```
1  class Fraction:
2      def __init__(self,top,bottom):
3          self.num = top
4          self.den = bottom
5
6      def __str__(self):
7          return str(self.num)+"/"+str(self.den)
8
9      def show(self):
10         print self.num,"/",self.den
11
12     def __add__(self,otherfraction):
13         newnum = self.num*otherfraction.den + \
14                     self.den*otherfraction.num
15         newden = self.den * otherfraction.den
16         common = gcd(newnum,newden)
17         return Fraction(newnum/common,newden/common)
18
19     def __cmp__(self,otherfraction):
20         num1 = self.num*otherfraction.den
21         num2 = self.den*otherfraction.num
22         if num1 < num2:
23             return -1
24         else:
25             if num1 == num2:
26                 return 0
27             else:
28                 return 1
```

Listing 1.8: Fraction Class

them is distinct based on whether the data is homogeneous and whether the collection is immutable. The children all gain from their parents but distinguish themselves by adding additional characteristics.

By organizing classes in this hierarchical fashion, object-oriented programming languages allow previously written code to be extended to meet the needs of a new situation. In addition, by organizing data in this hierarchical manner, we can better understand the relationships that exist. We can be more efficient in building our abstract representations.

To explore this idea further, we will construct a **simulation**, an application to simulate digital circuits. The basic building block for this simulation will be the logic gate. These electronic switches represent boolean algebra

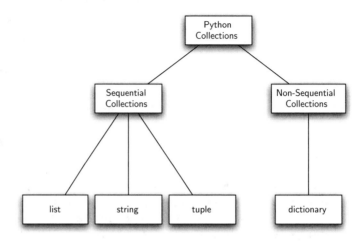

Figure 1.8: An Inheritance Hierarchy for Python Collections

relationships between their input and their output. In general, gates have a single output line. The value of the output is dependent on the values given on the input lines.

AND gates have two input lines, each of which can be either 0 or 1 (representing `False` or `True`, repectively). If both of the input lines have the value 1, the resulting output is 1. However, if either or both of the input lines is 0, the result is 0. OR gates also have two input lines and produce a 1 if one or both of the input values is a 1. In the case where both input lines are 0, the result is 0.

NOT gates differ from the other two gates in that they only have a single input line. The output value is simply the opposite of the input value. If 0 appears on the input, 1 is produced on the output. Similarly, 1 produces 0. Figure 1.9 shows how each of these gates is typically represented. Each gate also has a **truth table** of values showing the input-to-output mapping that is performed by the gate.

By combining these gates in various patterns and then applying a set of input values, we can build circuits that have logical functions. Figure 1.10 shows a circuit consisting of two AND gates, one OR gate, and a single NOT gate. The output lines from the two AND gates feed directly into the OR gate, and the resulting output from the OR gate is given to the NOT gate. If we apply a set of input values to the four input lines (two for each AND gate), the values are processed and a result appears at the output of the NOT gate. Figure 1.10 also shows an example with values.

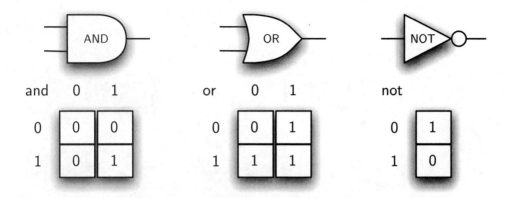

Figure 1.9: Three Types of Logic Gates

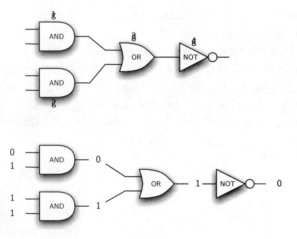

Figure 1.10: Circuit

In order to implement a circuit, we will first build a representation for logic gates. Logic gates are easily organized into a class inheritance hierarchy as shown in Figure 1.11. At the top of the hierarchy, the `LogicGate` class represents the most general characteristics of logic gates: namely, a label for the gate and an output line. The next level of subclasses breaks the logic gates into two families, those that have one input line and those that have two. Below that, the specific logic functions of each appear.

We can now start to implement the classes by starting with the most general, `LogicGate`. As noted earlier, each gate has a label for identification

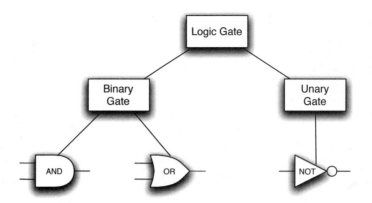

Figure 1.11: An Inheritance Hierarchy for Logic Gates

and a single output line. In addition, we need methods to allow a user of a gate to ask the gate for its label.

The other behavior that every logic gate needs is the ability to know its output value. This will require that the gate perform the appropriate logic based on the current input. In order to produce output, the gate needs to know specifically what that logic is. This means calling a method to perform the logic computation. The complete class is shown in Listing 1.9.

```python
class LogicGate:

    def __init__(self,n):
        self.label = n
        self.output = None

    def getLabel(self):
        return self.label

    def getOutput(self):
        self.output = self.performGateLogic()
        return self.output
```

Listing 1.9: Superclass `LogicGate`

At this point, we will not implement the `performGateLogic` function. The reason for this is that we do not know how each gate will perform its own logic operation. Those details will be included by each individual gate that is added to the hierarchy. This is a very powerful idea in object-oriented programming. We are writing a method that will use code that does not exist yet. The parameter self is a reference to the actual gate object invoking the method. Any new logic gate that gets added to the hierarchy will simply need to implement the performGateLogic function and it will be used at the appropriate time. Once done, the gate can provide its output value. This ability to extend a hierarchy that currently exists and provide the specific functions that the hierarchy needs to use the new class is extremely important for reusing existing code.

We categorized the logic gates based on the number of input lines. The AND gate has two input lines. The OR gate also has two input lines. NOT gates have one input line. The BinaryGate class will be a subclass of LogicGate and will add two input lines. The UnaryGate class will also subclass LogicGate but will have only a single input line. In computer circuit design, these lines are sometimes called "pins" so we will use that terminology in our implementation.

```
class BinaryGate(LogicGate):

    def __init__(self,n):
        LogicGate.__init__(self,n)

        self.pinA = None
        self.pinB = None

    def getPinA(self):
        return input("Enter Pin A input for gate "+ \
                            self.getLabel()+"-->")

    def getPinB(self):
        return input("Enter Pin B input for gate "+ \
                            self.getLabel()+"-->")
```

Listing 1.10: The BinaryGate Class

Listings 1.10 and 1.11 implement these two classes. The constructors in both of these classes start with an explicit call to the constructor of the parent class. When creating an instance of the BinaryGate class, we first want to initialize any data items that are inherited from LogicGate. In this case, that means the label for the gate. The constructor then goes on to add the two input lines (pinA and pinB). This is a very common pattern that you should always use when building class hierarchies. Child

```
1  class UnaryGate(LogicGate):
2
3      def __init__(self,n):
4          LogicGate.__init__(self,n)
5
6          self.pin = None
7
8      def getPin(self):
9          return input("Enter Pin input for gate "+ \
10                               self.getLabel()+"-->")
```

Listing 1.11: The UnaryGate Class

class constructors need to call parent class constructors and then move on
to their own distinguishing data.

The only behavior that the `BinaryGate` class adds is the ability to get the
values from the two input lines. Since these values come from some external
place, we will simply ask the user via an input statement to provide them.
The same implementation occurs for the `UnaryGate` class except that there
is only one input line.

Now that we have a general class for gates depending on the number
of input lines, we can build specific gates that have unique behavior. For
example, the `AndGate` class will be a subclass of `BinaryGate` since AND
gates have two input lines. As before, the first line of the constructor calls
upon the parent class constructor (`BinaryGate`), which in turn calls its
parent class constructor (`LogicGate`). Note that the `AndGate` class does not
provide any new data since it inherits two input lines, one output line, and
a label.

The only thing `AndGate` needs to add is the specific behavior that performs the boolean operation that was described earlier. This is the place
where we can provide the `performGateLogic` method. For an AND gate,
this method first must get the two input values and then only return 1 if
both input values are 1. The complete class is shown in Listing 1.12.

We can show the `AndGate` class in action by creating an instance and
asking it to compute its output. The following session shows an `AndGate`
object, `g1`, that has an internal label `"G1"`. When we invoke the `getOutput`
method, the object must first call its `performGateLogic` method which in
turn queries the two input lines. Once the values are provided, the correct
output is shown.

```
1  class AndGate(BinaryGate):
2
3      def __init__(self,n):
4          BinaryGate.__init__(self,n)
5
6      def performGateLogic(self):
7
8          a = self.getPinA()
9          b = self.getPinB()
10         if a==1 and b==1:
11             return 1
12         else:
13             return 0
```

Listing 1.12: The AndGate Class

```
>>> g1 = AndGate("G1")
>>> g1.getOutput()
Enter Pin A input for gate G1-->1
Enter Pin B input for gate G1-->0
0
```

The same development can be done for OR gates and NOT gates. The OrGate class will also be a subclass of BinaryGate and the NotGate class will extend the UnaryGate class. Both of these classes will need to provide their own performGateLogic functions, as this is their specific behavior.

We can use a single gate by first constructing an instance of one of the gate classes and then asking the gate for its output (which will in turn need inputs to be provided). For example:

```
>>> g2 = OrGate("G2")
>>> g2.getOutput()
Enter Pin A input for gate G2-->1
Enter Pin B input for gate G2-->1
1
>>> g2.getOutput()
Enter Pin A input for gate G2-->0
Enter Pin B input for gate G2-->0
0
>>> g3 = NotGate("G3")
```

```
>>> g3.getOutput()
Enter Pin input for gate G3-->0
1
```

Now that we have the basic gates working, we can turn our attention
to building circuits. In order to create a circuit, we need to connect gates
together, the output of one flowing into the input of another. To do this,
we will implement a new class called `Connector`.

The `Connector` class will not reside in the gate hierarchy. It will, however, use the gate hierarchy in that each connector will have two gates,
one on either end (see Figure 1.12). This relationship is very important in
object-oriented programming. It is called the **HAS-A** relationship. Recall
earlier that we used the phrase "IS-A relationship" to say that a child class
is related to a parent class, for example `UnaryGate` IS-A `LogicGate`.

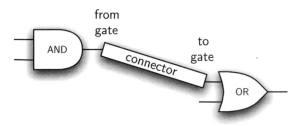

Figure 1.12: A Connector Connects the Output of One Gate to the Input of Another

Now, with the `Connector` class, we say that a `Connector` HAS-A `LogicGate`
meaning that connectors will have instances of the `LogicGate` class within
them but are not part of the hierarchy. When designing classes, it is very important to distinguish between those that have the IS-A relationship (which
requires inheritance) and those that have HAS-A relationships (with no inheritance).

Listing 1.13 shows the `Connector` class. The two gate instances within
each connector object will be referred to as the `fromgate` and the `togate`,
recognizing that data values will "flow" from the output of one gate into
an input line of the next. The call to `setNextPin` is very important for
making connections (see Listing 1.14). We need to add this method to our
gate classes so that each `togate` can choose the proper input line for the
connection.

In the `BinaryGate` class, for gates with two possible input lines, the
connector must be connected to only one line. If both of them are available,

```
 1  class Connector:
 2
 3      def __init__(self, fgate, tgate):
 4          self.fromgate = fgate
 5          self.togate = tgate
 6
 7          tgate.setNextPin(self)
 8
 9      def getFrom(self):
10          return self.fromgate
11
12      def getTo(self):
13          return self.togate
```

Listing 1.13: The Connector Class

we will choose pinA by default. If pinA is already connected, then we will choose pinB. It is not possible to connect to a gate with no available input lines.

```
 1      def setNextPin(self, source):
 2          if self.pinA == None:
 3              self.pinA = source
 4          else:
 5              if self.pinB == None:
 6                  self.pinB = source
 7              else:
 8                  print "Cannot Connect: NO EMPTY PINS"
```

Listing 1.14: The setNextPin Method

Now it is possible to get input from two places: externally, as before, and from the output of a gate that is connected to that input line. This requires a change to the getPinA and getPinB methods (see Listing 1.15). If the input line is not connected to anything (None), then ask the user externally as before. However, if there is a connection, the connection is accessed and fromgate's output value is retrieved. This in turn causes that gate to process its logic. This continues until all input is available and the final output value becomes the required input for the gate in question. In a sense, the circuit works backwards to find the input necessary to finally produce output.

```
1    def getPinA(self):
2        if self.pinA == None:
3            return input("Enter Pin A input for gate "+ \
4                              self.getName()+"-->")
5        else:
6            return self.pinA.getFrom().getOutput()
```

Listing 1.15: A Modified getPin Method

A complete listing of the circuit simulation classes is given in Listing 1.16. The following fragment constructs the circuit shown earlier in the section:

```
>>> g1 = AndGate("G1")
>>> g2 = AndGate("G2")
>>> g3 = OrGate("G3")
>>> g4 = NotGate("G4")
>>> c1 = Connector(g1,g3)
>>> c2 = Connector(g2,g3)
>>> c3 = Connector(g3,g4)
```

The outputs from the two AND gates (g1 and g2) are connected to the OR gate (g3) and that output is connected to the NOT gate (g4). The output from the NOT gate is the output of the entire circuit. For example:

```
>>> g4.getOutput()
Enter Pin A input for gate G1-->0
Enter Pin B input for gate G1-->1
Enter Pin A input for gate G2-->1
Enter Pin B input for gate G2-->1
0
>>>
```

```
1  class LogicGate:
2
3      def __init__(self,n):
4          self.label = n
5          self.output = None
6
7      def getLabel(self):
8          return self.label
9
```

```
10      def getOutput(self):
11          self.output = self.performGateLogic()
12          return self.output
13
14  class BinaryGate(LogicGate):
15
16      def __init__(self,n):
17          LogicGate.__init__(self,n)
18
19          self.pinA = None
20          self.pinB = None
21
22      def getPinA(self):
23          if self.pinA == None:
24              return input("Enter Pin A input for gate "+ \
25                                      self.getLabel()+"-->")
26          else:
27              return self.pinA.getFrom().getOutput()
28
29      def getPinB(self):
30          if self.pinB == None:
31              return input("Enter Pin B input for gate "+ \
32                                      self.getLabel()+"-->")
33          else:
34              return self.pinB.getFrom().getOutput()
35
36      def setNextPin(self,source):
37          if self.pinA == None:
38              self.pinA = source
39          else:
40              if self.pinB == None:
41                  self.pinB = source
42              else:
43                  print "Cannot Connect: NO EMPTY PINS"
44
45  class AndGate(BinaryGate):
46
47      def __init__(self,n):
48          BinaryGate.__init__(self,n)
49
50      def performGateLogic(self):
51
52          a = self.getPinA()
53          b = self.getPinB()
54          if a==1 and b==1:
```

```
55              return 1
56          else:
57              return 0
58
59  class OrGate(BinaryGate):
60
61      def __init__(self,n):
62          BinaryGate.__init__(self,n)
63
64      def performGateLogic(self):
65          a = self.getPinA()
66          b = self.getPinB()
67          if a ==1 or b==1:
68              return 1
69          else:
70              return 0
71
72  class UnaryGate(LogicGate):
73
74      def __init__(self,n):
75          LogicGate.__init__(self,n)
76
77          self.pin = None
78
79      def getPin(self):
80          if self.pin == None:
81              return input("Enter Pin input for gate "+ \
82                                  self.getLabel()+"-->")
83          else:
84              return self.pin.getFrom().getOutput()
85
86      def setNextPin(self,source):
87          if self.pin == None:
88              self.pin = source
89          else:
90              print "Cannot Connect: NO EMPTY PINS"
91
92  class NotGate(UnaryGate):
93
94      def __init__(self,n):
95          UnaryGate.__init__(self,n)
96
97      def performGateLogic(self):
98
99          if self.getPin():
```

```
100              return 0
101          else:
102              return 1
103
104  class Connector:
105
106      def __init__(self, fgate, tgate):
107          self.fromgate = fgate
108          self.togate = tgate
109
110          tgate.setNextPin(self)
111
112      def getFrom(self):
113          return self.fromgate
114
115      def getTo(self):
116          return self.togate
```

Listing 1.16: The Circuit Classes

1.5 Summary

- Computer science is the study of problem-solving.

- Computer science uses abstraction as a tool for representing both processes and data.

- Abstract data types allow programmers to manage the complexity of a problem domain by hiding the details of the data.

- Python is a powerful, yet easy-to-use, object-oriented language.

- Lists, tuples, and strings are built in Python sequential collections.

- Dictionaries are nonsequential collections of data.

- Classes allow programmers to implement abstract data types.

- Programmers can override standard methods as well as create new methods.

- Classes can be organized into hierarchies.

- A class constructor should always invoke the constructor of its parent before continuing on with its own data and behavior.

1.6   Key Terms

Abstract Data Type	Abstraction	Algorithm
Class	Computable	Data Type
Data Structure	Deep Equality	Dictionary
Encapsulation	HAS-A Relationship	Information Hiding
Inheritance	Inheritance Hierarchy	Interface
IS-A Relationship	Method	Mutability
Object	Procedural Abstraction	Programming
self	Shallow Equality	Simulation
Truth Table		

1.7   Discussion Questions

1. Construct a class hierarchy for people on a college campus. Include faculty, staff, and students. What do they have in common? What distinguishes them from one another?

2. Construct a class hierarchy for bank accounts.

3. Construct a class hierarchy for different types of computers.

4. Using the classes provided in the chapter, interactively construct a circuit and test it.

1.8   Programming Exercises

1. In many ways it would be better if all fractions were maintained in lowest terms right from the start. Modify the constructor for the Fraction class so that GCD is used to reduce fractions immediately. Notice that this means the __add__ function no longer needs to reduce. Make the necessary modifications.

2. In the definition of fractions we assumed that negative fractions have a negative numerator and a positive denominator. Using a negative denominator would cause the __cmp__ function to give incorrect results. In general, this is an unnecessary constraint. Modify the constructor

to allow the user to pass a negative denominator so that the __cmp__ function continues to work properly.

3. Complete the implementation of the **Fraction** class by overriding the methods for multiplication, subtraction, and division.

4. Research the __radd__ method. How does it differ from __add__? When is it used? Implement __radd__.

5. Repeat the last question but this time consider the __iadd__ method.

6. Research the __repr__ method. How does it differ from __str__? When is it used? Implement __repr__.

7. Research other types of gates that exist (such as NAND, NOR, and XOR). Add them to the circuit hierarchy. How much additional coding did you need to do?

8. The circuit simulation shown in this chapter works in a backward direction. In other words, given a circuit, the output is produced by working back through the input values, which in turn cause other outputs to be queried. This continues until external input lines are found, at which point the user is asked for values. Modify the implementation so that the action is in the forward direction; upon receiving inputs the circuit produces an output.

9. Design a class to represent a playing card. Now design a class to represent a deck of cards. Using these two classes, implement a favorite card game.

Chapter 2

Basic Data Structures

2.1 Objectives

- To understand the logical structure of the basic data structures stack, queue, and deque.

- To be able to implement the ADTs stack, queue, and deque using Python.

- To understand prefix, infix, and postfix expression formats.

- To use stacks to evaluate postfix expressions.

- To use stacks to convert expressions from infix to postfix.

- To use queues for basic timing simulations.

- To be able to recognize problem properties where stacks, queues, and deques are appropriate data structures.

2.2 What Are Linear Structures?

We will begin our study of data structures by considering three simple but very powerful concepts. Stacks, queues, and deques are examples of data collections whose items are ordered depending on how they are added or removed. Once an item is added, it stays in that position relative to the other elements that came before and came after it. Collections such as these are often referred to as **linear data structures**.

Linear structures can be thought of as having two ends. Sometimes these ends are referred to as the "left" and the "right" or in some cases the "front" and the "rear." You could also call them the "top" and the "bottom." The names given to the ends are not significant. What distinguishes one linear structure from another is the way in which items are added and removed, in particular the location where these additions and removals occur. For example, a structure might allow new items to be added at only one end. Some structures might allow items to be removed from either end.

These variations give rise to some of the most useful data structures in computer science. They appear in many algorithms and can be used to solve a variety of important problems.

2.3 Stacks

2.3.1 What is a Stack?

A **stack** (sometimes called a "push-down stack") is an ordered collection of items where the addition of new items and the removal of existing items always takes place at the same end. This end is commonly referred to as the "top." The end opposite the top is known as the "base."

The base of the stack is significant since items stored in the stack that are closer to the base represent those that have been in the stack the longest. The most recently added item is the one that is in position to be removed first. This ordering principle is sometimes called **LIFO, last-in first-out**. It provides an ordering based on length of time in the collection. Newer items are near the top, while older items are near the base.

Many examples of stacks occur in everyday situations. Almost any cafeteria has a stack of trays or plates where you take the one at the top, uncovering a new tray or plate for the next customer in line. Imagine a stack of books on a desk (Figure 2.1). The only book whose cover is visible is the one on top. To access others in the stack, we need to remove the ones that are sitting on top of them. Figure 2.2 shows another stack. This one contains a number of primitive Python data objects.

One of the most useful ideas related to stacks comes from the simple observation of items as they are added and then removed. Assume you start out with a clean desktop. Now place books one at a time on top of each other. You are constructing a stack. Consider what happens when you begin removing books. The order that they are removed is exactly the reverse of the order that they were placed. Stacks are fundamentally important, as they can be used to reverse the order of items. The order of insertion is the

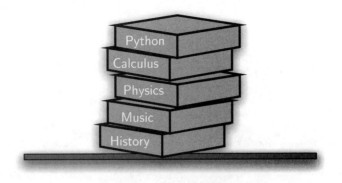

Figure 2.1: A Stack of Books

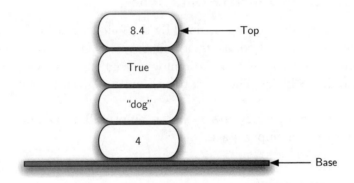

Figure 2.2: A Stack of Primitive Python Objects

reverse of the order of removal. Figure 2.3 shows the Python data object stack as it was created and then again as items are removed. Note the order of the objects.

Considering this reversal property, you can perhaps think of examples of stacks that occur as you use your computer. For example, every web browser has a Back button. As you navigate from web page to web page, those pages are placed on a stack (actually it is the URLs that are going on the stack). The current page that you are viewing is on the top and the first page you looked at is at the base. If you click on the Back button, you begin to move in reverse order through the pages.

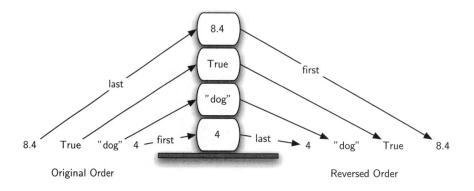

Figure 2.3: The Reversal Property of Stacks

The Stack Abstract Data Type

The stack abstract data type is defined by the following structure and operations. A stack is structured, as described above, as an ordered collection of items where items are added to and removed from the end called the "top." Stacks are ordered LIFO. The stack operations are given below.

- Stack() creates a new stack that is empty. It needs no parameters and returns an empty stack.

- push(item) adds a new item to the top of the stack. It needs the item and returns nothing.

- pop() removes the top item from the stack. It needs no parameters and returns the item. The stack is modified.

- peek() returns the top item from the stack but does not remove it. It needs no parameters. The stack is not modified.

- isEmpty() tests to see whether the stack is empty. It needs no parameters and returns a boolean value.

- size() returns the number of items on the stack. It needs no parameters and returns an integer.

For example, if s is a stack that has been created and starts out empty, then Table 2.1 shows the results of a sequence of stack operations. Under stack contents, the top item is listed at the far right.

Stack Operation	Stack Contents	Return Value
s.isEmpty()	[]	True
s.push(4)	[4]	
s.push('dog')	[4,'dog']	
s.peek()	[4,'dog']	'dog'
s.push(True)	[4,'dog',True]	
s.size()	[4,'dog',True]	3
s.isEmpty()	[4,'dog',True]	False
s.push(8.4)	[4,'dog',True,8.4]	
s.pop()	[4,'dog',True]	8.4
s.pop()	[4,'dog']	True
s.size()	[4,'dog']	2

Table 2.1: Sample Stack Operations

2.3.3 Implementing a Stack in Python

As we described in Chapter 1, in Python, as in any object-oriented programming language, the implementation of choice for an abstract data type such as a stack is the creation of a new class. The stack operations are implemented as methods. Further, to implement a stack, which is a collection of elements, it makes sense to utilize the power and simplicity of the primitive collections provided by Python. We will use a list.

Recall that the list class in Python provides an ordered collection mechanism and a set of methods. For example, if we have the list [2,5,3,6,7,4], we need only to decide which end of the list will be considered the top of the stack and which will be the base. Once that decision is made, the operations can be implemented using the list methods such as append and pop.

The following stack implementation (Listing 2.1) assumes that the end of the list will hold the top element of the stack. As the stack grows (as push operations occur), new items will be added on the end of the list. pop operations will manipulate that same end.

The following interactive Python session shows the Stack class in action as we perform the sequence of operations from Table 2.1.

```
>>> s=Stack()
>>> s.isEmpty()
True
>>> s.push(4)
>>> s.push('dog')
```

```
1  class Stack:
2      def __init__(self):
3          self.items = []
4
5      def isEmpty(self):
6          return self.items == []
7
8      def push(self, item):
9          self.items.append(item)
10
11     def pop(self):
12         return self.items.pop()
13
14     def peek(self):
15         return self.items[len(self.items)-1]
16
17     def size(self):
18         return len(self.items)
```

Listing 2.1: Stack Implementation in Python

```
>>> s.peek()
'dog'
>>> s.push(True)
>>> s.size()
3
>>> s.isEmpty()
False
>>> s.push(8.4)
>>> s.pop()
8.4
>>> s.pop()
True
>>> s.size()
2
>>>
```

It is important to note that we could have chosen to implement the stack using a list where the top is at the beginning instead of at the end. In this case, the previous pop and append methods would no longer work and we would have to index position 0 (the first item in the list) explicitly. The implementation is shown in Listing 2.2.

```
1  class Stack:
2      def __init__(self):
3          self.items = []
4
5      def isEmpty(self):
6          return self.items == []
7
8      def push(self, item):
9          self.items.insert(0,item)
10
11     def pop(self):
12         return self.items.pop(0)
13
14     def peek(self):
15         return self.items[0]
16
17     def size(self):
18         return len(self.items)
```

Listing 2.2: Alternative ADT Stack Implementation in Python

This ability to change the physical implementation of an abstract data type while maintaining the logical characteristics is an example of abstraction at work.

2.3.4 | Simple Balanced Parentheses

We now turn our attention to using stacks to solve real computer science problems. You have no doubt written arithmetic expressions such as $((5 + 6) * (7 + 8))/(4 + 3)$ where parentheses are used to order the performance of operations. You may also have some experience programming in a language such as Lisp with constructs like

```
(defun square(n)
    (* n n))
```

This defines a function called **square** that will return the square of its argument **n**. Lisp is notorious for using lots and lots of parentheses.

In both of these examples, parentheses must appear in a balanced fashion. **Balanced parentheses** means that each opening symbol has a corresponding closing symbol and the pairs of parentheses are properly nested. Consider the following correctly balanced strings of parentheses:

(() () () ())

((((()))))

(() ((()) ()))

Compare those with the following, which are not balanced:

((((((())

( )))

(() () (()

The ability to differentiate between parentheses that are correctly balanced and those that are unbalanced is an important part of recognizing many programming language structures.

The challenge then is to write an algorithm that will read a string of parentheses from left to right and decide whether the symbols are balanced. To solve this problem we need to make an important observation. As you process symbols from left to right, the most recent opening parenthesis must match the next closing symbol (see Figure 2.4). Also, the first opening symbol processed may have to wait until the very last symbol for its match. Closing symbols match opening symbols in the reverse order of their appearance; they match from the inside out. This is a clue that stacks can be used to solve the problem.

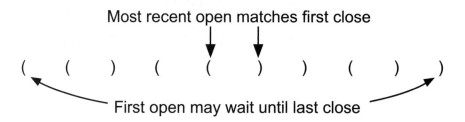

Figure 2.4: Matching Parentheses

Once you agree that a stack is the appropriate data structure for keeping the parentheses, the statement of the algorithm is straightforward. Starting with an empty stack, process the parenthesis strings from left to right. If a symbol is an opening parenthesis, push it on the stack as a signal that a corresponding closing symbol needs to appear later. If, on the other hand, a symbol is a closing parenthesis, pop the stack. As long as it is possible to pop the stack to match every closing symbol, the parentheses remain balanced. If at any time there is no opening symbol on the stack to match a closing symbol, the string is not balanced properly. At the end of the string, when all symbols have been processed, the stack should be empty. The Python code to implement this algorithm is shown in Listing 2.3.

```
1  def parChecker(symbolString):
2      s = Stack()
3
4      balanced = True
5      index = 0
6
7      while index < len(symbolString) and balanced:
8          symbol = symbolString[index]
9          if symbol == "(":
10             s.push(symbol)
11         else:
12             if s.isEmpty():
13                 balanced = False
14             else:
15                 s.pop()
16
17         index = index + 1
18
19     if balanced and s.isEmpty():
20         return True
21     else:
22         return False
```

Listing 2.3: Simple Balanced Parentheses

This function, parChecker, assumes that a Stack class is available and returns a boolean result as to whether the string of parentheses is balanced. Note that the boolean variable balanced is initialized to True as there is no reason to assume otherwise at the start. If the current symbol is (, then it is pushed on the stack (lines 9–10). Note also in line 15 that pop simply removes a symbol from the stack. The returned value is not used since we know it must be an opening symbol seen earlier. At the end (lines 19–22), as long as the expression is balanced and the stack has been completely cleaned off, the string represents a correctly balanced sequence of parentheses.

2.3.5 Balanced Symbols (A General Case)

The balanced parentheses problem shown above is a specific case of a more general situation that arises in many programming languages. The general problem of balancing and nesting different kinds of opening and closing symbols properly occurs frequently. For example, in Python, square brackets, [and], are used for lists; curly braces, { and }, are used for dictionaries; and parentheses, (and), are used for tuples and arithmetic expressions. It is possible to mix symbols as long as each maintains its own open and close relationship. Strings of symbols such as

{ { ([ ] [ ]) } ( ) }

[[{ { (( )) } }]]

[ ] [ ] [ ] ( ) { }

are properly balanced in that not only does each opening symbol have a corresponding closing symbol, but the types of symbols match as well.

Compare those with the following strings that are not balanced:

([ )]

((( )]))

[{ ( )]

The simple parentheses checker from the previous section can easily be extended to handle these new types of symbols. Recall that each opening symbol is simply pushed on the stack to wait for the matching closing symbol to appear later in the sequence. When a closing symbol does appear, the only difference is that we must check to be sure that it correctly matches the type of the opening symbol on top of the stack. If the two symbols do not match, the string is not balanced. Once again, if the entire string is processed and nothing is left on the stack, the string is correctly balanced.

The Python program to implement this is shown in Listing 2.4. The only change appears in line 17 where we call a helper function to assist with symbol-matching. Each symbol that is removed from the stack must be checked to see that it matches the current closing symbol. If a mismatch occurs, the boolean variable `balanced` is set to `False`.

```python
def parChecker(symbolString):

    s = Stack()

    balanced = True
    index = 0

    while index < len(symbolString) and balanced:
        symbol = symbolString[index]
        if symbol in "([{":
            s.push(symbol)
        else:
            if s.isEmpty():
                balanced = False
            else:
                top = s.pop()
                if not matches(top,symbol):
                    balanced = False

        index = index + 1

    if balanced and s.isEmpty():
        return True
    else:
        return False

def matches(open,close):
    opens = "([{"
    closers = ")]}"

    return opens.index(open) == closers.index(close)
```

Listing 2.4: Balanced Symbols–A General Case

These two examples show that stacks are very important data structures for the processing of language constructs in computer science. Almost any notation you can think of has some type of nested symbol that must be matched in a balanced order. There are a number of other important uses for stacks in computer science. We will continue to explore them next.

2.3.6 Converting Decimal Numbers to Binary Numbers

In your study of computer science, you have probably been exposed in one way or another to the idea of a binary number. Binary representation is important in computer science since all values stored within a computer exist as a string of binary digits, a string of 0s and 1s. Without the ability to convert back and forth between common representations and binary numbers, we would need to interact with computers in very awkward ways.

Integer values are common data items. They are used in computer programs and computation all the time. We learn about them in math class and of course represent them using the decimal number system, or base 10. The decimal number 233_{10} and its corresponding binary equivalent 11101001_2 are interpreted respectively as

$$2 \times 10^2 + 3 \times 10^1 + 3 \times 10^0$$

and

$$1 \times 2^7 + 1 \times 2^6 + 1 \times 2^5 + 0 \times 2^4 + 1 \times 2^3 + 0 \times 2^2 + 0 \times 2^1 + 1 \times 2^0$$

But how can we easily convert integer values into binary numbers? The answer is an algorithm called "Divide by 2" that uses a stack to keep track of the digits for the binary result.

The Divide by 2 algorithm assumes that we start with an integer greater than 0. A simple iteration then continually divides the decimal number by 2 and keeps track of the remainder. The first division by 2 gives information as to whether the value is even or odd. An even value will have a remainder of 0. It will have the digit 0 in the ones place. An odd value will have a remainder of 1 and will have the digit 1 in the ones place. We think about building our binary number as a sequence of digits; the first remainder we compute will actually be the last digit in the sequence. As shown in Figure 2.5, we again see the reversal property that signals that a stack is likely to be the appropriate data structure for solving the problem.

The Python code in Listing 2.5 implements the Divide by 2 algorithm. The function `divideBy2` takes an argument that is a decimal number and repeatedly divides it by 2. Line 6 uses the built-in modulo operator, %, to extract the remainder and line 7 then pushes it on the stack. After the division process reaches 0, a binary string is constructed in lines 10–12. Line 10 creates an empty string. The binary digits are popped from the stack one at a time and appended to the right-hand end of the string. The binary string is then returned.

The algorithm for binary conversion can easily be extended to perform the conversion for any base. In computer science it is common to use a number of different encodings. The most common of these are binary, octal

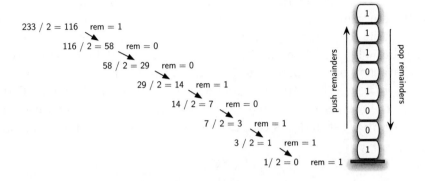

Figure 2.5: Decimal-to-Binary Conversion

```python
def divideBy2(decNumber):

    remstack = Stack()

    while decNumber > 0:
        rem = decNumber % 2
        remstack.push(rem)
        decNumber = decNumber / 2

    binString = ""
    while not remstack.isEmpty():
        binString = binString + str(remstack.pop())

    return binString
```

Listing 2.5: Decimal to Binary Conversion

(base 8), and hexadecimal (base 16).

The decimal number 233 and its corresponding octal and hexadecimal equivalents 351_8 and $E9_{16}$ are interpreted as

$$3 \times 8^2 + 5 \times 8^1 + 1 \times 8^0$$

and

$$15 \times 16^1 + 9 \times 16^0$$

The function `divideBy2` can be modified to accept not only a decimal value but also a base for the intended conversion. The "Divide by 2" idea is simply replaced with a more general "Divide by base." A new function called `baseConverter`, shown in Listing 2.6, takes a decimal number and any base between 2 and 16 as parameters. The remainders are still pushed onto the stack until the value being converted becomes 0. The same left-to-right string construction technique can be used with one slight change. Base 2 through base 10 numbers need a maximum of 10 digits, so the typical digit characters 0, 1, 2, 3, 4, 5, 6, 7, 8, and 9 work fine. The problem comes when we go beyond base 10. We can no longer simply use the remainders, as they are themselves represented as two-digit decimal numbers. Instead we need to create a set of digits that can be used to represent those remainders beyond 9.

```
def baseConverter(decNumber,base):

    digits = "0123456789ABCDEF"

    remstack = Stack()

    while decNumber > 0:
        rem = decNumber % base
        remstack.push(rem)
        decNumber = decNumber / base

    newString = ""
    while not remstack.isEmpty():
        newString = newString + digits[remstack.pop()]

    return newString
```

Listing 2.6: Conversion to Any Base

A solution to this problem is to extend the digit set to include some alphabet characters. For example, hexadecimal uses the ten decimal digits along with the first six alphabet characters for the 16 digits. To implement this, a digit string is created (line 3 in Listing 2.6) that stores the digits in their corresponding positions. 0 is at position 0, 1 is at position 1, A is at position 10, B is at position 11, and so on. When a remainder is removed from the stack, it can be used to index into the digit string and the correct resulting digit can be appended to the answer. For example, if the remainder 13 is removed from the stack, the digit D is appended to the resulting string.

2.3.7 Infix, Prefix and Postfix Expressions

When you write an arithmetic expression such as B * C, the form of the expression provides you with information so that you can interpret it correctly. In this case we know that the variable B is being multiplied by the variable C since the multiplication operator * appears between them in the expression. This type of notation is referred to as **infix** since the operator is *in between* the two operands that it is working on.

Consider another infix example, A + B * C. The operators + and * still appear between the operands, but there is a problem. Which operands do they work on? Does the + work on A and B or does the * take B and C? The expression seems ambiguous.

In fact, you have been reading and writing these types of expressions for a long time and they do not cause you any problem. The reason for this is that you know something about the operators + and *. Each operator has a **precedence** level. Operators of higher precedence are used before operators of lower precedence. The only thing that can change that order is the presence of parentheses. The precedence order for arithmetic operators places multiplication and division above addition and subtraction. If two operators of equal precedence appear, then a left-to-right ordering or associativity is used.

Let's interpret the troublesome expression A + B * C using precedence. B and C are multiplied first, and A is then added to that result. (A + B) * C would force the addition of A and B to be done first before the multiplication. In expression A + B + C, by precedence (via associativity), the leftmost + would be done first.

Although all this may be obvious to you, remember that computers need to know exactly what operators to perform and in what order. One way to write an expression that guarantees there will be no confusion with respect to the order of operations is to create what is called a **fully parenthesized** expression. This type of expression uses one pair of parentheses for each operator. The parentheses dictate the order of operations; there is no ambiguity. There is also no need to remember any precedence rules.

The expression A + B * C + D would be rewritten as ((A + (B * C)) + D) to show that the multiplication happens first, followed by the leftmost addition. A + B + C + D would be written as (((A + B) + C) + D) since the addition operations associate from left to right.

There are two other very important expression formats that may not seem obvious to you at first. Consider the infix expression A + B. What would happen if we moved the operator before the two operands? The resulting expression would be + A B. Likewise, we could move the operator to the end. We would get A B +. These look a bit strange.

These changes to the position of the operator with respect to the operands create two new expression formats, **prefix** and **postfix**. Prefix expression notation requires that all operators precede the two operands that they work on. Postfix, on the other hand, requires that its operators come after the corresponding operands. A few more examples should help to make this a bit clearer (see Table 2.2).

A + B * C would be written as + A * B C in prefix. The multiplication operator comes immediately before the operands B and C, denoting that * has precedence over +. The addition operator then appears before the A and the result of the multiplication.

In postfix, the expression would be A B C * +. Again, the order of operations is preserved since the * appears immediately after the B and the C, denoting that * has precedence, with + coming after. Although the operators moved and now appear either before or after their respective operands, the order of the operands stayed exactly the same relative to one another.

Infix Expression	Prefix Expression	Postfix Expression
A + B	+ A B	A B +
A + B * C	+ A * B C	A B C * +

Table 2.2: Examples of Infix, Prefix, and Postfix

Now consider the infix expression (A + B) * C. Recall that in this case, infix requires the parentheses to force the performance of the addition before the multiplication. However, when A + B was written in prefix, the addition symbol was simply moved before the operands, + A B. The result of this operation becomes the first operand for the multiplication. The multiplication symbol is moved in front of the entire expression, giving us * + A B C. Likewise, in postfix A B + forces the addition to happen first. The multiplication can be done to that result and the remaining operand C. The proper postfix expression is then A B + C *.

Consider these three expressions again (see Table 2.3). Something very important has happened. Where did the parentheses go? Why don't we need them in prefix and postfix? The answer is that the operators are no longer ambiguous with respect to the operands that they work on. Only infix notation requires the additional symbols. The order of operations within prefix and postfix expressions is completely determined by the position of the operator and nothing else. In many ways, this makes infix the least desirable notation to use.

Infix Expression	Prefix Expression	Postfix Expression
(A + B) * C	* + A B C	A B + C *

Table 2.3: An Expression with Parentheses

Table 2.4 shows some additional examples of infix expressions and the equivalent prefix and postfix expressions. Be sure that you understand how they are equivalent in terms of the order of the operations being performed.

2.3.7.1 Conversion of Infix Expressions to Prefix and Postfix

So far, we have used ad hoc methods to convert between infix expressions and the equivalent prefix and postfix expression notations. As you might expect, there are algorithmic ways to perform the conversion that allow any expression of any complexity to be correctly transformed.

The first technique that we will consider uses the notion of a fully parenthesized expression that was discussed earlier. Recall that A + B * C can be written as (A + (B * C)) to show explicitly that the multiplication has precedence over the addition. On closer observation, however, you can see that each parenthesis pair also denotes the beginning and the end of an operand pair with the corresponding operator in the middle.

Look at the right parenthesis in the subexpression (B * C) above. If we were to move the multiplication symbol to that position and remove the matching left parenthesis, giving us B C *, we would in effect have converted the subexpression to postfix notation. If the addition operator were also moved to its corresponding right parenthesis position and the matching left parenthesis were removed, the complete postfix expression would result (see Figure 2.6).

Infix Expression	Prefix Expression	Postfix Expression
A + B * C + D	+ + A * B C D	A B C * + D +
(A + B) * (C + D)	* + A B + C D	A B + C D + *
A * B + C * D	+ * A B * C D	A B * C D * +
A + B + C + D	+ + + A B C D	A B + C + D +

Table 2.4: Additional Examples of Infix, Prefix, and Postfix

Figure 2.6: Moving Operators to the Right for Postfix Notation

If we do the same thing but instead of moving the symbol to the position of the right parenthesis, we move it to the left, we get prefix notation (see Figure 2.7). The position of the parenthesis pair is actually a clue to the final position of the enclosed operator.

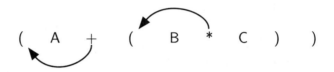

Figure 2.7: Moving Operators to the Left for Prefix Notation

So in order to convert an expression, no matter how complex, to either prefix or postfix notation, fully parenthesize the expression using the order of operations. Then move the enclosed operator to the position of either the left or the right parenthesis depending on whether you want prefix or postfix notation.

Here is a more complex expression: (A + B) * C - (D - E) * (F + G). Figure 2.8 shows the conversion to postfix and prefix notations.

2.3.7.2 General Infix-to-Postfix Conversion

We need to develop an algorithm to convert any infix expression to a postfix expression. To do this we will look closer at the conversion process.

Consider once again the expression A + B * C. As shown above, A B C * + is the postfix equivalent. We have already noted that the operands A, B, and C stay in their relative positions. It is only the operators that change position. Let's look again at the operators in the infix expression. The first operator that appears from left to right is +. However, in the postfix expression, + is at the end since the next operator, *, has precedence over

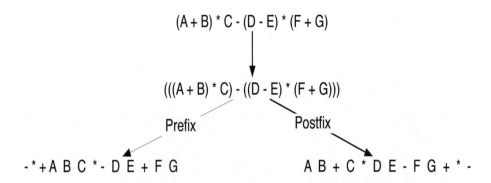

Figure 2.8: Converting a Complex Expression to Prefix and Postfix Notations

addition. The order of the operators in the original expression is reversed in the resulting postfix expression.

As we process the expression, the operators have to be saved somewhere since their corresponding right operands are not seen yet. Also, the order of these saved operators may need to be reversed due to their precedence. This is the case with the addition and the multiplication in this example. Since the addition operator comes before the multiplication operator and has lower precedence, it needs to appear after the multiplication operator is used. Because of this reversal of order, it makes sense to consider using a stack to keep the operators until they are needed.

What about (A + B) * C? Recall that A B + C * is the postfix equivalent. Again, processing this infix expression from left to right, we see + first. In this case, when we see *, + has already been placed in the result expression because it has precedence over * by virtue of the parentheses. We can now start to see how the conversion algorithm will work. When we see a left parenthesis, we will save it to denote that another operator of high precedence will be coming. That operator will need to wait until the corresponding right parenthesis appears to denote its position (recall the fully parenthesized technique). When that right parenthesis does appear, the operator can be popped from the stack.

As we scan the infix expression from left to right, we will use a stack to keep the operators. This will provide the reversal that we noted in the first example. The top of the stack will always be the most recently saved operator. Whenever we read a new operator, we will need to consider how that operator compares in precedence with the operators, if any, already on the stack.

Assume the infix expression is a string of tokens delimited by spaces. The operator tokens are *, /, +, and -, along with the left and right parentheses,

(and). The operand tokens are the single-character identifiers A, B, C, and so on. The following steps will produce a string of tokens in postfix order.

1. Create an empty stack called `opstack` for keeping operators. Create an empty list for output.

2. Convert the input infix string to a list by using the string method `split`.

3. Scan the token list from left to right.

   - If the token is an operand, append it to the end of the output list.
   - If the token is a left parenthesis, push it on the `opstack`.
   - If the token is a right parenthesis, pop the `opstack` until the corresponding left parenthesis is removed. Append each operator to the end of the output list.
   - If the token is an operator, *, /, +, or -, push it on the `opstack`. However, first remove any operators already on the `opstack` that have higher or equal precedence and append them to the output list.

4. When the input expression has been completely processed, check the `opstack`. Any operators still on the stack can be removed and appended to the end of the output list.

Figure 2.9 shows the conversion algorithm working on the expression A * B + C * D. Note that the first * operator is removed upon seeing the + operator. Also, + stays on the stack when the second * occurs, since multiplication has precedence over addition. At the end of the infix expression the stack is popped twice, removing both operators and placing + as the last operator in the postfix expression.

In order to code the algorithm in Python, we will use a dictionary called `prec` to hold the precedence values for the operators. This dictionary will map each operator to an integer that can be compared against the precedence levels of other operators (we have arbitrarily used the integers 3, 2, and 1). The left parenthesis will receive the lowest value possible. This way any operator that is compared against it will have higher precedence and will be placed on top of it. The complete conversion function is shown in Listing 2.7.

A few examples of execution in the Python shell are shown below.

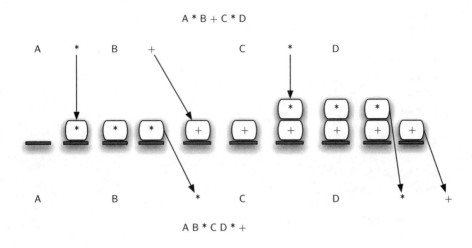

Figure 2.9: Converting A * B + C * D to Postfix Notation

```
>>> infixtopostfix("( A + B ) * ( C + D )")
'A B + C D + *'
>>> infixtopostfix("( A + B ) * C")
'A B + C *'
>>> infixtopostfix("A + B * C")
'A B C * +'
>>>
```

2.3.7.3   Postfix Evaluation

As a final stack example, we will consider the evaluation of an expression that is already in postfix notation. In this case, a stack is again the data structure of choice. However, as you scan the postfix expression, it is the operands that must wait, not the operators as in the conversion algorithm above. Another way to think about the solution is that whenever an operator is seen on the input, the two most recent operands will be used in the evaluation.

To see this in more detail, consider the postfix expression 4 5 6 * + . As you scan the expression from left to right, you first encounter the operands 4 and 5. At this point, you are still unsure what to do with them until you see the next symbol. Placing each on the stack ensures that they are available if an operator comes next.

In this case, the next symbol is another operand. So, as before, push it and check the next symbol. Now we see an operator, *. This means that the two most recent operands need to be used in a multiplication operation. By

```
 1  import string
 2  def infixToPostfix(infixexpr):
 3
 4      prec = {}
 5      prec["*"] = 3
 6      prec["/"] = 3
 7      prec["+"] = 2
 8      prec["-"] = 2
 9      prec["("] = 1
10
11      opStack = Stack()
12      postfixList = []
13
14      tokenList = infixexpr.split()
15
16      for token in tokenList:
17          if token in string.uppercase:
18              postfixList.append(token)
19          elif token == '(':
20              opStack.push(token)
21          elif token == ')':
22              topToken = opStack.pop()
23              while topToken != '(':
24                  postfixList.append(topToken)
25                  topToken = opStack.pop()
26
27          else:
28              while (not opStack.isEmpty()) and \
29                  (prec[opStack.peek()] >= prec[token]):
30                      postfixList.append(opStack.pop())
31
32              opStack.push(token)
33
34      while not opStack.isEmpty():
35          postfixList.append(opStack.pop())
36
37      return string.join(postfixList)
```

Listing 2.7: Converting Infix Expressions to Postfix Expressions

popping the stack twice, we can get the proper operands and then perform the multiplication (in this case getting the result 30).

We can now handle this result by placing it back on the stack so that it can be used as an operand for the later operators in the expression. When the final operator is processed, there will be only one value left on the stack. Pop and return it as the result of the expression. Figure 2.10 shows the stack contents as this entire example expression is being processed.

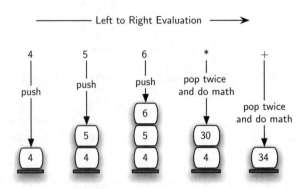

Figure 2.10: Stack Contents During Evaluation

Figure 2.11 shows a slightly more complex example, $7\,8 + 3\,2 + /$. There are two things to note in this example. First, the stack size grows, shrinks, and then grows again as the subexpressions are evaluated. Second, the division operation needs to be handled carefully. Recall that the operands in the postfix expression are in their original order since postfix changes only the placement of operators. When the operands for the division are popped from the stack, they are reversed. Since division is *not* a commutative operator, in other words 15/5 is not the same as 5/15, we must be sure that the order of the operands is not switched.

Assume the postfix expression is a string of tokens delimited by spaces. The operators are *, /, +, and - and the operands are assumed to be single-digit integer values. The output will be an integer result.

1. Create an empty stack called `operandStack`.

2. Convert the string to a list by using the string method `split`.

3. Scan the token list from left to right.

   - If the token is an operand, convert it from a string to an integer and push the value onto the `operandStack`.
   - If the token is an operator, *, /, +, or -, it will need two operands. Pop the `operandStack` twice. The first pop is the second operand

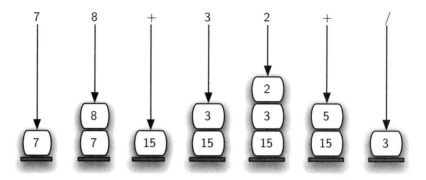

Figure 2.11: A More Complex Example of Evaluation

and the second pop is the first operand. Perform the arithmetic operation. Push the result back on the `operandStack`.

4. When the input expression has been completely processed, the result is on the stack. Pop the `operandStack` and return the value.

The complete function for the evaluation of postfix expressions is shown in Listing 2.8. To assist with the arithmetic, a helper function `doMath` is defined that will take two operands and an operator and then perform the proper arithmetic operation.

It is important to note that in both the postfix conversion and the postfix evaluation programs we assumed that there were no errors in the input expression. Using these programs as a starting point, you can easily see how error detection and reporting can be included. We leave this as an exercise at the end of the chapter.

2.4 Queues

We now turn our attention to another linear data structure. This one is called **queue**. Like stacks, queues are relatively simple and yet can be used to solve a wide range of important problems.

2.4.1 What Is a Queue?

A queue is an ordered collection of items where the addition of new items happens at one end, called the "rear," and the removal of existing items

```
 1  def postfixEval(postfixExpr):
 2
 3      operandStack = Stack()
 4
 5      tokenList = postfixExpr.split()
 6
 7      for token in tokenList:
 8          if token in "0123456789":
 9              operandStack.push(int(token))
10          else:
11              operand2 = operandStack.pop()
12              operand1 = operandStack.pop()
13              result = doMath(token,operand1,operand2)
14              operandStack.push(result)
15
16      return operandStack.pop()
17
18  def doMath(op, op1, op2):
19      if op == "*":
20          return op1 * op2
21      else:
22          if op == "/":
23              return op1 / op2
24          else:
25              if op == "+":
26                  return op1 + op2
27              else:
28                  return op1 - op2
```

Listing 2.8: Postfix Evaluation

occurs at the other end, commonly called the "front." As an element enters the queue it starts at the rear and makes its way toward the front, waiting until that time when it is the next element to be removed.

The most recently added item in the queue must wait at the end of the collection. The item that has been in the collection the longest is at the front. This ordering principle is sometimes called **FIFO, first-in first-out**. It is also known as "first-come first-served."

The simplest example of a queue is the typical line that we all participate in from time to time. We wait in a line for a movie, we wait in the check-out line at a grocery store, and we wait in the cafeteria line (so that we can pop the tray stack). Well-behaved lines, or queues, are very restrictive in that they have only one way in and only one way out. There is no jumping in the middle and no leaving before you have waited the necessary amount of time to get to the front. Figure 2.12 shows a simple queue of Python data objects.

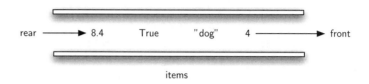

Figure 2.12: A Queue of Python Data Objects

Computer science also has common examples of queues. Our computer laboratory has 30 computers networked with a single printer. When students want to print, their print tasks "get in line" with all the other printing tasks that are waiting. The first task in is the next to be completed. If you are last in line, you must wait for all the other tasks to print ahead of you. We will explore this interesting example in more detail later.

In addition to printing queues, operating systems use a number of different queues to control processes within a computer. The scheduling of what gets done next is typically based on a queuing algorithm that tries to execute programs as quickly as possible and serve as many users as it can. Also, as we type, sometimes keystrokes get ahead of the characters that appear on the screen. This is due to the computer doing other work at that moment. The keystrokes are being placed in a queue-like buffer so that they can eventually be displayed on the screen in the proper order.

2.4.2 The Queue Abstract Data Type

The queue abstract data type is defined by the following structure and operations. A queue is structured, as described above, as an ordered collection of items which are added at one end, called the "rear," and removed from the other end, called the "front." Queues maintain a FIFO ordering property. The queue operations are given below.

- Queue() creates a new queue that is empty. It needs no parameters and returns an empty queue.

- enqueue(item) adds a new item to the rear of the queue. It needs the item and returns nothing.

- dequeue() removes the front item from the queue. It needs no parameters and returns the item. The queue is modified.

- isEmpty() tests to see whether the queue is empty. It needs no parameters and returns a boolean value.

- size() returns the number of items in the queue. It needs no parameters and returns an integer.

As an example, if we assume that q is a queue that has been created and is currently empty, then Table 2.5 shows the results of a sequence of queue operations. The queue contents are shown such that the front is on the right. 4 was the first item enqueued so it is the first item returned by dequeue.

Queue Operation	Queue Contents	Return Value
q.isEmpty()	[]	True
q.enqueue(4)	[4]	
q.enqueue('dog')	['dog',4,]	
q.enqueue(True)	[True,'dog',4]	
q.size()	[True,'dog',4]	3
q.isEmpty()	[True,'dog',3]	False
q.enqueue(8.4)	[8.4,True,'dog',4]	
q.dequeue()	[8.4,True,'dog']	4
q.dequeue()	[8.4,True]	'dog'
q.size()	[8.4,True]	2

Table 2.5: Example Queue Operations

2.4.3 Implementing a Queue in Python

It is again appropriate to create a new class for the implementation of the abstract data type queue. As before, we will use the power and simplicity of the list collection to build the internal representation of the queue.

We need to decide which end of the list to use as the rear and which to use as the front. The implementation shown in Listing 2.9 assumes that the rear is at position 0 in the list. This allows us to use the **insert** function on lists to add new elements to the rear of the queue. The **pop** operation can be used to remove the front element (the last element of the list).

The following interactive Python session shows the **Queue** class in action as we perform the sequence of operations from Table 2.5.

```
1  class Queue:
2      def __init__(self):
3          self.items = []
4
5      def isEmpty(self):
6          return self.items == []
7
8      def enqueue(self, item):
9          self.items.insert(0,item)
10
11      def dequeue(self):
12          return self.items.pop()
13
14      def size(self):
15          return len(self.items)
```

Listing 2.9: Queue Implementation in Python

```
>>> q=Queue()
>>> q.isEmpty()
True
>>> q.enqueue('dog')
>>> q.enqueue(4)
>>> q=Queue()
>>> q.isEmpty()
True
>>> q.enqueue(4)
>>> q.enqueue('dog')
>>> q.enqueue(True)
>>> q.size()
3
>>> q.isEmpty()
False
>>> q.enqueue(8.4)
>>> q.dequeue()
4
>>> q.dequeue()
'dog'
>>> q.size()
2
```

2.4.4 Simulation: Hot Potato

One of the typical applications for showing a queue in action is to simulate a real situation that requires data to be managed in a FIFO manner. To begin, let's consider the children's game Hot Potato. In this game (see Figure 2.13) children line up in a circle and pass an item from neighbor to neighbor as fast as they can. At a certain point in the game, the action is stopped and the child who has the item (the potato) is removed from the circle. Play continues until only one child is left.

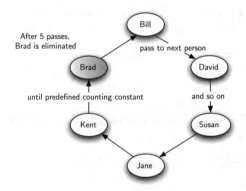

Figure 2.13: A Six Person Game of Hot Potato

This game is a modern-day equivalent of the famous Josephus problem. Based on a legend about the famous first-century historian Flavius Josephus, the story is told that in the Jewish revolt against Rome, Josephus and 39 of his comrades held out against the Romans in a cave. With defeat imminent, they decided that they would rather die than be slaves to the Romans. They arranged themselves in a circle. One man was designated as number one, and proceeding clockwise they killed every seventh man. Josephus, according to the legend, was among other things an accomplished mathematician. He instantly figured out where he ought to sit in order to be the last to go. When the time came, instead of killing himself, he joined the Roman side. You can find many different versions of this story. Some count every third man and some allow the last man to escape on a horse. In any case, the idea is the same.

We will implement a general simulation of Hot Potato. Our program will input a list of names and a constant, call it "N," to be used for counting. It will return the name of the last person remaining after repetitive counting by N. What happens to the names at that point is up to you.

To simulate the circle, we will use a queue (see Figure 2.14). Assume that the child holding the potato will be at the front of the queue. Upon passing the potato, the simulation will simply dequeue and then immediately enqueue that child, putting her at the end of the line. She will then wait until all the others have been at the front before it will be her turn again. After N dequeue/enqueue operations, the child at the front will be removed permanently and another cycle will begin. This process will continue until only one name remains (the size of the queue is 1).

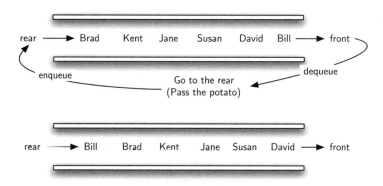

Figure 2.14: A Queue Implementation of Hot Potato

```
1  def hotPotato(namelist, N):
2
3      simqueue = Queue()
4      for name in namelist:
5          simqueue.enqueue(name)
6
7      while simqueue.size() > 1:
8          for i in range(N):
9              simqueue.enqueue(simqueue.dequeue())
10
11         simqueue.dequeue()
12
13     return simqueue.dequeue()
```

Listing 2.10: Hot Potato Simulation

The program is shown in Listing 2.10. A call to the `hotPotato` function using 7 as the counting constant shows:

```
>>> hotPotato(["Bill","David","Susan","Jane","Kent","Brad"],7)
'Susan'
>>>
```

Note that in this example the value of the counting constant is greater than the number of names in the list. This is not a problem since the queue acts like a circle and counting continues back at the beginning until the value is reached. Also, notice that the list is loaded into the queue such that the first name on the list will be at the front of the queue. Bill in this case is the first item in the list and therefore moves to the front of the queue. A variation of this implementation, described in the exercises, allows for a random counter.

2.4.5 Simulation: Printing Tasks

A more interesting simulation allows us to study the behavior of the printing queue described earlier in this section. Recall that as students send printing tasks to the shared printer, the tasks are placed in a queue to be processed in a first-come first-served manner. Many questions arise with this configuration. The most important of these might be whether the printer is capable of handling a certain amount of work. If it cannot, students will be waiting too long for printing and may miss their next class.

Consider the following situation in a computer science laboratory. On any average day about 10 students are working in the lab at any given hour. These students typically print up to twice during that time and the length of these tasks ranges from 1 to 20 pages. The printer in the lab is older, capable of processing 10 pages per minute of draft quality. The printer could be switched to give better quality, but then it would produce only five pages per minute. The slower printing speed could make students wait too long. What page rate should be used?

We could decide by building a simulation that models the laboratory. We will need to construct representations for students, printing tasks, and the printer (Figure 2.15). As students submit printing tasks, we will add them to a waiting list, a queue of print tasks attached to the printer. When the printer completes a task, it will look at the queue to see if there are any remaining tasks to process. Of interest for us is the average amount of time students will wait for their papers to be printed. This is equal to the average amount of time a task waits in the queue.

To model this situation we need to use some probabilities. For example, students may print a paper from 1 to 20 pages in length. If each length from 1 to 20 is equally likely, the actual length for a print task can be simulated

Lab Computers

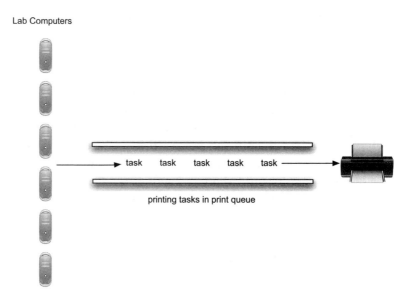

Figure 2.15: Computer Science Laboratory Printing Queue

by using a random number between 1 and 20 inclusive. This means that there is equal chance of any length from 1 to 20 appearing.

If there are 10 students in the lab and each prints twice, then there are 20 print tasks per hour on average. What is the chance that at any given second, a print task is going to be created? The way to answer this is to consider the ratio of tasks to time. Twenty tasks per hour means that on average there will be one task every 180 seconds:

$$\frac{20 \; tasks}{1 \; hour} \times \frac{1 \; hour}{60 \; minutes} \times \frac{1 \; minute}{60 \; seconds} = \frac{1 \; task}{180 \; seconds}$$

For every second we can simulate the chance that a print task occurs by generating a random number between 1 and 180 inclusive. If the number is 180, we say a task has been created. Note that it is possible that many tasks could be created in a row or we may wait quite a while for a task to appear. That is the nature of simulation. You want to simulate the real situation as closely as possible given that you know general parameters.

2.4.5.1   Main Simulation Steps

Here is the main simulation.

1. Create a queue of print tasks. Each task will be given a timestamp

upon its arrival. The queue is empty to start.

2. For each second (`currentSecond`):

- Does a new print task get created? If so, add it to the queue with the `currentSecond` as the timestamp.
- If the printer is not busy and if a task is waiting,
  - Remove the next task from the print queue and assign it to the printer.
  - Subtract the timestamp from the `currentSecond` to compute the waiting time for that task.
  - Append the waiting time for that task to a list for later processing.
  - Based on the number of pages in the print task, figure out how much time will be required.
- The printer now does one second of printing if necessary. It also subtracts one second from the time required for that task.
- If the task has been completed, in other words the time required has reached zero, the printer is no longer busy.

3. After the simulation is complete, compute the average waiting time from the list of waiting times generated.

2.4.5.2 Python Implementation

To design this simulation we will create classes for the three real-world objects described above: `Printer`, `Task`, and `PrintQueue`.

The `Printer` class (Listing 2.11) will need to track whether it has a current task. If it does, then it is busy (lines 13–17) and the amount of time needed can be computed from the number of pages in the task. The constructor will also allow the pages-per-minute setting to be initialized. The `tick` method decrements the internal timer and sets the printer to idle (line 11) if the task is completed.

The Task class (Listing 2.12) will represent a single printing task. When the task is created, a random number generator will provide a length from 1 to 20 pages. We have chosen to use the `randrange` function from the `random` module.

```python
class Printer:
    def __init__(self, pages):
        self.pagerate = pages
        self.currentTask = None
        self.timeRemaining = 0

    def tick(self):
        if self.currentTask != None:
            self.timeRemaining = self.timeRemaining - 1
            if self.timeRemaining == 0:
                self.currentTask = None

    def busy(self):
        if self.currentTask != None:
            return True
        else:
            return False

    def startNext(self, newtask):
        self.currentTask = newtask
        self.timeRemaining = newtask.getPages() \
                                  * 60/self.pagerate
```

Listing 2.11: Printer Queue Simulation–The Printer Class

```
>>> import random
>>> random.randrange(1,21)
18
>>> random.randrange(1,21)
8
>>>
```

Each task will also need to keep a timestamp to be used for computing waiting time. This timestamp will represent the time that the task was created and placed in the printer queue. The `waitTime` method can then be used to retrieve the amount of time spent in the queue before printing begins.

The main simulation (Listing 2.13) implements the algorithm described above. The `printQueue` object is an instance of our existing queue ADT. A boolean helper function, `newPrintTask`, decides whether a new printing task has been created. We have again chosen to use the `randrange` function from the `random` module to return a random integer between 1 and 180.

```
1  import random
2  class Task:
3      def __init__(self,time):
4          self.timestamp = time
5          self.pages = random.randrange(1,21)
6
7      def getStamp(self):
8          return self.timestamp
9
10     def getPages(self):
11         return self.pages
12
13     def waitTime(self, currenttime):
14         return currenttime - self.timestamp
```

Listing 2.12: Printer Queue Simulation–The Task Class

Print tasks arrive once every 180 seconds. By arbitrarily choosing 180 from the range of random integers (line 34), we can simulate this random event. The simulation function allows us to set the total time and the pages per minute for the printer.

When we run the simulation, we should not be concerned that the results are different each time. This is due to the probabilistic nature of the random numbers. We are interested in the trends that may be occurring as the parameters to the simulation are adjusted. Here are some results.

First, we will run the simulation for a period of 60 minutes (3,600 seconds) using a page rate of five pages per minute. In addition, we will run 10 independent trials.

```
>>>for i in range(10):
       simulation(3600,5)

Average Wait Time  34.82 seconds  Tasks Remaining 0
Average Wait Time 124.33 seconds  Tasks Remaining 2
Average Wait Time  49.44 seconds  Tasks Remaining 1
Average Wait Time 146.81 seconds  Tasks Remaining 2
Average Wait Time 301.46 seconds  Tasks Remaining 0
Average Wait Time  17.64 seconds  Tasks Remaining 0
Average Wait Time  59.46 seconds  Tasks Remaining 0
Average Wait Time 189.69 seconds  Tasks Remaining 2
Average Wait Time  85.44 seconds  Tasks Remaining 1
Average Wait Time  61.28 seconds  Tasks Remaining 0
```

```
1  from queue import *
2  from printer import *
3  from task import *
4
5  import random
6
7  def simulation(numSeconds, pagesPerMinute):
8
9      labprinter = Printer(pagesPerMinute)
10     printQueue = Queue()
11     waitingtimes = []
12
13     for currentSecond in range(numSeconds):
14
15       if newPrintTask():
16           task = Task(currentSecond)
17           printQueue.enqueue(task)
18
19       if (not labprinter.busy()) and \
20                 (not printQueue.isEmpty()):
21         nexttask = printQueue.dequeue()
22         waitingtimes.append( \
23             nexttask.waitTime(currentSecond))
24         labprinter.startNext(nexttask)
25
26       labprinter.tick()
27
28     averageWait=sum(waitingtimes)/float(len(waitingtimes))
29     print "Average Wait Time%6.2f seconds"%(averageWait),
30     print "Tasks Remaining %3d"%(printQueue.size())
31
32
33 def newPrintTask():
34     num = random.randrange(1,181)
35     if num == 180:
36         return True
37     else:
38         return False
```

Listing 2.13: Printer Queue Simulation–The Main Simulation

Now, we will adjust the page rate to 10 pages per minute, and run the 10 trials again.

```
>>>for i in range(10):
       simulation(3600,10)
```

```
Average Wait Time 19.33 seconds  Tasks Remaining 0
Average Wait Time  2.14 seconds  Tasks Remaining 0
Average Wait Time 14.47 seconds  Tasks Remaining 2
Average Wait Time 19.20 seconds  Tasks Remaining 0
Average Wait Time 11.96 seconds  Tasks Remaining 0
Average Wait Time 12.00 seconds  Tasks Remaining 0
Average Wait Time  5.31 seconds  Tasks Remaining 0
Average Wait Time  9.94 seconds  Tasks Remaining 0
Average Wait Time 15.12 seconds  Tasks Remaining 0
Average Wait Time 10.77 seconds  Tasks Remaining 0
```

2.4.5.3 Discussion

We were trying to answer a question about whether the current printer could handle the task load if it were set to print with a better quality but slower page rate. The approach we took was to write a simulation that modeled the printing tasks as random events of various lengths and arrival times.

The output above shows that with 5 pages per minute printing, the average waiting time varied from a low of 17 seconds to a high of 301 seconds (about 5 minutes). With a faster printing rate, the low value was 2 seconds with a high of only 19. In addition, in 5 out of 10 runs at 5 pages per minute there were print tasks still waiting in the queue at the end of the hour.

Therefore, we are perhaps persuaded that slowing the printer down to get better quality may not be a good idea. Students cannot afford to wait that long for their papers, especially when they need to be getting on to their next class. A five-minute wait would simply be too long.

This type of simulation analysis allows us to answer many questions, commonly known as "what if" questions. All we need to do is vary the parameters used by the simulation and we can simulate any number of interesting behaviors. For example,

- What if enrollment goes up and the average number of students increases by 20?

- What if it is Saturday and students are not needing to get to class? Can they afford to wait?

- What if the size of the average print task decreases since Python is such a powerful language and programs tend to be much shorter?

These questions could all be answered by modifying the above simulation. However, it is important to remember that the simulation is only as good as the assumptions that are used to build it. Real data about the number of print tasks per hour and the number of students per hour was necessary to construct a robust simulation.

2.5   Deque

We will conclude this introduction to basic data structures by looking at another variation on the theme of linear collections. However, unlike stack and queue, the deque (pronounced "deck") has very few restrictions. Also, be careful that you do not confuse the spelling of "deque" with the queue removal operation "dequeue."

2.5.1   What Is a Deque?

A **deque**, also known as a double-ended queue, is an ordered collection of items similar to the queue. It has two ends, a front and a rear, and the items remain positioned in the collection. What makes a deque different is the unrestrictive nature of adding and removing items. New items can be added at either the front or the rear. Likewise, existing items can be removed from either end. In a sense, this hybrid linear structure provides all the capabilities of stacks and queues in a single data structure. Figure 2.16 shows a deque of Python data objects.

It is important to note that even though the deque can assume many of the characteristics of stacks and queues, it does not require the LIFO and FIFO orderings that are enforced by those data structures. It is up to you to make consistent use of the addition and removal operations.

2.5.2   The Deque Abstract Data Type

The deque abstract data type is defined by the following structure and operations. A deque is structured, as described above, as an ordered collection of items where items are added and removed from either end, either front or rear. The deque operations are given below.

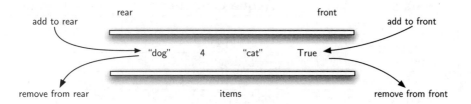

Figure 2.16: A Deque of Python Data Objects

- `Deque()` creates a new deque that is empty. It needs no parameters and returns an empty deque.

- `addFront(item)` adds a new item to the front of the deque. It needs the item and returns nothing.

- `addRear(item)` adds a new item to the rear of the deque. It needs the item and returns nothing.

- `removeFront()` removes the front item from the deque. It needs no parameters and returns the item. The deque is modified.

- `removeRear()` removes the rear item from the deque. It needs no parameters and returns the item. The deque is modified.

- `isEmpty()` tests to see whether the deque is empty. It needs no parameters and returns a boolean value.

- `size()` returns the number of items in the deque. It needs no parameters and returns an integer.

As an example, if we assume that d is a deque that has been created and is currently empty, then Table 2.6 shows the results of a sequence of deque operations. Note that the contents in front are listed on the right. It is very important to keep track of the front and the rear as you move items in and out of the collection as things can get a bit confusing.

2.5.3 Implementing a Deque in Python

As we have done in previous sections, we will create a new class for the implementation of the abstract data type deque. Again, the Python list will provide a very nice set of methods upon which to build the details of the

Deque Operation	Deque Contents	Return Value
d.isEmpty()	[]	True
d.addRear(4)	[4]	
d.addRear('dog')	['dog',4,]	
d.addFront('cat')	['dog',4,'cat']	
d.addFront(True)	['dog',4,'cat',True]	
d.size()	['dog',4,'cat',True]	4
d.isEmpty()	['dog',4,'cat',True]	False
d.addRear(8.4)	[8.4,'dog',4,'cat',True]	
d.removeRear()	['dog',4,'cat',True]	8.4
d.removeFront()	['dog',4,'cat']	True
d.size()	['dog',4,'cat']	3

Table 2.6: Examples of Deque Operations

deque. Our implementation (Listing 2.14) will assume that the rear of the deque is at position 0 in the list.

In removeFront we use the pop method to remove the last element from the list. However, in removeRear, the pop(0) method must remove the first element of the list. Likewise, we need to use the insert method (line 12) in addRear since the append method assumes the addition of a new element to the end of the list.

The following interactive Python session shows the Deque class in action as we perform the sequence of operations from Table 2.6.

```
>>> d=Deque()
>>> d.isEmpty()
True
>>> d.addRear(4)
>>> d.addRear('dog')
>>> d.addFront('cat')
>>> d.addFront(True)
>>> d.size()
4
>>> d.isEmpty()
False
>>> d.addRear(8.4)
>>> d.removeRear()
8.4
>>> d.removeFront()
```

```
1   class Deque:
2       def __init__(self):
3           self.items = []
4
5       def isEmpty(self):
6           return self.items == []
7
8       def addFront(self, item):
9           self.items.append(item)
10
11      def addRear(self, item):
12          self.items.insert(0,item)
13
14      def removeFront(self):
15          return self.items.pop()
16
17      def removeRear(self):
18          return self.items.pop(0)
19
20      def size(self):
21          return len(self.items)
```

Listing 2.14: Deque Implementation in Python

```
True
>>> d.size()
3
>>>
```

You can likely see many similarities to Python code already described for stacks and queues. This is to be expected given the common operations that appear for adding and removing items. Again, the important thing is to be certain that we know where the front and rear are assigned in the implementation.

2.5.4 Palindrome-Checker

An interesting problem that can be easily solved using the deque data structure is the classic palindrome problem. A **palindrome** is a string that reads the same forward and backward, for example, radar, toot, and madam. We would like to construct an algorithm to input a string of characters and check whether it is a palindrome.

The solution to this problem will use a deque to store the characters of the string. We will process the string from left to right and add each character to the rear of the deque. At this point, the deque will be acting very much like an ordinary queue. However, we can now make use of the dual functionality of the deque. The front of the deque will hold the first character of the string and the rear of the deque will hold the last character (see Figure 2.17).

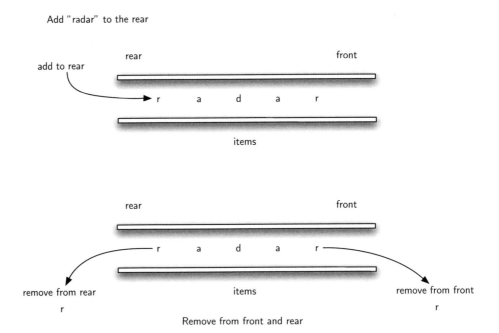

Figure 2.17: A Deque

Since we can remove both of them directly, we can compare them and continue only if they match. If we can keep matching first and the last items, we will eventually either run out of characters or be left with a deque of size 1 depending on whether the length of the original string was even or odd. In either case, the string must be a palindrome. The complete function for palindrome-checking appears in Listing 2.15.

A few sample invocations of the function should suffice to show how it works.

```
>>> palchecker("lsdkjfskf")
False
```

```
1   def palchecker(aString):
2
3       chardeque = Deque()
4
5       for ch in aString:
6           chardeque.addRear(ch)
7
8       stillEqual = True
9
10      while chardeque.size() > 1 and stillEqual:
11          first = chardeque.removeFront()
12          last = chardeque.removeRear()
13          if first != last:
14              stillEqual = False
15
16      return stillEqual
```

Listing 2.15: Palindrome Checker

```
>>> palchecker("toot")
True
>>> palchecker("radar")
True
>>>
```

2.6 Summary

- Linear data structures maintain their data in an ordered fashion.

- Stacks are simple data structures that maintain a LIFO, last-in first-out, ordering.

- The fundamental operations for a stack are push, pop, and isEmpty.

- Queues are simple data structures that maintain a FIFO, first-in first-out, ordering.

- The fundamental operations for a queue are enqueue, dequeue, and isEmpty.

- Prefix, infix, and postfix are all ways to write expressions.

- Stacks are very useful for designing algorithms to evaluate and translate expressions.

- Stacks can provide a reversal characteristic.

- Queues can assist in the construction of timing simulations.

- Simulations use random number generators to create a real-life situation and allow us to answer "what if" types of questions.

- Deques are data structures that allow hybrid behavior like that of stacks and queues.

- The fundamental operations for a deque are `addFront`, `addRear`, `removeFront`, `removeRear`, and `isEmpty`.

2.7 Key Terms

Balanced parentheses	Deque	First-in first-out (FIFO)
Infix	Last-in first-out (LIFO)	Linear data structure
Palindrome	Postfix	Precedence
Prefix	Queue	Simulation
Stack		

2.8 Discussion Questions

1. Convert the following values to binary using "divide by 2." Show the stack of remainders.

   - 17
   - 45
   - 96

2. Convert the following infix expressions to prefix (use full parentheses):

   - (A+B)*(C+D)*(E+F)
   - A+((B+C)*(D+E))

- A*B*C*D+E+F

3. Convert the above infix expressions to postfix (use full parentheses).

4. Convert the above infix expressions to postfix using the direct conversion algorithm. Show the stack as the conversion takes place.

5. Evaluate the following postfix expressions. Show the stack as each operand and operator is processed.

   - 2 3 * 4 +
   - 1 2 + 3 + 4 + 5 +
   - 1 2 3 4 5 * + * +

2.9 Programming Exercises

1. Modify the infix-to-postfix algorithm so that it can handle errors.

2. Modify the postfix evaluation algorithm so that it can handle errors.

3. Implement a direct infix evaluator that combines the functionality of infix-to-postfix conversion and the postfix evaluation algorithm. Your evaluator should process infix tokens from left to right and use two stacks, one for operators and one for operands, to perform the evaluation.

4. Turn your direct infix evaluator from the previous problem into a calculator.

5. Implement the Queue ADT, using a list such that the rear of the queue is at the end of the list.

6. Consider a real life situation. Formulate a question and then design a simulation that can help to answer it. Possible situations include:

   - Cars lined up at a car wash
   - Customers at a grocery store check-out
   - Airplanes taking off and landing on a runway
   - A bank teller

Be sure to state any assumptions that you make and provide any probabilistic data that must be considered as part of the scenario.

7. Modify the Hot Potato simulation to allow for a randomly chosen counting value so that each pass is not predictable from the previous one.

8. Implement a radix sorting machine. A radix sort for base 10 integers is a mechanical sorting technique that utilizes a collection of bins, one main bin and 10 digit bins. Each bin acts like a queue and maintains its values in the order that they arrive. The algorithm begins by placing each number in the main bin. Then it considers each value digit by digit. The first value is removed and placed in a digit bin corresponding to the digit being considered. For example, if the ones digit is being considered, 534 is placed in digit bin 4 and 667 is placed in digit bin 7. Once all the values are placed in the corresponding digit bins, the values are collected from bin 0 to bin 9 and placed back in the main bin. The process continues with the tens digit, the hundreds, and so on. After the last digit is processed, the main bin contains the values in order.

9. Another example of the parentheses matching problem comes from hypertext markup language (HTML). In HTML, tags exist in both opening and closing forms and must be balanced to properly describe a web document. This very simple HTML document:

```
<html>
   <head>
      <title>
         Example
      </title>
   </head>

   <body>
      <h1>Hello, world</h1>
   </body>
</html>
```

is intended only to show the matching and nesting structure for tags in the language. Write a program that can check an HTML document for proper opening and closing tags.

10. Extend the program from Listing 2.15 to handle palindromes with spaces. For example, I PREFER PI is a palindrome that reads the same forward and backward if you ignore the blank characters.

Chapter 3   Recursion

3.1 Objectives

The goals for this chapter are as follows:

- To understand that complex problems that may otherwise be difficult to solve may have a simple recursive solution.

- To learn how to formulate programs recursively.

- To understand and apply the three laws of recursion.

- To understand recursion as a form of iteration.

- To implement the recursive formulation of a problem.

- To understand how recursion is implemented by a computer system.

3.2 What Is Recursion?

Recursion is a method of solving problems that involves breaking a problem down into smaller and smaller subproblems until you get to a small enough problem that it can be solved trivially. Usually recursion involves a function calling itself. While it may not seem like much on the surface, recursion allows us to write elegant solutions to problems that may otherwise be very difficult to program.

3.2.1 Calculating the Sum of a List of Numbers

We will begin our investigation with a simple problem that you already know how to solve without using recursion. Suppose that you want to calculate the sum of a list of numbers such as: $[1, 3, 5, 7, 9]$. An iterative function that computes the sum is shown in Listing 3.1. The function uses an accumulator variable (theSum) to compute a running total of all the numbers in the list by starting with 0 and adding each number in the list.

```
def listsum(l):
    theSum = 0
    for i in l:
        theSum = theSum + i
    return theSum
```

Listing 3.1: The Iterative Sum Function

Pretend for a minute that you do not have **while** loops or **for** loops. How would you compute the sum of a list of numbers? If you were a mathematician you might start by recalling that addition is a function that is defined for two parameters, a pair of numbers. To redefine the problem from adding a list to adding pairs of numbers, we could rewrite the list as a fully parenthesized expression. Such an expression looks like this: $((((1 + 3) + 5) + 7) + 9)$. We can also parenthesize the expression the other way around, $(1 + (3 + (5 + (7 + 9))))$. Notice that the innermost set of parentheses, $(7 + 9)$, is a problem that we can solve without a loop or any special constructs. In fact, we can use the following sequence of simplifications to compute a final sum.

$$total = (1 + (3 + (5 + (7 + 9))))$$
$$total = (1 + (3 + (5 + 16)))$$
$$total = (1 + (3 + 21))$$
$$total = (1 + 24)$$
$$total = 25$$

How can we take this idea and turn it into a Python program? First, let's restate the sum problem in terms of Python lists. We might say the the sum of the list numList is the sum of the first element of the list (numList[0]), and the sum of the numbers in the rest of the list (numList[1:]). To state it in a functional form:

$$listSum(numList) = first(numList) + listSum(rest(numList))$$

In this equation $first(numList)$ returns the first element of the list and $rest(numList)$ returns a list of everything but the first element. This is easily expressed in Python as shown in Listing 3.2.

```
1  def listsum(l):
2      if len(l) == 1:
3          return l[0]
4      else:
5          return l[0] + listsum(l[1:])
```

Listing 3.2: Recursive listSum

There are a few key ideas in this listing to look at. First, on line 2 we are checking to see if the list is one element long. This check is crucial and is our escape clause from the function. The sum of a list of length 1 is trivial; it is just the number in the list. Second, on line 5 our function calls itself! This is the reason that we call the `listsum` algorithm recursive. A recursive function is a function that calls itself.

Figure 3.1 shows the series of **recursive calls** that are needed to sum the list $[1, 3, 5, 7, 9]$. You should think of this series of calls as a series of simplifications. Each time we make a recursive call we are solving a smaller problem, until we reach the point where the problem cannot get any smaller.

When we reach the point where the problem is as simple as it can get, we begin to piece together the solutions of each of the small problems until the initial problem is solved. Figure 3.2 shows the additions that are performed as `listsum` works its way backward through the series of calls. When `listsum` returns from the topmost problem, we have the solution to the whole problem.

3.2.2 The Three Laws of Recursion

Like the robots of Asimov, all recursive algorithms must obey three important laws:

1. A recursive algorithm must have a **base case**.

2. A recursive algorithm must change its state and move toward the base case.

3. A recursive algorithm must call itself, recursively.

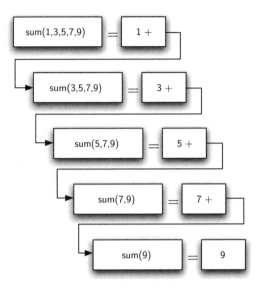

Figure 3.1: Series of Recursive Calls Adding a List of Numbers

Let's look at each one of these laws in more detail and see how it was used in the `listsum` algorithm. First, a base case is the condition that allows the algorithm to stop recursing. A base case is typically a problem that is small enough to solve directly. In the `listsum` algorithm the base case is a list of length 1.

To obey the second law, we must arrange for a change of state that moves the algorithm toward the base case. A change of state means that some data that the algorithm is using is modified. Usually the data that represents our problem gets smaller in some way. In the `listsum` algorithm our primary data structure is a list, so we must focus our state-changing efforts on the list. Since the base case is a list of length 1, a natural progression toward the base case is to shorten the list. This is exactly what happens on line 5 of Listing 3.2 when we call `listsum` with a shorter list.

The final law is that the algorithm must call itself. This is the very definition of recursion. Recursion is a confusing concept to many beginning programmers. As a novice programmer, you have learned that functions are good because you can take a large problem and break it up into smaller problems. The smaller problems can be solved by writing a function to solve each problem. When we talk about recursion it may seem that we are

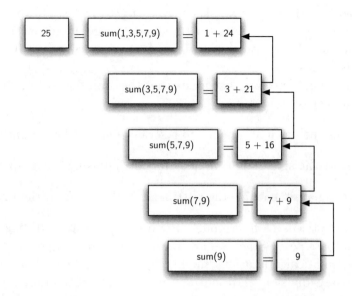

Figure 3.2: Series of Recursive Returns from Adding a List of Numbers

talking ourselves in circles. We have a problem to solve with a function, but that function solves the problem by calling itself! But the logic is not circular at all; the logic of recursion is an elegant expression of solving a problem by breaking it down into a smaller and easier problems.

In the remainder of this chapter we will look at more examples of recursion. In each case we will focus on designing a solution to a problem by using the three laws of recursion.

3.2.3 Converting an Integer to a String in Any Base

Suppose you want to convert an integer to a string in some base between binary and hexadecimal. For example, convert the integer 10 to its string representation in decimal as "10", or to its string representation in binary as "1010". While there are many algorithms to solve this problem, including the algorithm discussed in section 2.3.6, the recursive formulation of the problem is very elegant.

Let's look at a concrete example using base 10 and the number 769. Suppose we have a sequence of characters corresponding to the first 10 digits, like convString = "0123456789". It is easy to convert a number less than 10 to its string equivalent by looking it up in the sequence. For example, if the number is 9, then the string is `convString[9]` or `"9"`. If we can arrange to break up the number 769 into three single-digit numbers, 7, 6, and 9, then converting it to a string is simple. A number less than 10 sounds like a good base case.

Knowing what our base is suggests that the overall algorithm will involve three components:

1. Reduce the original number to a series of single-digit numbers.

2. Convert the single digit-number to a string using a lookup.

3. Concatenate the single-digit strings together to form the final result.

The next step is to figure out how to change state and make progress toward the base case. Since we are working with an integer, let's consider what mathematical operations might reduce a number. The most likely candidates are division and subtraction. While subtraction might work, it is unclear what we should subtract from what. Integer division with remainders gives us a clear direction. Let's look at what happens if we divide a number by the base we are trying to convert to.

Using integer division to divide 769 by 10, we get 76 with a remainder of 9. This gives us two good results. First, the remainder is a number less than our base that can be converted to a string immediately by lookup. Second, we get a number that is smaller than our original and moves us toward the base case of having a single number less than our base. Now our job is to convert 76 to its string representation. Again we will use integer division plus remainder to get results of 7 and 6 respectively. Finally, we have reduced the problem to converting 7, which we can do easily since it satisfies the base case condition of $n < base$, where $base = 10$. The series of operations we have just performed is illustrated in Figure 3.3. Notice that the numbers we want to remember are in the remainder boxes along the right side of the diagram.

Listing 3.3 shows the Python code that implements the algorithm outlined above for any base between 2 and 16.

Notice that in line 4 we check for the base case where n is less than the base we are converting to. When we detect the base case, we stop recursing and simply return the string from the `convertString` sequence. In line 7 we satisfy both the second and third laws–by making the recursive call and by reducing the problem size–using division.

Let's trace the algorithm again; this time we will convert the number 10 to its base 2 string representation (`"1010"`).

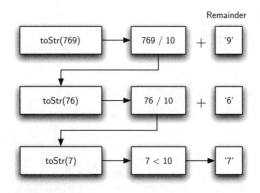

Figure 3.3: Converting an Integer to a String in Base 10

```
1  convertString = "0123456789ABCDEF"
2
3  def toStr(n,base):
4      if n < base:
5          return convertString[n]
6      else:
7          return toStr(n / base,base) + convertString[n%base]
```

Listing 3.3: Converting an Integer to a String in Base 2–16

Figure 3.4 shows that we get the results we are looking for, but it looks like the digits are in the wrong order. The algorithm works correctly because we make the recursive call first on line 7, then we add the string representation of the remainder. If we reversed returning the `convertString` lookup and returning the `toStr` call, the resulting string would be backward! But by delaying the concatenation operation until after the recursive call has returned, we get the result in the proper order. This should remind you of our discussion of stacks back in Chapter 2.

3.3 Stack Frames: Implementing Recursion

Suppose that instead of concatenating the result of the recursive call to `toStr` with the string from `convertString`, we modified our algorithm to push the strings onto a stack prior to making the recursive call. The code for this modified algorithm is shown in Listing 3.4.

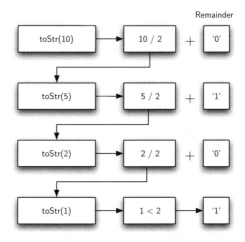

Figure 3.4: Converting the Number 10 to its Base 2 String Representation

```
1  convertString = "0123456789 ABCDEF"
2  rStack = Stack ()
3
4  def toStr (n,base):
5      if n < base:
6          rStack.push(convertString[n])
7      else:
8          rStack.push(convertString[n%base])
9          toStr(n / base,base)
```

Listing 3.4: Pushing the Strings onto a Stack

Each time we make a call to **toStr**, we push a character on the stack. Returning to the previous example we can see that after the fourth call to **toStr** the stack would look like Figure 3.5. Notice that now we can simply pop the characters off the stack and concatenate them into the final result, "1010".

The previous example gives us some insight into how Python implements a recursive function call. When a function is called in Python, a **stack frame** is allocated to handle the local variables of the function. When the function returns, the return value is left on top of the stack for the calling function to access. Figure 3.6 illustrates the call stack after the return statement on line 4.

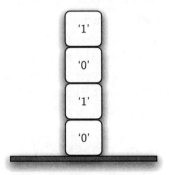

Figure 3.5: Strings Placed on the Stack During Conversion

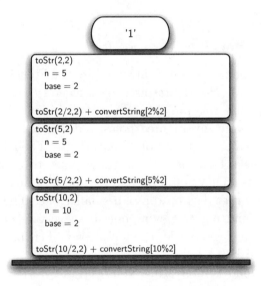

Figure 3.6: Call Stack Generated from `toStr(10,2)`

Notice that the call to `toStr(2/2,2)` leaves a return value of `"1"` on the stack. This return value is then used in place of the function call (`toStr(1,2)`) in the expression `"1" + convertString[2%2]`, which will leave the string `"10"` on the top of the stack. In this way, the Python call stack takes the place of the stack we used explicitly in Listing 3.4. In our list summing example, you can think of the return value on the stack taking the place of an accumulator variable.

The stack frames also provide a scope for the variables used by the function. Even though we are calling the same function over and over, each call creates a new scope for the variables that are local to the function.

If you keep this idea of the stack in your head, you will find it much easier to write a proper recursive function.

3.4 Complex Recursive Problems

In the previous section we looked at a couple of problems that are relatively easy to solve using either a recursive or an iterative solution. In this section we will look at some problems that are really difficult to solve using an iterative programming style but are very elegant and easy to solve using recursion.

3.4.1 Tower of Hanoi

The Tower of Hanoi puzzle was first invented by the French mathematician Edouard Lucas in 1883. He was inspired by a legend that tells of a Hindu temple where the puzzle was presented to young priests. At the beginning of time, the priests were given three poles and a stack of 64 gold disks, each disk a little smaller than the one beneath it. Their assignment was to transfer all 64 disks from one of the three poles to another, with two important constraints. They could only move one disk at a time, and they could never place a larger disk on top of a smaller one. The priests worked very efficiently, day and night, moving one disk every second. When they finished their work, the legend said, the temple would crumble into dust and the world would vanish.

Although the legend is interesting, you need not worry about the world ending any time soon. The number of moves required to correctly move a tower of 64 disks is $2^{64} - 1 = 18,446,744,073,709,551,615$. At a rate of one move per second, that is 584,942,417,355 years! Clearly there is more to this puzzle than meets the eye.

Figure 3.7 shows an example of a configuration of disks in the middle of a move from the first peg to the third. Notice that, as the rules specify, the disks on each peg are stacked so that smaller disks are always on top of the larger disks. If you have not tried to solve this puzzle before, you should try it now. You do not need fancy disks and poles–a pile of books or pieces of paper will work.

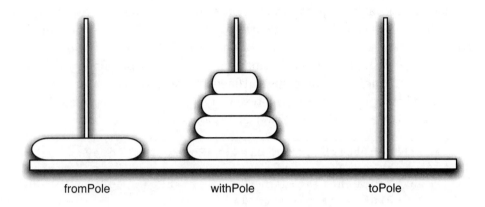

fromPole   withPole   toPole

Figure 3.7: An Example Arrangement of Disks for the Tower of Hanoi

How do we go about solving this problem recursively? How would you go about solving this problem at all? What is our base case? Let's think about this problem from the bottom up. Suppose you have a tower of five disks, originally on peg one. If you already knew how to move a tower of four disks to peg two, you could then easily move the bottom disk to peg three, and then move the tower of four from peg two to peg three. But what if you do not know how to move a tower of height four? Suppose that you knew how to move a tower of height three to peg three; then it would be easy to move the fourth disk to peg two and move the three from peg three on top of it. But what if you do not know how to move a tower of three? How about moving a tower of two disks to peg two and then moving the third disk to peg three, and then moving the tower of height two on top of it? But what if you still do not know how to do this? Surely you would agree that moving a single disk to peg three is easy enough, trivial you might even say. This sounds like a base case in the making.

Here is a high-level outline of how to move a tower from the starting pole, to the goal pole, using an intermediate pole:

1. Move a tower of height-1 to an intermediate pole, using the final pole.

2. Move the remaining disk to the final pole.

3. Move the tower of height-1 from the intermediate pole to the final pole using the original pole.

As long as we always obey the rule that the larger disks remain on the bottom of the stack, we can use the three steps above recursively, treating any larger disks as though they were not even there. The only thing missing from the outline above is the identification of a base case. The simplest Tower of Hanoi problem is a tower of one disk. In this case, we need move only a single disk to its final destination. A tower of one disk will be our base case. In addition, the steps outlined above move us toward the base case by reducing the height of the tower in steps 1 and 3. Listing 3.5 shows the Python code to solve the Tower of Hanoi puzzle.

```
def moveTower(height,fromPole, toPole, withPole):
    if height >= 1:
        moveTower(height-1,fromPole,withPole,toPole)
        moveDisk(fromPole,toPole)
        moveTower(height-1,withPole,toPole,fromPole)
```

Listing 3.5: Python Code for the Tower of Hanoi

Notice that the code in Listing 3.5 is almost identical to the English description. The key to the simplicity of the algorithm is that we make two different recursive calls, one on line 3 and a second on line 5. On line 3 we move all but the bottom disk on the initial tower to an intermediate pole. The next line simply moves the bottom disk to its final resting place. Then on line 5 we move the tower from the intermediate pole to the top of the largest disk. The base case is detected when the tower height is 0; in this case there is nothing to do, so the moveTower function simply returns. The important thing to remember about handling the base case this way is that simply returning from moveTower is what finally allows the moveDisk function to be called.

The function moveDisk, shown in Listing 3.6, is very simple. All it does is print out that it is moving a disk from one pole to another. If you type in and run the moveTower program you can see that it gives you a very efficient solution to the puzzle.

```
def moveDisk(fp,tp):
    print "moving disk from %d to %d\n" % (fp,tp)
```

Listing 3.6: Python Code to Move One Disk

Now that you have seen the code for both moveTower and moveDisk, you may be wondering why we do not have a data structure that explicitly keeps track of what disks are on what poles. Here is a hint: if you were

going to explicitly keep track of the disks, you would probably use three
`Stack` objects, one for each pole. The answer is that Python provides the
stacks that we need implicitly through the call stack, just like it did in the
`toStr` problem.

3.4.2 Sierpinski Triangle

A **fractal** is a geometric object which is rough or irregular at many different
levels of magnification, and so which appears to be "broken up" in a radical
way. Some of the best examples can be divided into parts, each of which
is similar to the original object. Fractals are said to possess infinite detail,
and they may have a self-similar structure that occurs at different levels of
magnification. A fractal can be generated by a repeating pattern, typically
using a recursive or iterative algorithm. The term fractal was coined in 1975
by Benoit Mandelbrot, from the Latin fractus or "broken."

Figure 3.8: The Sierpinski Triangle

One simple fractal that exhibits this property of self-similarity is the
Sierpinski triangle, shown in Figure 3.8. The Sierpinski triangle illustrates
a three-way recursive algorithm. The procedure for drawing a Sierpinski

triangle by hand is simple. Start with a single large triangle. Divide this large triangle into four new triangles by connecting the midpoint of each side. Ignoring the middle triangle that you just created, apply the same procedure to each of the three corner triangles. Each time you create a new set of triangles, you recursively apply this procedure to the three smaller corner triangles. You can continue to apply this procedure indefinitely if you have a sharp enough pencil. Before you continue reading, you may want to try drawing the Sierpinski triangle yourself, using the method described.

Since we can continue to apply the algorithm indefinitely, what is the base case? We will see that the base case is set arbitrarily as the number of times we want to divide the triangle into pieces. Sometimes we call this number the "degree" of the fractal. Each time we make a recursive call, we subtract 1 from the degree until we reach 0. When we reach a degree of 0, we stop making recursive calls. The code that generated the Sierpinski Triangle in Figure 3.8 is shown in Listing 3.7.

The program in Listing 3.7 follows the ideas outlined above. The first thing sierpinskiT does is draw the outer triangle. Next, there are three recursive calls, one for each of the new corner triangles we get when we connect the midpoints. In appendix A you will find a short list of some of the graphics packages available to use with Python.

Look at the code and think about the order in which the triangles will be drawn. While the exact order of the corners depends upon how the initial set is specified, let's assume that the corners are ordered lower left, top, lower right. Because of the way the sierpinskiT function calls itself, sierpinskiT works its way to the smallest allowed triangle in the lower-left corner, and then begins to fill out the rest of the triangles working back. Then it fills in the triangles in the top corner by working toward the smallest, topmost triangle. Finally, it fills in the lower-right corner, working its way toward the smallest triangle in the lower right.

Sometimes it is helpful to think of a recursive algorithm in terms of a diagram of function calls. Figure 3.9 shows that the recursive calls are always made going to the left. The active functions are outlined in black, and the inactive function calls are in gray. The farther you go toward the bottom of Figure 3.9, the smaller the triangles. The function finishes drawing one level at a time; once it is finished with the bottom left it moves to the bottom middle, and so on.

The sirepinskiT function relies heavily on the getMid function. getMid takes as arguments two endpoints and returns the point halfway between them. In addition, Listing 3.7 creates a filled polygon so that each new level of triangles is drawn in a different color.

```python
def sierpinskiT(points,level,win):
    colormap = ['blue','red','green','white',
                'yellow','violet','orange']
    p = Polygon(points)
    p.setFill(colormap[level])
    p.draw(win)
    if level > 0:
        sierpinskiT([points[0],
                    getMid(points[0],points[1]),
                    getMid(points[0],points[2])],level-1,win)
        sierpinskiT([points[1],
                    getMid(points[0],points[1]),
                    getMid(points[1],points[2])],level-1,win)
        sierpinskiT([points[2],
                    getMid(points[2],points[1]),
                    getMid(points[0],points[2])],level-1,win)

def getMid(p1,p2):
    return Point( ((p1.getX()+p2.getX()) / 2.0),
                  ((p1.getY()+p2.getY()) / 2.0) )

if __name__ == '__main__':
    win = GraphWin('st',500,500)
    win.setCoords(20,-10,80,50)
    myPoints = [Point(25,0),Point(50,43.3),Point(75,0)]
    sierpinskiT(myPoints,6,win)
```

Listing 3.7: Code for the Sierpinski Triangle

3.4.3 Cryptography and Modular Arithmetic

One of the most common uses of numerical computing today is in the field of cryptography. Each time you check your bank account, sign on to a secure web site to purchase something, or sign on to your computer, you are using cryptography. In a general sense, **cryptography** is concerned with encrypting and decrypting information that you do not want other people to see. In this section we will look at some functions that are used in everyday cryptographic programming. In practice there may be faster ways to implement these functions, but each of them has an interesting recursive implementation.

The algorithms in this section make use of Python's modulo operator (%). Remember that a % b is what is left over after a is divided by b, for

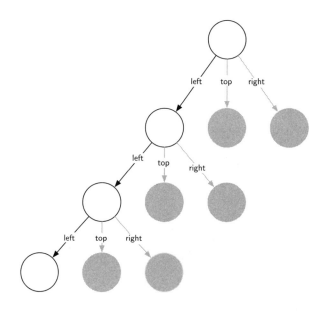

Figure 3.9: Building a Sierpinski Triangle

example 10 % 7 = 3. When we compute the result of any mathematical expression modulo 10, the only possible results are 0–9.

One of the earliest forms of cryptography used only simple modular arithmetic. Take the string `"uryybjbeyq"` for example. Can you guess what message is encrypted? Listing 3.8 shows you the function that produced the message. Look at the listing and see if you can figure it out.

```python
def encrypt(m):
    s = 'abcdefghijklmnopqrstuvwxyz'
    n = ''
    for i in m:
        j = (s.find(i)+13)%26
        n = n + s[j]
    return n
```

Listing 3.8: A Simple Modular Encryption Function

The `encrypt` function illustrates a form of encryption known as the "Caesar Cipher." It also goes by the name `rot13`, which is a bit more descriptive. `encrypt` simply takes each letter in the message and adds 13 to its ordinal position in the alphabet. If the position goes past the end of the alphabet, it wraps around. This wraparound function is easily accomplished using the modulo operator. In addition, since there are 26 letters in the alphabet, this function is symmetric. The symmetry allows us to use the function to encrypt and decrypt the same message. If you pass the string `"uryybjbeyg"` to the `encrypt` function it returns `"helloworld"`.

Rotations by amounts other than 13 are possible; however, they are not symmetric with respect to encrypting and decrypting. Asymmetry would require us to write a separate decrypt algorithm that subtracted the amount to rotate. In that case, we could generalize both the `encrypt` and `decrypt` functions to take the amount of rotation as a parameter. In cryptographic terms, the rotation parameter is called the "key" and would be the number of positions to rotate. Given the message and the key, the encryption and decryption algorithms can do their jobs. Listing 3.9 shows the decryption algorithm that takes the amount of rotation as a parameter. As an exercise you should be able to modify Listing 3.8 to accept a parameter that specifies a key.

```
1  def decrypt(m,k):
2      s = 'abcdefghijklmnopqrstuvwxyz'
3      n = ''
4      for i in m:
5          j = (s.find(i)26-k)%26
6          n = n + s[j]
7      return n
```

Listing 3.9: Decryption Using a Simple Key

Even if you keep the number k from everyone except the person you are sending the message to, this simple form of encryption is not going to stop anyone from stealing your secrets for very long. In the remainder of this section, we will build up to a much more secure form of encryption, the RSA public key encryption algorithm.

3.4.3.1 Modular Arithmetic Theorems

If two numbers, a and b, give the same remainder when divided by n, we say that a and b are "congruent modulo n", in shorthand we write $a \equiv b$ (mod n). The algorithms in this section make use of three important theorems:

1. If $a \equiv b \pmod{n}$ then $\forall c, a + c \equiv b + c \pmod{n}$.

2. If $a \equiv b \pmod{n}$ then $\forall c, ac \equiv bc \pmod{n}$.

3. If $a \equiv b \pmod{n}$ then $\forall p, p > 0, a^p \equiv b^p \pmod{n}$.

3.4.3.2   Modular Exponentiation

Suppose we wanted to know the last digit of $3^{1,254,906}$. Not only is that a large computation problem, but using Python's "infinite precision" integers the number has 598,743 digits! All we want to know is the value of the rightmost digit. There are really two problems here. First, how do we compute x^n efficiently? Second, how can we compute $x^n \pmod{p}$ without first calculating all 598,743 digits and then looking at the last one?

The answer to the second question is easy, given the third theorem from above.

1. Initialize `result` to 1.

2. Repeat **n** times:

    (a) Multiply `result` by **x**.

    (b) Apply modulo operation to `result`.

The above approach makes the computation simpler because we are keeping the result smaller rather than following it out to its full precision. However, we can do even better using a recursive approach.

$$x^n = \begin{cases} (x \cdot x)^{n/2} & \text{if n is even} \\ (x \cdot x^{n-1}) = x \cdot (x \cdot x)^{\lfloor n/2 \rfloor} & \text{if n is odd} \end{cases}$$

Remember that for a floating point number n the floor operation, $\lfloor n \rfloor$, results in the largest integer smaller than n. Python's integer division operator returns the floor of the result of the division, so we do not need to do anything special in our code to achieve the results we want. The above equation gives us a very nice recursive definition for computing x^n. All we need now is a base case. Recall that for any number x, $x^0 = 1$. Since we are reducing the size of our exponent in each recursive call, checking for the condition $n = 0$ is a good base case.

Notice that in the above equation both the even and odd cases include a factor of $(x \cdot x)^{\lfloor n/2 \rfloor}$, so we compute that unconditionally and store it in the variable `tmp`. Also note that since we are computing modulo **p** we still

```
1   def modexp(x,n,p):
2       if n == 0:
3           return 1
4       t = (x*x)%p
5       tmp = modexp(t,n/2,p)
6       if n%2 != 0:
7           tmp = (tmp * x) % p
8       return tmp
```

Listing 3.10: Recursive Definition for $x^n \pmod p$

apply the modulo operator at each step of the calculation. The solution in Listing 3.10 keeps the result size small and uses many fewer multiplications than a purely iterative approach.

3.4.3.3 The Greatest Common Divisor and Multiplicative Inverses

A **multiplicative inverse** of a positive integer x modulo m is any number a such that $ax \equiv 1 \pmod m$. For example let $x = 3$ and let $m = 7$, and $a = 5$ $3 * 5 = 15$ and $15 \% 7 = 1$, so 5 is a multiplicative inverse of 3 modulo 7. The idea of multiplicative inverses in the world of modulo arithmetic may seem very confusing at first. How did we select 5 in the previous example? Is 5 the only multiplicative inverse of 3 modulo 7? Do all numbers a have a multiplicative inverse for any given m?

Let's look at an example that may shed some light on the first question: how did we select 5 as the multiplicative inverse of 3, modulo 7? Look at the following Python session:

```
>>> for i in range(1,40):
...     if (3*i)%7 == 1:
...         print i
...
5
12
19
26
33
```

This little experiment tells us that there are many multiplicative inverses (modulo 7) for $x = 3$ and $m = 7$, namely $5, 12, 19, 26, 33$, and so on. Do

you notice anything interesting about the sequence? Each number in the
sequence is two less than a multiple of seven.

Do all pairs of numbers x and m, have a multiplicative inverse? Let's
look at another example. Consider $x = 4$ and $m = 8$. Plugging 4 and 8
into the loop in the previous example gives us no output. If we take out
the conditional and print out the results of $(4 * i)$ % 8, we get the sequence
(0,4,0,4,0,4...). Here we have a case where the remainder alternates between
0 and 4 repeatedly. Clearly the result is never going to be 1. How can we
know that ahead of time?

The answer is that a number x has a multiplicative inverse, modulo m,
if and only if m and x are relatively prime. Two numbers are relatively
prime if $gcd(m, x) = 1$. Recall that the greatest common divisor (**GCD**)is
the largest integer that divides both numbers. The next question is, how
can we compute the greatest common divisor for a pair of numbers?

Given two numbers a and b we can find the GCD by repeatedly sub-
tracting b from a until $a < b$. When $a < b$, we switch roles for a and b. At
some point $a - b$ becomes 0, so we swap a and b one more time. At that
point we have $gcd(a, 0) = a$. This algorithm was first described more than
2,000 years ago and is called **Euclid's Algorithm**.

In terms of recursive algorithm design, Euclid's Algorithm is very straightforward. The base case is when $b = 0$. There are two possibilities for a
recursive call: when $a < b$, we swap a and b and make a recursive call.
Otherwise, we can make a recursive call passing $a - b$ in place of a. Euclid's
Algorithm is shown in Listing 3.11.

```
1  def gcd(a,b):
2      if b == 0:
3          return a
4      elif a < b:
5          return gcd(b,a)
6      else:
7          return gcd(a-b,b)
```

Listing 3.11: Euclid's Algorithm for GCD

Although Euclid's Algorithm is quite easy to understand and program,
it is not as efficient as we would like, particularly if $a >> b$. Once again,
modular arithmetic comes to our rescue. Notice that the result of the last
subtraction (when $a-b < b$) is really the same as the remainder of a divided
by b. With that in mind, we can cut out all of the subtractions and combine
the swap of a and b in one recursive call. A revised algorithm is shown in
Listing 3.12.

```
1  def gcd(a,b):
2      if b == 0:
3          return a
4      else:
5          return gcd(b, a % b)
```

Listing 3.12: An Improved Euclid's Algorithm

Now that we have a way to know whether two numbers x and m will have a multiplicative inverse, our next task is to write an efficient algorithm to compute the inverse. Suppose that for any pair of numbers x and y we could compute both $gcd(x, y)$ and a pair of integers a and b such that $d = gcd(x, y) = ax + by$. For example, $1 = gcd(3, 7) = -2 * 3 + 1 * 7$, so here $a = -2$ and $b = 1$ are possible values for a and b. Rather than any numbers x and y, let's use m and x from our previous examples. Now we have $1 = gcd(m, x) = am + bx$. From the discussion at the beginning of this section we know that $bx = 1 \mod m$, so b is a multiplicative inverse of x modulo m.

We have reduced the problem of computing inverses to the problem of finding integers a and b that satisfy the equation $d = gcd(x, y) = ax + by$. Since we started this problem with the gcd algorithm, we can finish it with an extension of this algorithm as well. We will take two numbers $x >= y$ and return a tuple (d, a, b) such that $d = gcd(x, y)$ and $d = ax + by$. The extension to Euclid's Algorithm is shown in listing 3.13.

```
1  def ext_gcd(x,y):
2      if y == 0:
3          return(x,1,0)
4      else:
5          (d,a,b) = ext_gcd(y, x%y)
6          return(d,b,a-(x/y)*b)
```

Listing 3.13: Extended GCD

To understand how our extended GCD algorithm works, let's start with an example: let $x = 25$ and $y = 9$. Figure 3.10 illustrates the call and return values for the recursive function.

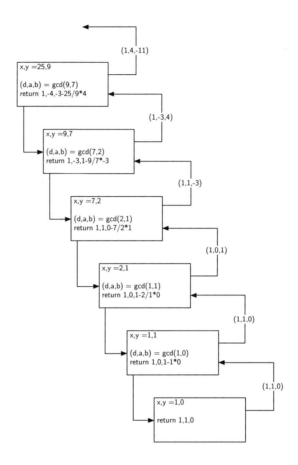

Figure 3.10: Call Tree for Extended GCD Algorithm

Notice that when we get the base case $y = 0$, we return $d = x$ just like the original Euclid's algorithm. However, we return two additional values $a = 1$ and $b = 0$. Together these three values satisfy the equation $d = ax + by$. If $y > 0$, then we recursively compute values (d, a, b) such that $d = gcd(y, x \bmod y)$ and $d = ay + b(x \bmod y)$. Like in the original algorithm, $d = gcd(x, y)$. But what about the other two values, a and b? We know that a and b must be integers, so let's call them A and B. Further, we know that $d = Ax + By$. To figure out what A and B should be, let's rearrange the equation as follows:

$$d = ay + b(x \mod y)$$
$$= ay + b(x - \lfloor x/y \rfloor y)$$
$$= bx + (a - \lfloor x/y \rfloor b)y$$

Note the substitution made in the second line, $x \mod y = x - \lfloor x/y \rfloor$. This is legal because this is how we would normally calculate the remainder of x / y ($x \mod y$). Looking at the rearranged equation, we can see that $A = b$ and $B = a - \lfloor x/y \rfloor b$. Notice that this is exactly what line 6 does! To check this, note that at each return step in the algorithm the return values satisfy the equation $d = ax + by$.

3.4.3.4 RSA Algorithm

Now we have all the tools we need to write the RSA encryption algorithm. The RSA algorithm is perhaps the easiest to understand of all the public-key encryption algorithms. Public-key cryptography was invented by Whitfield Diffie and Martin Hellman and independently by Ralph Merkle. The major contribution of public-key cryptography was the idea that keys could come in pairs: an encryption key to convert the plaintext message to ciphertext, and a decryption key to convert the ciphertext back to plaintext (or vice versa). The keys only work one way so that a message encrypted with the private key can only be decrypted with the public key, and vice versa.

RSA gets its security from the difficulty of factoring large numbers. The public and private keys are derived from a pair of large (100–200 digits) prime numbers. Since long integers are native to Python, this is a fun and easy algorithm to implement.

To generate the two keys, choose two large prime numbers p and q. Then compute the product

$$n = p \times q$$

The next step is to randomly choose the encryption key e such that e and $(p - 1) \cdot (q - 1)$ are relatively prime, that is the

$$gcd(e, (p - 1) \times (q - 1)) = 1$$

Finally, the decryption key d is simply the multiplicative inverse of e modulo $(p - 1) \times (q - 1)$. For this we can use our extended version of Euclid's Algorithm.

The numbers e and n taken together are the public key. The number d is the private key. Once we have computed n, e, and d, the original primes p and q are no longer needed. However, they should not be revealed.

To encrypt a message we simply use the equation $c = m^e \pmod n$. To decrypt the message we use $m = c^d \pmod n$.

It is easy to see that this works when you remember that d is the multiplicative inverse of $e \pmod n$.

$$
\begin{aligned}
c^d &= (m^e)^d \pmod n \\
&= m^{ed} \pmod n \\
&= m^1 \pmod n \\
&= m \pmod n
\end{aligned}
$$

Before we turn all these equations into Python code, we need to talk about a couple of other details. First, how do we take a text message like `'hello world'` and turn it into a number? The easiest way is to simply use the ASCII values associated with each character and concatenate all the numbers together. For example:

h	e	l	l	o		w	o	r	l	d
104	101	108	108	111	32	119	111	114	108	100

Putting all the numbers together gives us

$$m = 10410110810811132119111114108100$$

Python can handle this large number just fine. However, there are two reasons that real programs using RSA encryption break the message up into smaller chunks and encrypt each chunk. The first reason is performance. Even a relatively short email message, say 1k of text, will generate a number with 2,000 to 3,000 digits! If we raise that to a power of d which has 10 digits, we are talking about a very long number indeed!

The second reason for breaking the message into chunks is the restriction that $m \leq n$. We must be sure that the message has a unique representation modulo n. With binary data, choose the largest power of two less than n. For example, let's choose p and q to be 5563, and 8191. So $n = 5563 \times 8191 = 45,566,533$. To keep the integer value of our chunks less than m, we will divide up our word into chunks that are seven digits long (one less than the number of digits in m):

$$m_1 = 1041011$$
$$m_2 = 0810811$$
$$m_3 = 1321191$$
$$m_4 = 1111410$$
$$m_5 = 8100$$

Now let's choose a value for e. We can select values randomly and use the GCD algorithm to test them against $(p-1) \times (q-1) = 45552780$. Remember that we are looking for an e that is relatively prime to 45,552,780. The number 1,471 will work nicely for this example.

$$d = ext\_gcd(45552780, 1471)$$
$$= -11705609$$
$$= 45552780 - 11705609$$
$$= 33847171$$

Let's use this information to encrypt the first chunk of our message:

$$c = 1041011^{1471} \pmod{45566533} = 28713328$$

To check our work, let's decrypt c to make sure we recover the original value:

$$m = 28713328^{33847171} \pmod{45566533} = 1041011$$

The remaining chunks of the message can be encrypted using the same procedure and sent all together as the encrypted message.

Finally, let's look at three Python functions. RSAgenkeys creates a public and private key, given p and q. RSAencrypt takes a message, the public key, and n and returns an encrypted version of the message. RSAdecrypt takes the encrypted message, the private key, and n and returns the original message.

Here is an example of running the code above. The two helper functions toChunks, and chunksToPlain are left as an exercise for the reader.

```
>>> e,d,n = RSAgenKeys(5563,8191)
>>> c = RSAencrypt('goodbye girl',e,n)
>>> c
[24656386L, 1510798L, 10814034L, 20328277L, 5134670L, 41536563L]
```

```
1  def RSAgenKeys(p,q):
2      n = p * q
3      pqminus = (p-1) * (q-1)
4      e = int(random.random() * n)
5      while gcd(pqminus,e) != 1:
6          e = int(random.random() * n)
7      d,a,b = ext_gcd(pqminus,e)
8      if b < 0:
9          d = pqminus+b
10     else:
11         d = b
12     return ((e,d,n))
13
14 def RSAencrypt(m,e,n):
15     ndigits = len(str(n))
16     chunkSize = ndigits - 1
17     chunks = toChunks(m,chunkSize)
18     encList = []
19     for messChunk in chunks:
20         print messChunk
21         c = modexp(messChunk,e,n)
22         encList.append(c)
23     return encList
24
25 def RSAdecrypt(clist,d,n):
26     rList = []
27     for c in clist:
28         m = modexp(c,d,n)
29         rList.append(m)
30     return rList
```

Listing 3.14: RSA Algorithm

```
>>> m = RSAdecrypt(c,d,n)
>>> m
[1031111L, 1110009L, 8121101L, 321031L, 511410L, 8L]
>>> chunksToPlain(m)
'goodbye girl'
```

3.5 Summary

In this chapter we have looked at examples of several recursive algorithms. These algorithms were chosen to expose you to several different problems where recursion is an effective problem-solving technique. The key points to remember from this chapter are as follows:

- All recursive algorithms must have a base case.

- A recursive algorithm must change its state and make progress toward the base case.

- A recursive algorithm must call itself (recursively).

- Recursion can take the place of iteration in some cases.

- Recursive algorithms often map very naturally to a formal expression of the problem you are trying to solve.

- Recursion is not always the answer. Sometimes a recursive solution may be more computationally expensive than an alternative algorithm.

3.6 Key Terms

Base case	Cryptography
Decrypt	Encrypt
Euclid's Algorithm	Fractal
Greatest common divisor (GCD)	Multiplicative inverse
Public-Key Cryptography	Recursion
Recursive call	Stack frame

3.7 Discussion Questions

1. Draw a call stack for the Towers of Hanoi problem. Assume that you start with a stack of three disks.

2. In order to keep your lucky number (18) a secret, you have decided to employ the RSA encryption algorithm. Pick two prime numbers greater than 500 and use them to encrypt your lucky number.

3.8 Programming Exercises

1. Write a recursive function to compute the factorial of a number.

2. Write a recursive function to reverse a list.

3. Given a representation of a maze that looks like the following:

```
11 22
++ +++ +++++++++++++++
+    +   ++ ++
        +          +++++ ++
+ +     ++  ++++ + + ++
+ +   + + ++     +++   +
            ++   ++   + +
+++++ + +        ++   + +
+++++ +++  + +  ++    +
+              + +  S +   +
+++++ +  + + +      + +
+++++++++ +++++++++++
```

A + character indicates a wall in the maze, and the S indicates the starting point. Write a program that reads in a maze like the one above, and prints a path out of the maze. For example, one path out of the maze looks like the following:

```
++ +++0+++++++++++++++
+    + 00++ ++
        +000      +++++ ++
+ +     ++0 ++++ + + ++
+ +   + +0++ 00 +++   +
            00++00++  + +
+++++ + + 00000++   + +
+++++ +++  + +00++    +
+             + + 0S +   +
+++++ +  + + + 00  + +
+++++++++ +++++++++++
```

4. Write a recursive function to compute the Fibonacci sequence. How does the performance of the recursive function compare to that of an iterative version?

5. Implement a solution to the Towers of Hanoi using three stacks to keep track of the disks.

6. Using a graphics package, write a recursive program to display a Hilbert curve.

7. Using a graphics package, write a recursive program to display a Koch snowflake.

8. Write a program to solve the following problem: You have two jugs: a 4-gallon jug and a 3-gallon jug. Neither of the jugs have markings on them. There is a pump that can be used to fill the jugs with water. How can you get exactly two gallons of water in the 4-gallon jug?

9. Generalize the problem above so that the parameters to your solution include the sizes of each jug and the final amount of water to be left in the larger jug.

10. Write a program that solves the following problem: Three missionaries and three cannibals come to a river and find a boat that holds two people. Everyone must get across the river to continue on the journey. However, if the cannibals ever outnumber the missionaries on either bank, the missionaries will be eaten. Find a series of crossings that will get everyone safely to the other side of the river.

11. Pascal's triangle is a number triangle with numbers arranged in staggered rows such that

$$a_{nr} = \frac{n!}{r!(n-r)!}$$

This equation is the equation for a binomial coefficient. You can build Pascal's triangle by adding the two numbers that are diagonally above a number in the triangle. An example of Pascal's triangle is shown below.

```
          1
        1   1
      1   2   1
    1   3   3   1
  1   4   6   4   1
```

Write a program that prints out Pascal's triangle. Your program should accept a parameter that tells how many rows of the triangle to print.

Chapter 4   Algorithm Analysis

4.1   Objectives

- To understand why algorithm analysis is important.

- To be able to use "Big-O" to describe execution time.

- To understand how different algorithms for solving the same problem can be compared to one another.

- To be able to explain and implement sequential search and binary search.

- To be able to explain and implement selection sort, bubble sort, merge sort, quick sort, insertion sort, and shell sort.

- To understand the idea of hashing as a search technique.

- To understand when and how Python objects use hashing.

4.2   What Is Algorithm Analysis?

It is very common for beginning computer science students to compare their programs with one another. You may have noticed that it is not uncommon for computer programs to look very similar, especially the simple ones. An interesting question often arises. When two programs solve the same problem but look different, is one program better than the other?

In order to answer this question, we need to remember that there is an important difference between a program and the underlying algorithm that the program is representing. As we stated in Chapter 1, an algorithm is a

129

generic, step-by-step list of instructions for solving a problem. It is a method for solving any instance of the problem such that given a particular input, the algorithm produces the desired result. A program, on the other hand, is an algorithm that has been encoded into some programming language. There may be many programs for the same algorithm, depending on the programmer and the programming language being used.

To explore this difference further, consider the function shown in Listing 4.1. This function solves a familiar problem, computing the sum of the first n integers. The algorithm uses the idea of an accumulator variable that is initialized to 0. The solution then iterates through the n integers, adding each to the accumulator.

```
1  def sumOfN(n):
2      theSum = 0
3      for i in range(1,n+1):
4          theSum = theSum + i
5
6      return theSum
```

Listing 4.1: Summation of the First n Integers

Now look at the function in Listing 4.2. At first glance it may look strange, but upon further inspection you can see that this function is essentially doing the same thing as the previous one. The reason this is not obvious is poor coding. We did not use good identifier names to assist with readability, and we used an extra assignment statement during the accumulation step that was not really necessary.

```
1  def foo(tom):
2      fred = 0
3      for bill in range(1,tom+1):
4          barney = bill
5          fred = fred + barney
6
7      return fred
```

Listing 4.2: Another Summation of the First n Integers

The question we raised earlier asked whether one function is better than another. The answer depends on your criteria. The function sumOfN is certainly better than the function foo if you are concerned with readability. In fact, you have probably seen many examples of this in your introductory programming course since one of the goals there is to help you write programs that are easy to read and easy to understand. In this course, however, we are also interested in characterizing the algorithm itself. (We certainly hope that you will continue to strive to write readable, understandable code.)

Algorithm analysis is concerned with comparing algorithms based upon the amount of computing resources that each algorithm uses. We want to be able to consider two algorithms and say that one is better than the other because it is more efficient in its use of those resources or perhaps because it simply uses fewer. From this prospective, the two functions above seem very similar. They both use essentially the same algorithm to solve the summation problem.

At this point, it is important to think more about what we really mean by computing resources. There are two different ways to look at this. First, we can consider the amount of space or memory an algorithm requires to solve the problem. Unfortunately, there is often not much one can do about this. The amount of space required by a problem is typically dictated by the problem instance itself. Every so often, however, there are algorithms that have very specific space requirements and in those cases we will be very careful to explain the variations.

Second, we can analyze and compare algorithms based on the amount of time they require to execute. This measure is sometimes referred to as the "execution time" or "running time" of the algorithm. One way we can measure the execution time for the function sumOfN is to do a benchmark analysis. This means that we will track the actual time required for the program to compute its result. In Python, we can benchmark a function by noting the starting time and ending time with respect to the system we are using. In the time module there is a function called clock that will return the current system clock time. By calling this function twice, at the beginning and at the end, and then computing the difference, we can get an exact number of seconds (fractions in most cases) for execution.

Listing 4.3 shows the original sumOfN function with the timing calls embedded before and after the summation. The function returns a tuple consisting of the result and the amount of time (in seconds) required for the calculation. If we perform invocations of the function, each computing the sum of the first 100 integers, we get the following:

```
>>> print "Sum is %d required %f10 seconds"%sumOfN(100)
Sum is 5050 required 0.00006810 seconds
>>> print "Sum is %d required %f10 seconds"%sumOfN(100)
Sum is 5050 required 0.00007010 seconds
```

```
1  import time
2
3  def sumOfN(n):
4      start = time.clock()
5
6      theSum = 0
7      for i in range(1,n+1):
8          theSum = theSum + i
9
10     end = time.clock()
11
12     return theSum,end-start
```

Listing 4.3: Timing the Summation

In fact, if we continue to execute this function, we discover that it takes on average about 0.000069 seconds to sum the first 100 integers. What if we run the function adding the first 1,000 integers?

```
>>>print "Sum is %d required %f10 seconds"%sumOfN(1000)
Sum is 500500 required 0.00046610 seconds
>>>print "Sum is %d required %f10 seconds"%sumOfN(1000)
Sum is 500500 required 0.00047310 seconds
>>>
```

Again, the time required for each run, although longer, is very consistent, averaging 0.00047 seconds. For n equal to 10,000 we get:

```
>>> print "Sum is %d required %f10 seconds"%sumOfN(10000)
Sum is 50005000 required 0.00478410 seconds
>>> print "Sum is %d required %f10 seconds"%sumOfN(10000)
Sum is 50005000 required 0.00449010 seconds
```

In this case, the average turns out to be 0.0046 seconds.

Now consider Listing 4.4, which shows a different means of solving the summation problem. This function, sumOfN3, takes advantage of a closed equation

$$\sum_{i=1}^{n} i = \frac{(n)(n+1)}{2}$$

to compute the sum of the first n integers without iterating.

If we do the same benchmark measurement for sumOfN3, using the three different values for n (100, 1,000, and 10,000), we get the following results:

```
1   def sumOfN3(n):
2       return (n*(n+1))/2
```

Listing 4.4: Summation Without Iteration

```
>>> print "Sum is %d required %f10 seconds"%sumOfN3(100)
Sum is 5050 required 0.00000910 seconds
>>> print "Sum is %d required %f10 seconds"%sumOfN3(100)
Sum is 5050 required 0.00000910 seconds
>>> print "Sum is %d required %f10 seconds"%sumOfN3(1000)
Sum is 500500 required 0.00000810 seconds
>>> print "Sum is %d required %f10 seconds"%sumOfN3(1000)
Sum is 500500 required 0.00000910 seconds
>>> print "Sum is %d required %f10 seconds"%sumOfN3(10000)
Sum is 50005000 required 0.00000910 seconds
>>> print "Sum is %d required %f10 seconds"%sumOfN3(10000)
Sum is 50005000 required 0.00000810 seconds
>>> print "Sum is %d required %f10 seconds"%sumOfN3(10000)
Sum is 50005000 required 0.00000910 seconds
>>>
```

There are two important things to notice about this output. First, the times recorded above are shorter than any of the previous examples. Second, they are very consistent no matter what the value of n. It appears that sumOfN3 is hardly impacted by the number of integers being added.

But what does this benchmark really tell us? Intuitively, we can see that the iterative solutions seem to be doing more work since some program steps are being repeated. This is likely the reason it is taking longer. Also, the time required for the iterative solution seems to increase as we increase the value of n. However, there is a problem. If we ran the same function on a different computer or used a different programming language, we would likely get different results. It could take even longer to perform sumOfN3 if the computer were older.

We need a better way to characterize these algorithms with respect to execution time. The benchmark technique computes the actual time to execute. It does not really provide us with a useful measurement, because it is dependent on a particular machine, program, time of day, compiler, and programming language. Instead, we would like to have a characterization that is independent of the program or computer being used. This measure would then be useful for judging the algorithm alone and could be used to compare algorithms across implementations.

4.2.1 Big-O Notation

When trying to characterize an algorithm's efficiency in terms of execution time, independent of any particular program or computer, it is important to quantify the number of operations or steps that the algorithm will require. If each of these steps is considered to be a basic unit of computation, then the execution time for an algorithm can be expressed as the number of steps required to solve the problem.

A good basic unit of computation for comparing the summation algorithms shown earlier might be to count the number of assignment statements performed to compute the sum. In the function sumOfN, the number of assignment statements is 1 $(theSum = 0)$ plus the value of n (the number of times we perform $theSum = theSum + i$). We can denote this by a function, call it T, where $T(n) = 1 + n$. The parameter n is often referred to as the "size of the problem," and we can read this as "$T(n)$ is the time it takes to solve a problem of size n, namely $1+n$ steps."

In the summation functions given above, it makes sense to use the number of terms in the summation to denote the size of the problem. We can then say that the sum of the first 100,000 integers is a bigger instance of the summation problem than the sum of the first 1,000. Because of this, it might seem reasonable that the time required to solve the larger case would be greater than for the smaller case. Our goal then is to show how the algorithm's execution time changes with respect to the size of the problem.

Computer scientists prefer to take this analysis technique one step further. It turns out that the exact number of operations is not as important as determining the most dominant part of the $T(n)$ function. In other words, as the problem gets larger, some portion of the $T(n)$ function tends to overpower the rest. This dominant term is what, in the end, is used for comparison. The **order of magnitude** function describes the part of $T(n)$ that increases the fastest as the value of n increases. Order of magnitude is often called **Big-O** notation (for "order") and written as $O(f(n))$. It provides a useful approximation to the actual number of steps in the computation. The function $f(n)$ provides a simple representation of the dominant part of the original $T(n)$.

In the above example, $T(n) = 1 + n$. As n gets large, the constant 1 will become less and less significant to the final result. If we are looking for an approximation for $T(n)$, then we can drop the 1 and simply say that the running time is $O(n)$. It is important to note that the 1 is certainly significant for $T(n)$. However, as n gets large, our approximation will be just as accurate without it.

As another example, suppose that for some algorithm, the exact number of steps is $T(n) = 5n^2 + 27n + 1005$. When n is small, say 1 or 2, the constant 1005 seems to be the dominant part of the function. However, as n gets larger, the n^2 term becomes the most important. In fact, when n is really large, the other two terms become insignificant in the role that they play in determining the final result. Again, to approximate $T(n)$ as n gets large, we can ignore the other terms and focus on $5n^2$. In addition, the coefficient 5 becomes insignificant as n gets large. We would say then that the function $T(n)$ has an order of magnitude $f(n) = n^2$, or simply that it is $O(n^2)$.

More formally, we say that a function $T(n)$ is $O(f(n))$ if there exist two constants, c_0 and n_0, such that $T(n) \leq c_0 f(n)$ for all $n \geq n_0$. For example, $T(n) = 3n + 2$ is $O(n)$ since $3n + 2 \leq 4n$ for all $n \geq 2$. Likewise, we can say that $T(n) = 2n^2 + 6n + 3$ is $O(n^2)$ since $2n^2 + 6n + 3 \leq 3n^2$ for all $n \geq 6$.

A number of very common order of magnitude functions will come up over and over as you study algorithms. These are shown in Table 4.1. In order to decide which of these functions is the dominant part of any $T(n)$ function, we must see how they compare with one another as n gets large. Figure 4.1 shows graphs of the common functions from Table 4.1. Notice that when n is small, the functions are not very well defined with respect to one another. It is hard to tell which is dominant. However, as n grows, there is a definite relationship and it is easy to see how they compare with one another.

f(n)	Name
1	Constant
$\log n$	Logarithmic
n	Linear
$n \log n$	Log Linear
n^2	Quadratic
n^3	Cubic
2^n	Exponential

Table 4.1: Common Functions for Big-O

As a final example, suppose that we have the fragment of Python code shown in Listing 4.5. Although this program does not really do anything, it is instructive to see how we can take actual code and analyze performance.

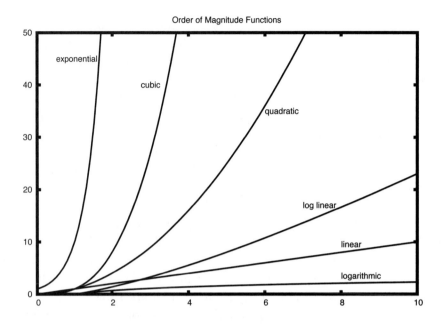

Figure 4.1: Plot of Common Big-O Functions

The number of assignment operations is the sum of four terms. The first term is the constant 3, representing the three assignment statements at the start of the fragment. The second term is $3n^2$, since there are three statements that are performed n^2 times due to the nested iteration. The third term is $2n$, two statements iterated n times. Finally, the fourth term is the constant 1, representing the final assignment statement. This gives us $T(n) = 3 + 3n^2 + 2n + 1 = 3n^2 + 2n + 4$. By looking at the exponents, we can easily see that the n^2 term will be dominant and therefore this fragment of code is $O(n^2)$. Note that all of the other terms as well as the coefficient on the dominant term can be ignored as n grows larger.

4.2.2 An Anagram Example

A good example problem for showing algorithms with different orders of magnitude is the classic anagram problem for strings. One string is an anagram of another if the second is simply a rearrangement of the first. For

```
1  a=5
2  b=6
3  c=10
4  for i in range(n):
5      for j in range(n):
6          x = i * i
7          y = j * j
8          z = i * j
9  for k in range(n):
10     w = a*k + 45
11     v = b*b
12 d = 33
```

Listing 4.5: Example Python Code

example, 'heart' and 'earth' are anagrams. The strings 'python' and 'typhon' are anagrams as well. For the sake of simplicity, we will assume that the two strings in question are of equal length and that they are made up of symbols from the set of 26 lowercase alphabetic characters. Our goal is to write a boolean function that will take two strings and return whether they are anagrams.

4.2.2.1 Solution 1: Checking Off

Our first solution to the anagram problem will check to see that each character in the first string actually occurs in the second. If it is possible to "checkoff" each character, then the two strings must be anagrams. Checking off a character will be accomplished by replacing it with the special Python value None. However, since strings in Python are immutable, the first step in the process will be to convert the second string to a list. Each character from the first string can be checked against the characters in the list and if found, checked off by replacement. Listing 4.6 shows this function.

To analyze this algorithm, we need to note that each of the n characters in s1 will cause an iteration through up to n characters in the list from s2. Each of the n positions in the list will be visited once to match a character from s1. The number of visits then becomes the sum of the integers from 1 to n. We stated earlier that this can be written as

$$\sum_{i=1}^{n} i = \frac{n(n+1)}{2} = \frac{1}{2}n^2 + \frac{1}{2}n$$

```
 1  def anagramSolution1(s1,s2):
 2      alist = list(s2)
 3
 4      pos1 = 0
 5      stillOK = True
 6
 7      while pos1 < len(s1) and stillOK:
 8          pos2 = 0
 9          found = False
10          while pos2 < len(alist) and not found:
11              if s1[pos1] == alist[pos2]:
12                  found = True
13              else:
14                  pos2 = pos2 + 1
15
16          if found:
17              alist[pos2] = None
18          else:
19              stillOK = False
20
21          pos1 = pos1 + 1
22
23      return stillOK
```

Listing 4.6: Checking Off

As n gets large, the n^2 term will dominate the n term and the $\frac{1}{2}$ can be ignored. Therefore, this solution is $O(n^2)$.

4.2.2.2 Solution 2: Sort and Compare

Another solution to the anagram problem will make use of the fact that even though s1 and s2 are different, they are anagrams only if they consist of exactly the same characters. So, if we begin by sorting each string alphabetically, from a to z, we will end up with the same string if the original two strings are anagrams. Listing 4.7 shows this solution. Again, in Python we can use the built-in sort method on lists by simply converting each string to a list at the start.

At first glance you may be tempted to think that this algorithm is $O(n)$, since there is one simple iteration to compare the n characters after the sorting process. However, the two calls to the Python sort method are

```
1   def anagramSolution2(s1,s2):
2       alist1 = list(s1)
3       alist2 = list(s2)
4
5       alist1.sort()
6       alist2.sort()
7
8       pos = 0
9       matches = True
10
11      while pos < len(s1) and matches:
12          if alist1[pos]==alist2[pos]:
13              pos = pos + 1
14          else:
15              matches = False
16
17      return matches
```

Listing 4.7: Sort and Compare

not without their own cost. As we will see later in this chapter, sorting is typically either $O(n^2)$ or $O(n \log n)$, so the sorting operations dominate the iteration. In the end, this algorithm will have the same order of magnitude as that of the sorting process.

4.2.2.3 Solution 3: Brute Force

A brute force technique for solving a problem typically tries to exhaust all possibilities. For the anagram problem, we can simply generate a list of all possible anagrams for s1 and then see if s2 occurs. However, there is a difficulty with this approach. When generating all possible anagrams for s1, there are n possible first characters, $n-1$ possible characters for the second position, $n-2$ for the third, and so on. The total number of anagrams for a string of length n is $n * (n - 1) * (n - 2) * ... * 3 * 2 * 1$, which is $n!$.

It turns out that $n!$ grows even faster than 2^n as n gets large. In fact, if s1 were 20 characters long, there would be $20! = 2432902008176640000$ possible anagrams. If we processed one possibility every second, it would still take us 77,146,816,596 years to go through the entire list. This is probably not going to be a good solution.

Solution 4: Count and Compare

Our final solution to the anagram problem takes advantage of the fact that any two anagrams will have the same number of a's, the same number of b's, the same number of c's, and so on. In order to decide whether two strings are anagrams, we will first count the number of times each character occurs. Since there are 26 possible characters, we can use a list of 26 counters, one for each possible character. Each time we see a particular character, we will increment the counter at that position. In the end, if the two lists of counters are identical, the strings must be anagrams. Listing 4.8 shows this solution.

```
1  def anagramSolution4(s1,s2):
2      c1 = [0]*26
3      c2 = [0]*26
4
5      for i in range(len(s1)):
6          pos = ord(s1[i])-ord('a')
7          c1[pos] = c1[pos] + 1
8
9      for i in range(len(s2)):
10         pos = ord(s2[i])-ord('a')
11         c2[pos] = c2[pos] + 1
12
13     j = 0
14     stillOK = True
15     while j<26 and stillOK:
16         if c1[j]==c2[j]:
17             j = j + 1
18         else:
19             stillOK = False
20
21     return stillOK
```

Listing 4.8: Count and Compare

Again, the solution has a number of iterations. However, unlike the first solution, none of them are nested. The first two iterations used to count the characters are both based on n. The third iteration, comparing the two lists of counts, always takes 26 steps since there are 26 possible characters in the strings. Adding it all up gives us $T(n) = 2n + 26$ steps. That is $O(n)$. We have found a linear order of magnitude algorithm for solving this problem.

Before leaving this example, we need to say something about space requirements. Although the last solution was able to run in linear time, it could only do so by using additional storage to keep the two lists of character counts. In other words, this algorithm sacrificed space in order to gain time. The other solutions did not require any additional space beyond that used for the original strings.

This is a common occurrence. On many occasions you will need to make decisions between time and space trade-offs. In this case, the amount of extra space is not significant. However, if the underlying alphabet had millions of characters, there would be more concern. As a computer scientist, when given a choice of algorithms, it will be up to you to determine the best use of computing resources given a particular problem.

4.3 Searching

We will now turn our attention to some of the most common problems that arise in computing, those of searching and sorting. In this section we will study searching. We will return to sorting later in the chapter. Searching is the algorithmic process of finding a particular item in a collection of items. A search typically answers either `True` or `False` as to whether the item is present. On occasion it may be modified to return where the item is found. For our purposes here, we will simply concern ourselves with the question of membership.

In Python, there is a very easy way to ask whether an item is in a list of items. We use the `in` operator.

```
>>> 15 in [3,5,2,4,1]
False
>>> 3 in [3,5,2,4,1]
True
>>>
```

Even though this is easy to write, an underlying process must be carried out to answer the question. It turns out that there are many different ways to search for the item. What we are interested in here is how these algorithms work and how they compare to one another.

4.3.1 The Sequential Search

When data items are stored in a collection such as a list, we say that they have a linear or sequential relationship. Each data item is stored in a position relative to the others. In Python lists, these relative positions are the index values of the individual items. Since these index values are ordered, it is possible for us to visit them in sequence. This process gives rise to our first searching technique, the **sequential search**.

Figure 4.2 shows how this search works. Starting at the first item in the list, we simply move from item to item, following the underlying sequential ordering until we either find what we are looking for or run out of items. If we run out of items, we have discovered that the item we were searching for was not present.

Figure 4.2: Sequential Search of a List of Integers

The Python implementation for this algorithm is shown in Listing 4.9. The function needs the list and the item we are looking for and returns a boolean value as to whether it is present. The boolean variable `found` is initialized to `False` and is assigned the value `True` if we discover the item in the list.

```python
def sequentialSearch(alist, item):
    pos = 0
    found = False

    while pos < len(alist) and not found:
        if alist[pos] == item:
            found = True
        else:
            pos = pos+1

    return found
```

Listing 4.9: Sequential Search of an Unordered List

To analyze searching algorithms, we need to decide on a basic unit of computation. Recall that this is typically the common step that must be repeated in order to solve the problem. For searching, it makes sense to count the number of comparisons performed. Each comparison may or may not discover the item we are looking for. In addition, we make another assumption here. The list of items is not ordered in any way. The items have been placed randomly into the list. In other words, the probability that the item we are looking for is in any particular position is exactly the same for each position of the list.

If the item is not in the list, the only way to know it is to compare it against every item present. If there are n items, then the sequential search requires n comparisons to discover that the item is not there. In the case where the item is in the list, the analysis is not so straightforward. There are actually three different scenarios that can occur. In the best case we will find the item in the first place we look, at the beginning of the list. We will need only one comparison. In the worst case, we will not discover the item until the very last comparison, the nth comparison.

What about the average case? On average, we will find the item about halfway into the list; that is, we will compare against $\frac{n}{2}$ items. Recall, however, that as n gets large, the coefficients, no matter what they are, become insignificant in our approximation, so the complexity of the sequential search, is $O(n)$. Table 4.2 summarizes these results.

	Best Case	**Worst Case**	**Average Case**
item is present	1	n	$\frac{n}{2}$
item is not present	n	n	n

Table 4.2: Comparisons Used in a Sequential Search of an Unordered List

We assumed earlier that the items in our collection had been randomly placed so that there is no relative order between the items. What would happen to the sequential search if the items were ordered in some way? Would we be able to gain any efficiency in our search technique?

Assume that the list of items was constructed so that the items were in ascending order, from low to high. If the item we are looking for is present in the list, the chance of it being in any one of the n positions is still the same as before. We will still have the same number of comparisons to find the item. However, if the item is not present there is a slight advantage. Figure 4.3 shows this process as the algorithm looks for the item 50. Notice that items are still compared in sequence until 54. At this point, however, we know something extra. Not only is 54 not the item we are looking for, but no other elements beyond 54 can work either since the list is sorted. In this case, the algorithm does not have to continue looking through all of the items to report that the item was not found. It can stop immediately. Listing 4.10 shows this variation of the sequential search function.

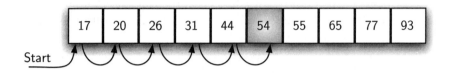

Figure 4.3: Sequential Search of an Ordered List of Integers

```
1  def orderedSequentialSearch(alist, item):
2      pos = 0
3      found = False
4      stop = False
5      while pos < len(alist) and not found and not stop:
6          if alist[pos] == item:
7              found = True
8          else:
9              if alist[pos] > item:
10                 stop = True
11             else:
12                 pos = pos+1
13
14     return found
```

Listing 4.10: Sequential Search of an Ordered List

Table 4.3 summarizes these results. Note that in the best case we might discover that the item is not in the list by looking at only one item. On average, we will know after looking through only $\frac{n}{2}$ items. However, this technique is still $O(n)$. In summary, a sequential search is improved by ordering the list only in the case where we do not find the item.

	Best Case	Worst Case	Average Case
item is present	1	n	$\frac{n}{2}$
item is not present	1	n	$\frac{n}{2}$

Table 4.3: Comparisons Used in Sequential Search of an Ordered List

4.3.2 | The Binary Search

It is possible to take greater advantage of the ordered list if we are clever with our comparisons. In the sequential search, when we compare against the first item, there are at most $n - 1$ more items to look through if the first item is not what we are looking for. Instead of searching the list in sequence, a **binary search** will start by examining the middle item. If that item is the one we are searching for, we are done. If it is not the correct item, we can use the ordered nature of the list to eliminate half of the remaining items. If the item we are searching for is greater than the middle item, we know that the entire lower half of the list as well as the middle item can be eliminated from further consideration. The item, if it is in the list, must be in the upper half.

We can then repeat the process with the upper half. Start at the middle item and compare it against what we are looking for. Again, we either find it or split the list in half, therefore eliminating another large part of our possible search space. Figure 4.4 shows how this algorithm can quickly find the value 54. The complete function is shown in Listing 4.11.

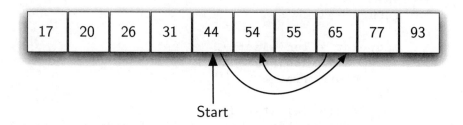

Figure 4.4: Binary search of an ordered list of integers

Before we move on to the analysis, we should note that this algorithm is a great example of a divide and conquer strategy described earlier in Chapter 3. When we perform a binary search of a list, we first check the middle item. If the item we are searching for is less than the middle item, we can simply perform a binary search of the left half of the original list. Likewise, if the item is greater, we can perform a binary search of the right half. Either way, this is a recursive call to the binary search function passing a smaller list. Listing 4.12 shows this recursive version.

To analyze the binary search algorithm, we need to recall that each comparison eliminates about half of the remaining items from consideration.

```
1  def binarySearch(alist, item):
2      first = 0
3      last = len(alist)-1
4      found = False
5
6      while first<=last and not found:
7          midpoint = (first + last)/2
8          if alist[midpoint] == item:
9              found = True
10         else:
11             if item < alist[midpoint]:
12                 last = midpoint-1
13             else:
14                 first = midpoint+1
15
16     return found
```

Listing 4.11: Binary Search of an Ordered List

```
1  def binarySearch(alist, item):
2      if len(alist) == 0:
3          return False
4      else:
5          midpoint = len(alist)/2
6          if alist[midpoint]==item:
7              return True
8          else:
9              if item<alist[midpoint]:
10                 return binarySearch(alist[:midpoint],item)
11             else:
12                 return binarySearch(alist[midpoint+1:],item)
```

Listing 4.12: A Binary Search–Recursive Version

What is the maximum number of comparisons this algorithm will require to check the entire list? If we start with n items, about $\frac{n}{2}$ items will be left after the first comparison. After the second comparison, there will be about $\frac{n}{4}$. Then $\frac{n}{8}$, $\frac{n}{16}$, and so on. How many times can we split the list? Table 4.4 helps us to see the answer.

When we split the list enough times, we end up with a list that has just one item. Either that is the item we are looking for or it is not. Either way,

Comparisons	Approximate Number of Items Left
1	$\frac{n}{2}$
2	$\frac{n}{4}$
3	$\frac{n}{8}$
...	
i	$\frac{n}{2^i}$

Table 4.4: Tabular Analysis for a Binary Search

we are done. The number of comparisons necessary to get to this point is i where $\frac{n}{2^i} = 1$. Solving for i gives us $i = \log n$. The maximum number of comparisons is logarithmic with respect to the number of items in the list. Therefore, the binary search is $O(\log n)$.

Even though a binary search is generally better than a sequential search, it is important to note that for small values of n, the additional cost of sorting is probably not worth it. In fact, we should always consider whether it is cost effective to take on the extra work of sorting to gain searching benefits. If we can sort once and then search many times, the cost of the sort is not so significant. However, for large lists, sorting even once can be so expensive that simply performing a sequential search from the start may be the best choice.

4.3.3   Hashing

In previous sections we were able to make improvements in our search algorithms by taking advantage of information about where items are stored in the collection with respect to one another. For example, by knowing that a list was ordered, we could search in logarithmic time using a binary search. In this section we will attempt to go one step further by building a data structure that can be searched in $O(1)$ time. This concept is referred to as **hashing**.

In order to do this, we will need to know even more about where the items might be when we go to look for them in the collection. If every item is where it should be, then the search can use a single comparison to discover the presence of an item. We will see, however, that this is typically not the case.

A **hash table** is a collection of items which are stored in such a way as to make it easy to find them later. Each position of the hash table, often called a **slot**, can hold an item and is named by an integer value starting at 0. For example, we will have a slot named 0, a slot named 1, a slot named 2, and so on. Initially, the hash table contains no items so every slot is empty. We can implement a hash table by using a list with each element initialized to the special Python value None. Figure 4.5 shows a hash table of size $m = 11$. In other words, there are m slots in the table, named 0 through 10.

Figure 4.5: Hash Table with 11 Empty Slots

The mapping between an item and the slot where that item belongs in the hash table is called the **hash function**. The hash function will take any item in the collection and return an integer in the range of slot names, between 0 and m-1. Assume that we have the set of integer items 54, 26, 93, 17, 77, and 31. Our first hash function, sometimes referred to as the "remainder method," simply takes an item and divides it by the table size, returning the remainder as its hash value ($h(item) = item\%11$). Table 4.5 gives all of the hash values for our example items. Note that this remainder method (modulo arithmetic) will typically be present in some form in all hash functions, since the result must be in the range of slot names.

Item	Hash Value
54	10
26	4
93	5
17	6
77	0
31	9

Table 4.5: Simple Hash Function Using Remainders

Once the hash values have been computed, we can insert each item into the hash table at the designated position as shown in Figure 4.6. Note that 6 of the 11 slots are now occupied. This is referred to as the **load factor**, and is commonly denoted by $\lambda = \frac{number of items}{tablesize}$. For this example, $\lambda = \frac{6}{11}$.

Now when we want to search for an item, we simply use the hash function to compute the slot name for the item and then check the hash table to see

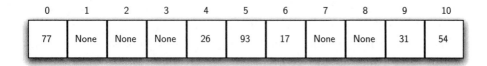

Figure 4.6: Hash Table with Six Items

if it is present. This searching operation is $O(1)$, since a constant amount of time is required to compute the hash value and then index the hash table at that location. If everything is where it should be, we have found a constant time search algorithm.

You can probably already see that this technique is going to work only if each item maps to a unique location in the hash table. For example, if the item 44 had been the next item in our collection, it would have a hash value of 0 ($44\%11 == 0$). Since 77 also had a hash value of 0, we would have a problem. According to the hash function, two or more items would need to be in the same slot. This is referred to as a **collision** (it may also be called a "clash"). Clearly, collisions create a problem for the hashing technique. We will discuss them in detail later.

4.3.3.1 Hash Functions

Given a collection of items, a hash function that maps each item into a unique slot is referred to as a **perfect hash function**. If we know the items and the collection will never change, then it is possible to construct a perfect hash function (refer to the exercises for more about perfect hash functions). Unfortunately, given an arbitrary collection of items, there is no systematic way to construct a perfect hash function. Luckily, we do not need the hash function to be perfect to still gain performance efficiency.

One way to always have a perfect hash function is to increase the size of the hash table so that each possible value in the item range can be accommodated. This guarantees that each item will have a unique slot. Although this is practical for small numbers of items, it is not feasible when the number of possible items is large. For example, if the items were nine-digit Social Security numbers, this method would require almost one billion slots. If we only want to store data for a class of 25 students, we will be wasting an enormous amount of memory.

Our goal is to create a hash function that minimizes the number of collisions, is easy to compute, and evenly distributes the items in the hash table. There are a number of common ways to extend the simple remainder method. We will consider a few of them here.

The **folding method** for constructing hash functions begins by dividing the item into equal-size pieces (the last piece may not be of equal size). These pieces are then added together to give the resulting hash value. For example, if our item was the phone number 436-555-4601, we would take the digits and divide them into groups of 2 (43,65,55,46,01). After the addition, $43 + 65 + 55 + 46 + 01$, we get 210. If we assume our hash table has 11 slots, then we need to perform the extra step of dividing by 11 and keeping the remainder. In this case 210 % 11 is 1, so the phone number 436-555-4601 hashes to slot 1. Some folding methods go one step further and reverse every other piece before the addition. For the above example, we get $43 + 56 + 55 + 64 + 01 = 219$; 219 % 11 = 10.

Another numerical technique for constructing a hash function is called the **mid-square method**. We first square the item, and then extract some portion of the resulting digits. For example, if the item were 44, we would first compute $44^2 = 1,936$. By extracting the middle two digits, 93, and performing the remainder step, we get 5 (93 % 11). Table 4.6 shows items under both the remainder method and the mid-square method. You should verify that you understand how these values were computed.

Item	Remainder	Mid-Square
54	10	3
26	4	7
93	5	9
17	6	8
77	0	4
31	9	6

Table 4.6: Comparison of Remainder and Mid-Square Methods

We can also create hash functions for character-based items such as strings. The word "cat" can be thought of as a sequence of ordinal values.

```
>>> ord('c')
99
>>> ord('a')
97
>>> ord('t')
116
```

We can then take these three ordinal values, add them up, and use the remainder method to get a `hash` value (see Figure 4.7). Listing 4.13 shows a function called `hash` that takes a string and a table size and returns the hash value in the range from 0 to `tablesize`-1.

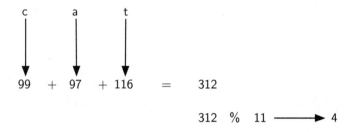

Figure 4.7: Hashing a String Using Ordinal Values

```
1 def hash(astring, tablesize):
2     sum = 0
3     for pos in range(len(astring)):
4         sum = sum + ord(astring[pos])
5
6     return sum%tablesize
```

Listing 4.13: Simple Hash Function for Strings

It is interesting to note that when using this hash function, anagrams will always be given the same hash value. To remedy this, we could use the position of the character as a weight. Figure 4.8 shows one possible way to use the positional value as a weighting factor. The modification to the `hash` function is left as an exercise.

You may be able to think of a number of additional ways to compute hash values for items in a collection. The important thing to remember is that the hash function has to be efficient so that it does not become the dominant part of the storage and search process. If the hash function is too complex, then it becomes more work to compute the slot name than it would be to simply do a basic sequential or binary search as described earlier. This would quickly defeat the purpose of hashing.

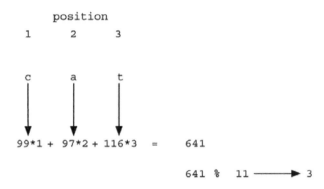

Figure 4.8: Hashing a String Using Ordinal Values with Weighting

4.3.3.2 Collision Resolution

We now return to the problem of collisions. When two items hash to the same slot, we must have a systematic method for placing the second item in the hash table. This process is called **collision resolution**. As we stated earlier, if the hash function is perfect, collisions will never occur. However, since this is often not possible, collision resolution becomes a very important part of hashing.

One method for resolving collisions looks into the hash table and tries to find another open slot to hold the item that caused the collision. A simple way to do this is to start at the original hash value position and then move in a sequential manner through the slots until we encounter the first slot that is empty. Note that we may need to go back to the first slot (circularly) to cover the entire hash table. This collision resolution process is referred to as **open addressing** in that it tries to find the next open slot or address in the hash table. By systematically visiting each slot one at a time, we are performing an open addressing technique called **linear probing**.

Figure 4.9 shows an extended set of integer items under the simple remainder method hash function (54,26,93,17,77,31,44,55,20). Table 4.5 above shows the hash values for the original items. Figure 4.6 shows the original contents. When we attempt to place 44 into slot 0, a collision occurs. Under linear probing, we look sequentially, slot by slot, until we find an open position. In this case, we find slot 1.

Again, 55 should go in slot 0 but must be placed in slot 2 since it is the next open position. The final value of 20 hashes to slot 9. Since slot 9 is full, we begin to do linear probing. We visit slots 10, 0, 1, and 2, and finally find an empty slot at position 3.

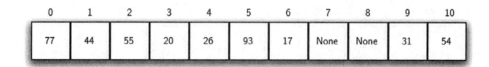

Figure 4.9: Collision Resolution with Linear Probing

Once we have built a hash table using open addressing and linear probing, it is essential that we utilize the same methods to search for items. Assume we want to look up the item 93. When we compute the hash value, we get 5. Looking in slot 5 reveals 93, and we can return **True**. What if we are looking for 20? Now the hash value is 9, and slot 9 is currently holding 31. We cannot simply return **False** since we know that there could have been collisions. We are now forced to do a sequential search, starting at position 10, looking until either we find the item 20 or we find an empty slot.

A disadvantage to linear probing is the tendency for **clustering**; items become clustered in the table. This means that if many collisions occur at the same hash value, a number of surrounding slots will be filled by the linear probing resolution. This will have an impact on other items that are being inserted, as we saw when we tried to add the item 20 above. A cluster of values hashing to 0 had to be skipped to finally find an open position. This cluster is shown in Figure 4.10.

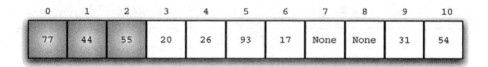

Figure 4.10: A Cluster of Items for Slot 0

One way to deal with clustering is to extend the linear probing technique so that instead of looking sequentially for the next open slot, we skip slots, thereby more evenly distributing the items that have caused collisions. This will potentially reduce the clustering that occurs. Figure 4.11 shows the items when collision resolution is done with a "plus 3" probe. This means that once a collision occurs, we will look at every third slot until we find one that is empty.

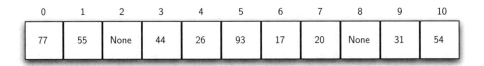

Figure 4.11: Collision Resolution Using "Plus 3"

The general name for this process of looking for another slot after a collision is **rehashing**. With simple linear probing, the rehash function is $newhashvalue = rehash(oldhashvalue)$ where $rehash(pos) = (pos + 1)\%sizeoftable$. The "plus 3" rehash can be defined as $rehash(pos) = (pos+3)\%sizeoftable$. In general, $rehash(pos) = (pos+skip)\%sizeoftable$. It is important to note that the size of the "skip" must be such that all the slots in the table will eventually be visited. Otherwise, part of the table will be unused. To ensure this, it is often suggested that the table size be a prime number. This is the reason we have been using 11 in our examples.

A variation of the linear probing idea is called **quadratic probing**. Instead of using a constant "skip" value, we use a rehash function that increments the hash value by 1, 3, 5, 7, 9, and so on. This means that if the first hash value is h, the successive values are $h+1$, $h+4$, $h+9$, $h+16$, and so on. In other words, quadratic probing uses a skip consisting of successive perfect squares. Figure 4.12 shows our example values after they are placed using this technique.

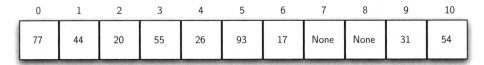

Figure 4.12: Collision Resolution with Quadratic Probing

An alternative method for handling the collision problem is to allow each slot to hold a reference to a collection (or chain) of items. **Chaining** allows many items to exist at the same location in the hash table. When collisions happen, the item is still placed in the proper slot of the hash table. As more and more items hash to the same location, the difficulty of searching for the item in the collection increases. Figure 4.13 shows the items as they are added to a hash table that uses chaining to resolve collisions.

When we want to search for an item, we use the hash function to generate

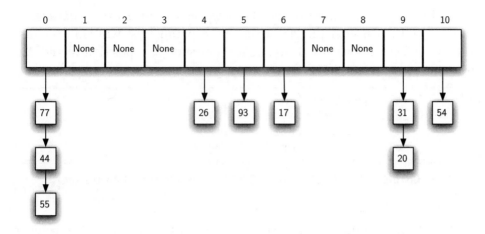

Figure 4.13: Collision Resolution with Chaining

the slot where it should reside. Since each slot holds a collection, we use a searching technique to decide whether the item is present. The advantage is that on the average there are likely to be many fewer items in each slot, so the search is perhaps more efficient. We will look at the analysis for hashing at the end of this section.

4.3.3.3 The HashTable Class

We will now implement the ideas described above by building a Python HashTable class. The HashTable abstract data type is defined by the structure that was described above. In addition, we will implement our hash table so that it can behave like a dictionary. Each slot will have an item, or key, and a corresponding data value. The operations are given below. You should note that collisions need to be resolved as part of the store operation, and the search operation needs to use the same method.

- HashTable(size) creates a new hash table. It needs the size and returns a hash table with size empty slots named 0 through size-1.

- store(item, data) stores a new piece of data in the hash table using the item as the key location. It needs the item and the associated data. It returns nothing.

- search(item) returns the data value associated with the key item. It returns None if the key is not in the hash table.

In Listing 4.14 we use two lists to implement the hash table data structure. One list will hold the key items and a parallel list will hold the data values. When we look up an item, the corresponding position in the data list will hold the associated data value.

```
1  class HashTable:
2      def __init__(self,size):
3          self.slots = [None] * size
4          self.data = [None] * size
```

Listing 4.14: HashTable Implementation in Python–Constructor

`hashfunction` implements the simple remainder method. The collision resolution technique is linear probing with a "plus 1" rehash function. The `store` function (see Listing 4.15) assumes that there will eventually be an empty slot. It computes the original hash value and if that slot is not empty, iterates the `rehash` function until an empty slot occurs.

```
1      def store(self,item,data):
2          hashvalue = self.hashfunction(item,len(self.slots))
3
4          if self.slots[hashvalue] == None:
5              self.slots[hashvalue] = item
6              self.data[hashvalue] = data
7          else:
8              nextslot = self.rehash(hashvalue,len(self.slots))
9              while self.slots[nextslot] != None:
10                 nextslot = self.rehash(nextslot,len(self.slots))
11
12             self.slots[nextslot]=item
13             self.data[nextslot]=data
14
15     def hashfunction(self,item,size):
16         return item%size
17
18     def rehash(self,oldhash,size):
19         return (oldhash+1)%size
```

Listing 4.15: HashTable Implementation in Python–Store Method

Likewise, the `search` function (see Listing 4.16) begins by computing the initial hash value. If the value is not in the initial slot, `rehash` is used to locate the next possible position. Notice that line 15 guarantees that the search will terminate by checking to make sure that we have not returned to the initial slot. If that happens, we have exhausted all possible slots and the item must not be present. In addition, we overload the __getitem__ and __setitem__ methods to allow access using [].

```
1   def search(self,item):
2       startslot = self.hashfunction(item,len(self.slots))
3
4       data = None
5       stop = False
6       found = False
7       position = startslot
8       while self.slots[position] != None and  \
9                           not found and not stop:
10          if self.slots[position] == item:
11              found = True
12              data = self.data[position]
13          else:
14              position=self.rehash(position,len(self.slots))
15              if position == startslot:
16                  stop = True
17      return data
18
19  def __getitem__(self,item):
20      return self.search(item)
21
22  def __setitem__(self,item,data):
23      self.store(item,data)
```

Listing 4.16: HashTable Implementation in Python–Search Method

The following session shows the **HashTable** class storing integer key items and string data values.

```
>>> H=HashTable(11)
>>> H[54]="cat"
>>> H[26]="dog"
>>> H[93]="lion"
>>> H[17]="tiger"
>>> H[77]="bird"
>>> H[31]="cow"
```

```
>>> H[44]="goat"
>>> H[55]="pig"
>>> H[20]="chicken"
>>> H.slots
[77, 44, 55, 20, 26, 93, 17, None, None, 31, 54]
>>> H.data
['bird', 'goat', 'pig', 'chicken', 'dog', 'lion',
       'tiger', None, None, 'cow', 'cat']
>>> H[20]
'chicken'
>>> H[17]
'tiger'
>>>
```

4.3.3.4   Analysis of Hashing

We stated earlier that in the best case hashing would provide a $O(1)$, constant time search technique. However, due to collisions, the number of comparisons is typically not so simple. Even though a complete analysis of hashing is beyond the scope of this text, we can state some well-known results that approximate the number of comparisons necessary to search for an item.

The most important piece of information we need to analyze the use of a hash table is the load factor, λ. Conceptually, if λ is small, then there is a lower chance of collisions, meaning that items are more likely to be in the slots where they belong. If λ is large, meaning that the table is filling up, then there are more and more collisions. This means that collision resolution is more difficult, requiring more comparisons to find an empty slot. With chaining, increased collisions means an increased number of items on each chain.

As before, we will have a result for both a successful and an unsuccessful search. For a successful search using open addressing with linear probing, the average number of comparisons is approximately

$$\frac{1}{2}\left(1 + \frac{1}{1-\lambda}\right)$$

and an unsuccessful search gives

$$\frac{1}{2}\left(1 + \left(\frac{1}{1-\lambda}\right)^2\right)$$

If we are using chaining, the average number of comparisons is

$$1 + \frac{\lambda}{2}$$

for the successful case, and simply λ comparisons if the search is unsuccessful.

4.4 Sorting

Sorting is the process of placing elements from a collection in some kind of order. For example, a list of words could be sorted alphabetically or by length. A list of cities could be sorted by population, by area, or by zip code. We have already seen a number of algorithms that were able to benefit from having a sorted list (recall the final anagram example and the binary search).

There are many, many sorting algorithms that have been developed and analyzed. This suggests that sorting is an important area of study in computer science. Sorting a large number of items can take a substantial amount of computing resources. Like searching, the efficiency of a sorting algorithm is related to the number of items being processed. For small collections, a complex sorting method may be more trouble than it is worth. The overhead may be too high. On the other hand, for larger collections, we want to take advantage of as many improvements as possible. In this section we will discuss several sorting techniques and compare them with respect to their running time.

Before getting into specific algorithms, we should think about the operations that can be used to analyze a sorting process. First, it will be necessary to compare two values to see which is smaller (or larger). In order to sort a collection, it will be necessary to have some systematic way to compare values to see if they are out of order. The total number of comparisons will be the most common way to measure a sort procedure. Second, when values are not in the correct position with respect to one another, it may be necessary to exchange them. This exchange is a costly operation and the total number of exchanges will also be important for evaluating the overall efficiency of the algorithm.

4.4.1 The Bubble Sort

The **bubble sort** makes multiple passes through a list. It compares adjacent items and exchanges those that are out of order. Each pass through the list places the next largest value in its proper place. In essence, each item "bubbles" up to the location where it belongs.

Figure 4.14 shows the first pass of a bubble sort. The shaded items are being compared to see if they are out of order. If there are n items in the list, then there are $n - 1$ pairs of items that need to be compared on the first pass. It is important to note that once the largest value in the list is part of a pair, it will continually be moved along until the pass is complete.

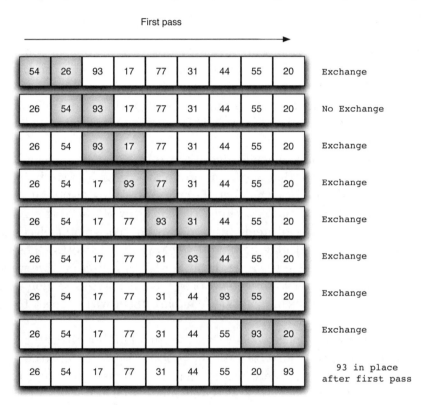

Figure 4.14: bubbleSort: The First Pass

At the start of the second pass, the largest value is now in place. There are $n - 1$ items left to sort, meaning that there will be $n - 2$ pairs. Since each pass places the next largest value in place, the total number of passes necessary will be $n - 1$. After completing the $n - 1$ passes, the smallest item must be in the correct position with no further processing required. Listing 4.17 shows the complete bubbleSort function. It takes the list as a parameter, and modifies it by exchanging items as necessary.

The exchange operation, sometimes called a "swap," is slightly different in Python than in most other programming languages. Typically, swapping two elements in a list requires a temporary storage location (an additional memory location). A code fragment such as

```
temp = alist[i]
alist[i] = alist[j]
alist[j] = temp
```

will exchange the ith and jth items in the list. Without the temporary storage, one of the values would be overwritten.

In Python, simultaneous assignment is possible. The statement `a,b=b,a` will result in two assignment statements being done at the same time (see Figure 4.15). Listing 4.17 shows the complete Python implementation. Line 5 performs the simultaneous assignment to exchange the i and $(i+1)$th items.

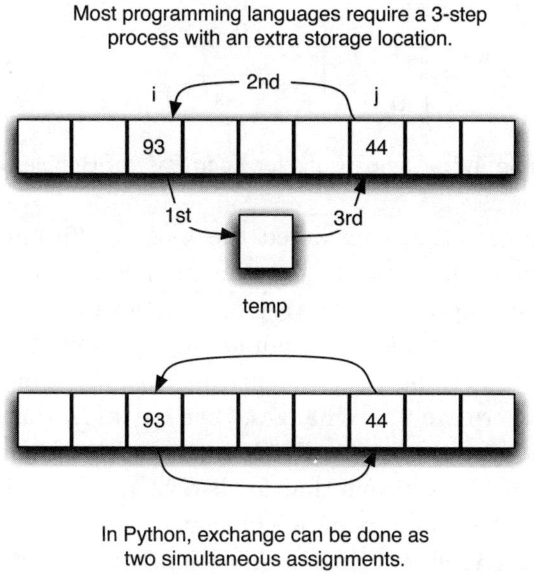

Most programming languages require a 3-step
process with an extra storage location.

Figure 4.15: Exchanging Two Values in Python

To analyze the bubble sort, we should note that regardless of how the items are arranged in the initial list, n-1 passes will be made to sort a list of size n. Table 4.7 shows the number of comparisons for each pass. The total number of comparisons is the sum of the first $n - 1$ integers. Recall that the sum of the first n integers is $\frac{1}{2}n^2 + \frac{1}{2}n$. The sum of the first $n - 1$ integers is $\frac{1}{2}n^2 + \frac{1}{2}n - n$, which is $\frac{1}{2}n^2 - \frac{1}{2}n$. This is still $O(n^2)$ comparisons. In the best case, if the list is already ordered, no exchanges will be made.

```
1  def bubbleSort(alist):
2      for passnum in range(len(alist)-1,0,-1):
3          for i in range(passnum):
4              if alist[i]>alist[i+1]:
5                  alist[i],alist[i+1]=alist[i+1],alist[i]
```

Listing 4.17: A Bubble Sort

However, in the worst case, every comparison will cause an exchange. On average, we exchange half of the time.

Pass	Comparisons
1	$n - 1$
2	$n - 2$
3	$n - 3$
...	
$n - 1$	1

Table 4.7: Comparisons for Each Pass of Bubble Sort

A bubble sort is often considered the most inefficient sorting method since it must exchange items before the final location is known. These "wasted" exchange operations are very costly. However, because the bubble sort makes passes through the entire unsorted portion of the list, it has the capability to do something most sorting algorithms cannot. In particular, if during a pass there are no exchanges, then we know that the list must be sorted. A bubble sort can be modified to stop early if it finds that the list has become sorted. This means that for lists that require just a few passes, a bubble sort may have an advantage in that it will recognize the sorted list and stop. Listing 4.18 shows this modification, which is often referred to as the **short bubble**.

4.4.2 The Selection Sort

The **selection sort** improves on the bubble sort by making only one exchange for every pass through the list. In order to do this, a selection sort looks for the largest value as it makes a pass and, after completing the pass, places it in the proper location. As with a bubble sort, after the first pass, the largest item is in the correct place. After the second pass, the next largest is in place. This process continues and requires $n - 1$ passes to sort

```
1  def shortBubbleSort(alist):
2      exchanges = True
3      passnum = len(alist)-1
4      while passnum > 0 and exchanges:
5          exchanges = False
6          for i in range(passnum):
7              if alist[i]>alist[i+1]:
8                  exchanges = True
9                  alist[i],alist[i+1]=alist[i+1],alist[i]
10         passnum = passnum-1
```

Listing 4.18: A Modified Bubble Sort

n items, since the final item must be in place after the $(n-1)$st pass.

Figure 4.16 shows the entire sorting process. On each pass, the largest remaining item is selected and then placed in its proper location. The first pass places 93, the second pass places 77, the third places 55, and so on. The function is shown in Listing 4.19.

```
1  def selectionSort(alist):
2      for fillslot in range(len(alist)-1,0,-1):
3          positionOfMax=0
4          for location in range(1,fillslot+1):
5              if alist[location]>alist[positionOfMax]:
6                  positionOfMax = location
7
8          alist[positionOfMax],alist[fillslot] = \
9                  alist[fillslot],alist[positionOfMax]
```

Listing 4.19: A Selection Sort

You may see that the selection sort makes the same number of comparisons as the bubble sort and is therefore also $O(n^2)$. However, due to the reduction in the number of exchanges, the selection sort typically executes faster in benchmark studies. In fact, for our list, the bubble sort makes 20 exchanges, while the selection sort makes only 8.

4.4.3 The Insertion Sort

The **insertion sort**, although still $O(n^2)$, works in a slightly different way. It always maintains a sorted sublist in the lower positions of the list. Each

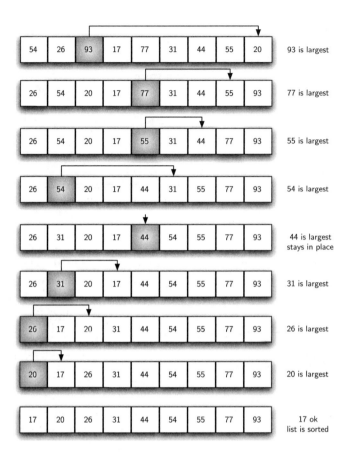

Figure 4.16: `selectionSort`

new item is then "inserted" back into the previous sublist such that the sorted sublist is one item larger. Figure 4.17 shows the insertion sorting process. The shaded items represent the ordered sublists as the algorithm makes each pass.

We begin by assuming that a list with one item (position 0) is already sorted. On each pass, one for each item 1 through $n - 1$, the current item is checked against those in the already sorted sublist. As we look back into the already sorted sublist, we shift those items that are greater to the right. When we reach a smaller item or the end of the sublist, the current item can be inserted.

Figure 4.18 shows the fifth pass in detail. At this point in the algorithm, a sorted sublist of five items consisting of 17, 26, 54, 77, and 93 exists. We

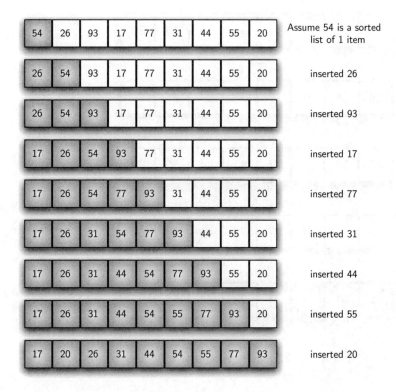

Figure 4.17: `insertionSort`

want to insert 31 back into the already sorted items. The first comparison against 93 causes 93 to be shifted to the right. 77 and 54 are also shifted. When the item 26 is encountered, the shifting process stops and 31 is placed in the open position. Now we have a sorted sublist of six items.

The implementation of `insertionSort` (Listing 4.20) shows that there are again $n - 1$ passes to sort n items. The iteration starts at position 1 and moves through position $n - 1$, as these are the items that need to be inserted back into the sorted sublists. Line 8 performs the shift operation that moves a value up one position in the list, making room behind it for the insertion. Remember that this is not a complete exchange as was performed in the previous algorithms.

The maximum number of comparisons for an insertion sort is the sum of the first $n - 1$ integers. Again, this is $O(n^2)$. However, in the best case, only one comparison needs to be done on each pass. This would be the case for an already sorted list.

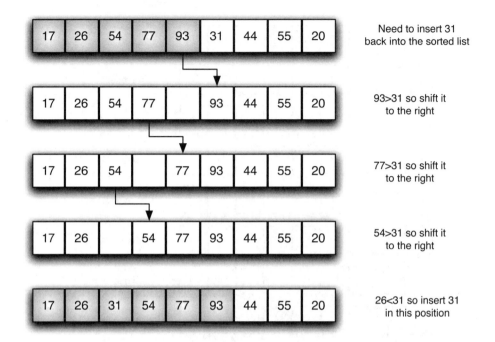

Figure 4.18: insertionSort: Fifth Pass of the Sort

One note about shifting versus exchanging is also important. In general, a shift operation requires approximately a third of the processing work of an exchange since only one assignment is performed. In benchmark studies, insertion sort will show very good performance.

```
 1  def insertionSort(alist):
 2      for index in range(1,len(alist)):
 3
 4          currentvalue = alist[index]
 5          position = index
 6
 7          while position>0 and alist[position-1]>currentvalue:
 8              alist[position]=alist[position-1]
 9              position = position-1
10
11          alist[position]=currentvalue
```

Listing 4.20: insertionSort

4.4.4   The Shell Sort

The **shell sort**, sometimes called the "diminishing increment sort," improves on the insertion sort by breaking the original list into a number of smaller sublists, each of which is sorted using an insertion sort. The unique way that these sublists are chosen is the key to the shell sort. Instead of breaking the list into sublists of contiguous items, the shell sort uses an increment i, sometimes called the **gap**, to create a sublist by choosing all items that are i items apart.

This can be seen in Figure 4.19. This list has nine items. If we use an increment of three, there are three sublists, each of which can be sorted by an insertion sort. After completing these sorts, we get the list shown in Figure 4.20. Although this list is not completely sorted, something very interesting has happened. By sorting the sublists, we have moved the items closer to where they actually belong.

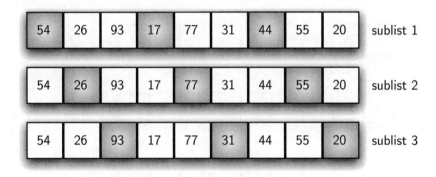

Figure 4.19: A Shell Sort with Increments of Three

Figure 4.21 shows a final insertion sort using an increment of one; in other words, a standard insertion sort. Note that by performing the earlier sublist sorts, we have now reduced the total number of shifting operations necessary to put the list in its final order. For this case, we need only four more shifts to complete the process.

We said earlier that the way in which the increments are chosen is the unique feature of the shell sort. The function shown in Listing 4.21 uses a different set of increments. In this case, we begin with $\frac{n}{2}$ sublists. On the next pass, $\frac{n}{4}$ sublists are sorted. Eventually, a single list is sorted with the basic insertion sort. Figure 4.22 shows the first sublists for our example using this increment.

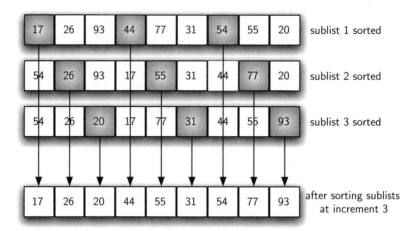

Figure 4.20: A Shell Sort after Sorting Each Sublist

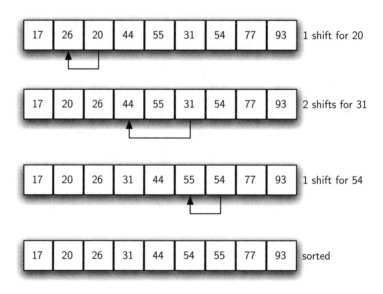

Figure 4.21: ShellSort: A Final Insertion Sort with Increment of 1

The following invocation of the **shellSort** function shows the partially sorted lists after each increment, with the final sort being an insertion sort with an increment of one.

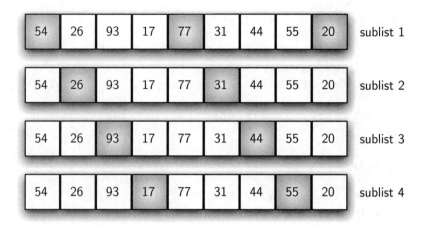

Figure 4.22: Initial Sublists for a Shell Sort

```
>>> alist=[54,26,93,17,77,31,44,55,20]
>>> shellSort(alist)
After increments of size 4 the list is
        [20, 26, 44, 17, 54, 31, 93, 55, 77]
After increments of size 2 the list is
        [20, 17, 44, 26, 54, 31, 77, 55, 93]
After increments of size 1 the list is
        [17, 20, 26, 31, 44, 54, 55, 77, 93]
```

At first glance you may think that a shell sort cannot be better than an insertion sort, since it does a complete insertion sort as the last step. It turns out, however, that this final insertion sort does not need to do very many comparisons (or shifts) since the list has been pre-sorted by earlier incremental insertion sorts, as described above. In other words, each pass produces a list that is "more sorted" than the previous one. This makes the final pass very efficient.

Although a general analysis of the shell sort is well beyond the scope of this text, we can say that it tends to fall somewhere between $O(n)$ and $O(n^2)$, based on the behavior described above. For the increments shown in Listing 4.21, the performance is $O(n^2)$. By changing the increment, for example using $2^k - 1$ (1, 3, 7, 15, 31, and so on), a shell sort can perform at $O(n^{\frac{3}{2}})$.

```
1  def shellSort(alist):
2      sublistcount = len(alist)/2
3      while sublistcount > 0:
4
5          for startposition in range(sublistcount):
6              gapInsertionSort(alist,startposition,sublistcount)
7
8          print "After increments of size",sublistcount,
9                              "The list is",alist
10
11         sublistcount = sublistcount / 2
12
13 def gapInsertionSort(alist,start,gap):
14     for i in range(start+gap,len(alist),gap):
15
16         currentvalue = alist[i]
17         position = i
18
19         while position>=gap and \
20                 alist[position-gap]>currentvalue:
21             alist[position]=alist[position-gap]
22             position = position-gap
23
24         alist[position]=currentvalue
```

Listing 4.21: shellSort

4.4.5 The Merge Sort

We now turn our attention to using a divide and conquer strategy as a way to improve the performance of sorting algorithms. The first algorithm we will study is the **merge sort**. Merge sort is a recursive algorithm that continually splits a list in half. If the list is empty or has one item, it is sorted by definition (the base case). If the list has more than one item, we split the list and recursively invoke a merge sort on both halves. Once the two halves are sorted, the fundamental operation, called a **merge**, is performed. Merging is the process of taking two smaller sorted lists and combining them together into a single, sorted, new list. Figure 4.23(a) shows our familiar example list as it is being split by mergeSort. Figure 4.23(b) shows the simple lists, now sorted, as they are merged back together.

The mergeSort function shown in Listing 4.22 begins by asking the base case question. If the length of the list is less than or equal to one, then we already have a sorted list and no more processing is necessary. If, on the

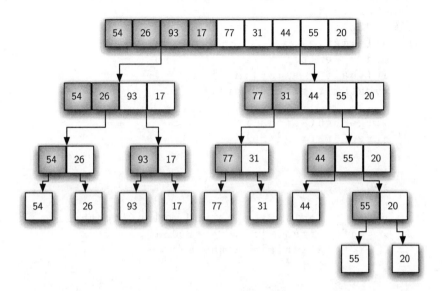

(a) Splitting the List in a Merge Sort

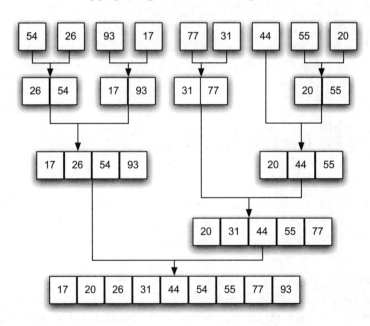

(b) Lists as They Are Merged Together

Figure 4.23: Splitting and Merging in a Merge Sort

```
1   def mergeSort(alist):
2       print "Splitting ",alist
3       if len(alist)>1:
4           mid = len(alist)/2
5           lefthalf = alist[:mid]
6           righthalf = alist[mid:]
7
8           mergeSort(lefthalf)
9           mergeSort(righthalf)
10
11          i=0
12          j=0
13          k=0
14          while i<len(lefthalf) and j<len(righthalf):
15              if lefthalf[i]<righthalf[j]:
16                  alist[k]=lefthalf[i]
17                  i=i+1
18              else:
19                  alist[k]=righthalf[j]
20                  j=j+1
21              k=k+1
22
23          while i<len(lefthalf):
24              alist[k]=lefthalf[i]
25              i=i+1
26              k=k+1
27
28          while j<len(righthalf):
29              alist[k]=righthalf[j]
30              j=j+1
31              k=k+1
32      print "Merging ",alist
```

Listing 4.22: mergeSort

other hand, the length is greater than one, then we use the Python slice
operation to extract the left and right halves. It is important to note that
the list may not have an even number of items. That does not matter, as
the lengths will differ by at most one.

Once the mergeSort function is invoked on the left half and the right
half (lines 8–9), it is assumed they are sorted. The rest of the function

```
>>> b=[54,26,93,17,77,31,44,55,20]
>>> mergeSort(b)
Splitting   [54, 26, 93, 17, 77, 31, 44, 55, 20]
Splitting   [54, 26, 93, 17]
Splitting   [54, 26]
Splitting   [54]
Merging   [54]
Splitting   [26]
Merging   [26]
Merging   [26, 54]
Splitting   [93, 17]
Splitting   [93]
Merging   [93]
Splitting   [17]
Merging   [17]
Merging   [17, 93]
Merging   [17, 26, 54, 93]
Splitting   [77, 31, 44, 55, 20]
Splitting   [77, 31]
Splitting   [77]
Merging   [77]
Splitting   [31]
Merging   [31]
Merging   [31, 77]
Splitting   [44, 55, 20]
Splitting   [44]
Merging   [44]
Splitting   [55, 20]
Splitting   [55]
Merging   [55]
Splitting   [20]
Merging   [20]
Merging   [20, 55]
Merging   [20, 44, 55]
Merging   [20, 31, 44, 55, 77]
Merging   [17, 20, 26, 31, 44, 54, 55, 77, 93]
>>>
```

(lines 11–31) is responsible for merging the two smaller sorted lists into a larger sorted list. Notice that the merge operation places the items back into the original list (`alist`) one at a time by repeatedly taking the smallest item from the sorted lists.

The `mergeSort` function has been augmented with a `print` statement (line 2) to show the contents of the list being sorted at the start of each invocation. There is also a `print` statement (line 32) to show the merging process. The transcript shows the result of executing the function on our example list. Note that the list with 44, 55, and 20 will not divide evenly. The first split gives [44] and the second gives [55,20]. It is easy to see how the splitting process eventually yields a list that can be immediately merged with other sorted lists.

In order to analyze the `mergeSort` function, we need to consider the two distinct processes that make it up. First, the list is split into halves. We already computed (in a binary search) that we can divide a list in half $\log_2 n$ times where n is the length of the list. The second process is the merge. Each item in the list will eventually be processed and placed on the sorted list. So the merge operation which results in a list of size n requires n operations. The result of this analysis is that $\log n$ splits, each of which costs n for a total of $n \log n$ operations. A merge sort is an $O(n \log n)$ algorithm.

It is important to notice that the `mergeSort` function does require extra space to hold the two halves as they are extracted with the slicing operations. This additional space can be a critical factor if the list is large and can make this sort problematic when working on large data sets.

4.4.6   The Quick Sort

The **quick sort** uses divide and conquer to gain the same advantages as the merge sort, while not using additional storage. As a trade-off, however, it is possible that the list may not be divided in half. When this happens, we will see that performance is diminished.

A quick sort first selects a value, which is called the **pivot value**. Although there are many different ways to choose the pivot value, we will simply use the first item in the list. The role of the pivot value is to assist with splitting the list. The actual position where the pivot value belongs in the final sorted list, commonly called the **split point**, will be used to divide the list for subsequent calls to the quick sort.

Figure 4.24 shows that 54 will serve as our first pivot value. Since we have looked at this example a few times already, we know that 54 will eventually end up in the position currently holding 31. The **partition** process will happen next. It will find the split point and at the same time move other items to the appropriate side of the list, either less than the pivot value or greater than.

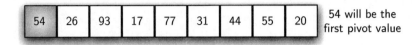

Figure 4.24: The First Pivot Value for a Quick Sort

Partitioning begins by locating two position markers–let's call them `leftmark` and `rightmark`–at the beginning and end of the remaining items in the list (positions 1 and 8 in Figure 4.25). The goal of the partition process is to move items that are on the wrong side with respect to the pivot value while also converging on the split point. Figure 4.25 shows this process as we locate the position of 54.

We begin by incrementing `leftmark` until we locate a value that is greater than the pivot value. We then decrement `rightmark` until we find a value that is less than the pivot value. At this point we have discovered two items that are out of place with respect to the eventual split point. For our example, this occurs at 93 and 20. Now we can exchange these two items and then repeat the process again.

At the point where `rightmark` becomes less than `leftmark`, we stop. The position of `rightmark` is now the split point. The pivot value can be exchanged with the contents of the split point and the pivot value is now in place (Figure 4.26). In addition, all the items to the left of the split point are less than the pivot value, and all the items to the right of the split point are greater than the pivot value. The list can now be divided at the split point and the quick sort can be invoked recursively on the two halves.

The `quickSort` function shown in Listing 4.23 invokes a recursive function, `quickSortHelper`. `quickSortHelper` begins with the same base case as the merge sort. If the length of the list is less than or equal to one, it is already sorted. If it is greater, then it can be partitioned and recursively sorted. The `partition` function implements the process described earlier.

To analyze the `quickSort` function, note that for a list of length n, if the partition always occurs in the middle of the list, there will again be $\log n$ divisions. In order to find the split point, each of the n items needs to be checked against the pivot value. The result is $n \log n$. In addition, there is no need for additional memory as in the merge sort process.

Unfortunately, in the worst case, the split points may not be in the

```
1  def quickSort(alist):
2      quickSortHelper(alist,0,len(alist)-1)
3
4  def quickSortHelper(alist,first,last):
5      if first<last:
6
7          splitpoint = partition(alist,first,last)
8
9          quickSortHelper(alist,first,splitpoint-1)
10         quickSortHelper(alist,splitpoint+1,last)
11
12
13 def partition(alist,first,last):
14     pivotvalue = alist[first]
15
16     leftmark = first+1
17     rightmark = last
18
19     done = False
20     while not done:
21
22         while leftmark <= rightmark and \
23                 alist[leftmark] <= pivotvalue:
24             leftmark = leftmark + 1
25
26         while alist[rightmark] >= pivotvalue and \
27                 rightmark >= leftmark:
28             rightmark = rightmark -1
29
30         if rightmark < leftmark:
31             done = True
32         else:
33             alist[leftmark],alist[rightmark]= \
34                         alist[rightmark],alist[leftmark]
35
36     alist[first],alist[rightmark]= \
37                 alist[rightmark],alist[first]
38
39     return rightmark
```

Listing 4.23: A Quick Sort

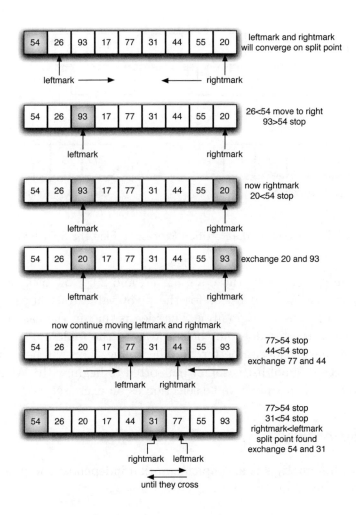

Figure 4.25: Finding the Split Point for 54

middle and can be very skewed to the left or the right, leaving a very uneven division. In this case, sorting a list of n items divides into sorting a list of 0 items and a list of $n - 1$ items. Then sorting a list of $n - 1$ divides into a list of size 0 and a list of size $n - 2$, and so on. The result is an $O(n^2)$ sort with all of the overhead that recursion requires.

We mentioned earlier that there are different ways to choose the pivot value. In particular, we can attempt to alleviate some of the potential for an uneven division by using a technique called **median of three**. To choose the pivot value, we will consider the first, the middle, and the last element

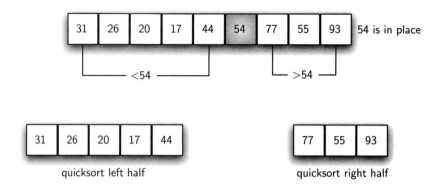

Figure 4.26: Completing the Partition Process to Find the Split Point for 54

in the list. In our example, those are 54, 77, and 20. Now pick the median value, in our case 54, and use it for the pivot value (of course, that was the pivot value we used originally). The idea is that in the case where the the first item in the list does not belong toward the middle of the list, the median of three will choose a better "middle" value. This will be particularly useful when the original list is somewhat sorted to begin with. We leave the implementation of this pivot value selection as an exercise.

4.5 Summary

- Algorithm analysis is an implementation-independent way of measuring an algorithm.

- Big-O notation allows algorithms to be classified by their dominant process with respect to the size of the problem.

- A sequential search is $O(n)$ for ordered and unordered lists.

- A binary search of an ordered list is $O(\log n)$ in the worst case.

- Hash tables can provide constant time searching.

- A bubble sort, a selection sort, and an insertion sort are $O(n^2)$ algorithms.

- A shell sort improves on the insertion sort by sorting incremental sublists. It falls between $O(n)$ and $O(n^2)$.

- A merge sort is $O(n \log n)$, but requires additional space for the merging process.

- A quick sort is $O(n \log n)$, but may degrade to $O(n^2)$ if the split points are not near the middle of the list. It does not require additional space.

4.6 Key Terms

Big-O Notation	Binary Search	Bubble Sort
Chaining	Clustering	Collision
Collision resolution	Exponential	Folding method
Gap	Hash function	Hash table
Hashing	Insertion sort	Linear
Linear probing	Load factor	Log linear
Logarithmic	Median of three	Merge
Merge sort	Mid-square method	Open addressing
Order of magnitude	Partition	Perfect hash function
Pivot value	Quadratic	Quadratic probing
Quick sort	Rehashing	Selection sort
Sequential search	Shell sort	Short bubble
Slot	Split point	

4.7 Discussion Questions

1. Using the hash table performance formulas given in the chapter, compute the average number of comparisons necessary when the table is

   - 10% full
   - 25% full
   - 50% full
   - 75% full
   - 90% full
   - 99% full

   At what point do you think the hash table is too small? Explain.

2. Modify the hash function for strings to use positional weightings.

3. We used a hash function for strings that weighted the characters by position. Devise an alternative weighting scheme. What are the biases that exist with these functions?

4. Research perfect hash functions. Using a list of names (classmates, family members, etc.), generate the hash values using the perfect hash algorithm.

5. Generate a random list of integers. Show how this list is sorted by the following algorithms:

   - bubble sort
   - selection sort
   - insertion sort
   - shell sort (you decide on the increments)
   - merge sort
   - quick sort (you decide on the pivot value)

6. Consider the following list of integers: [1,2,3,4,5,6,7,8,9,10]. Show how this list is sorted by the following algorithms:

   - bubble sort
   - selection sort
   - insertion sort
   - shell sort (you decide on the increments)
   - merge sort
   - quick sort (you decide on the pivot value)

7. Consider the following list of integers: [10,9,8,7,6,5,4,3,2,1]. Show how this list is sorted by the following algorithms:

   - bubble sort
   - selection sort
   - insertion sort
   - shell sort (you decide on the increments)
   - merge sort

   - quick sort (you decide on the pivot value)

8. Consider the list of characters: ['P','Y','T','H','O','N']. Show how this list is sorted using the following algorithms:

   - bubble sort
   - selection sort
   - insertion sort
   - shell sort (you decide on the increments)
   - merge sort
   - quick sort (you decide on the pivot value)

9. Devise alternative strategies for choosing the pivot value in quick sort. For example, pick the middle item. Re-implement the algorithm and then execute it on random data sets. Under what criteria does your new strategy perform better or worse than the strategy from this chapter?

4.8 Programming Exercises

1. Set up a random experiment to test the difference between a sequential search and a binary search on a list of integers.

2. Implement the binary search as a recursive function and an iterative function. Generate a random, ordered list of integers and do a benchmark analysis. What are your results? Can you explain them?

3. How can you delete items from a hash table that uses chaining for collision resolution? How about if open addressing is used? What are the special circumstances that must be handled? Implement the delete method for the HashTable class.

4. Implement quadratic probing as a rehash technique.

5. Using a random number generator, create a list of 500 integers. Perform a benchmark analysis using some of the sorting algorithms from this chapter. What is the difference in execution speed?

6. A bubble sort can be modified to "bubble" in both directions. The first pass moves "up" the list, and the second pass moves "down." This alternating pattern continues until no more passes are necessary. Implement this variation and describe under what circumstances it might be appropriate.

7. Perform a benchmark analysis for a shell sort, using different increment sets on the same list.

8. One way to improve the quick sort is to use an insertion sort on lists that have a small length (call it the "partition limit"). Why does this make sense? Reimplement the quick sort and use it to sort a random list of integers. Perform an analysis using different list sizes for the partition limit.

9. Implement the median-of-three method for selecting a pivot value as a modification to `quickSort`. Run an experiment to compare the two techniques.

Chapter 5   Trees

5.1   Objectives

- To understand what a tree data structure is and how it is used.

- To see how trees can be used to implement a map data structure.

- To implement trees using a list.

- To implement trees using classes and references.

- To implement trees as a recursive data structure.

- To implement a priority queue using a heap.

5.2   Examples of Trees

Now that we have studied linear data structures like stacks and queues and have some experience with recursion, we will look at a common data structure called the **tree**. Trees are used in many areas of computer science, including operating systems, graphics, database systems, and computer networking. Tree data structures have many things in common with their botanical cousins. A tree data structure has a root, branches, and leaves. The difference between a tree in nature and a tree in computer science is that a tree data structure has its root at the top and its leaves on the bottom.

Before we begin our study of tree data structures, let's look at a few common examples. Our first example of a tree is a classification tree from biology. Figure 5.1 shows an example of the biological classification of some animals. From this simple example, we can learn about several properties of trees. The first property this example demonstrates is that trees are hierarchical. By hierarchical, we mean that trees are structured in layers with the more general things near the top and the more specific things near the bottom. The top of the hierarchy is the Kingdom, the next layer of the tree (the "children" of the layer above) is the Phylum, then the Class, and so on. However, no matter how deep we go in the classification tree, all the organisms are still animals.

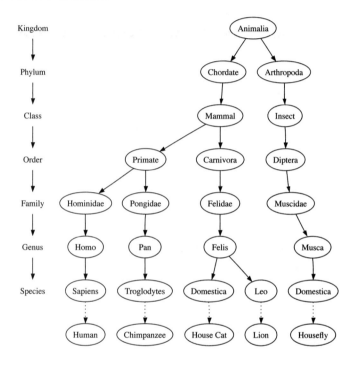

Figure 5.1: Taxonomy of Some Common Animals Shown as a Tree

Notice that you can start at the top of the tree and follow a path made of circles and arrows all the way to the bottom. At each level of the tree we might ask ourselves a question and then follow the path that agrees with our answer. For example we might ask, "Is this animal a Chordate or an Arthropod?" If the answer is "Chordate" then we follow that path and ask, "Is this Chordate a Mammal?" If not, we are stuck (but only in this simplified example). When we are at the Mammal level we ask, "Is this Mammal a Primate or a Carnivore?" We can keep following paths until we get to the very bottom of the tree where we have the common name.

A second property of trees is that all of the children of one node are independent of the children of another node. For example, the Genus Felis has the children Domestica and Leo. The Genus Musca also has a child named Domestica, but it is a different node and is independent of the Domestica child of Felis. This means that we can change the node that is the child of Musca without affecting the child of Felis.

A third property is that each leaf node is unique. We can specify a path from the root of the tree to a leaf that uniquely identifies each species in the animal kingdom; for example, Animalia → Chordate → Mammal → Carnivora → Felidae →Felis→ Domestica.

Another example of a tree structure that you probably use every day is a file system. In a file system, directories, or folders, are structured as a tree. Figure 5.2 illustrates a small part of a Unix file system hierarchy.

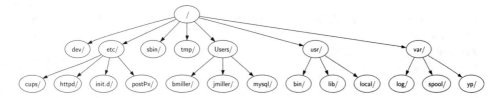

Figure 5.2: A Small Part of the Unix File System Hierarchy

The file system tree has much in common with the biological classification tree. You can follow a path from the root to any directory. That path will uniquely identify that subdirectory (and all the files in it). Another important property of trees, derived from their hierarchical nature, is that you can move entire sections of a tree (called a **subtree**) to a different position in the tree without affecting the lower levels of the hierarchy. For example, we could take the entire subtree staring with /etc/, detach etc/ from the root and reattach it under usr/. This would change the unique pathname to httpd from /etc/httpd to /usr/etc/httpd, but would not affect the contents or any children of the httpd directory.

A final example of a tree is a web page. The following is an example of a simple web page written using HTML. Figure 5.3 shows the tree that corresponds to each of the HTML tags used to create the page.

The HTML source code and the tree accompanying the source illustrate another hierarchy. Notice that each level of the tree corresponds to a level of nesting inside the HTML tags. The first tag in the source is <html> and the last is </html> All the rest of the tags in the page are inside the pair. If you check, you will see that this nesting property is true at all levels of the tree.

```
<html xmlns="http://www.w3.org/1999/xhtml"
      xml:lang="en" lang="en">
<head>
   <meta http-equiv="Content-Type"
         content="text/html; charset=utf-8" />
   <title>simple</title>
</head>
<body>
<h1>A simple web page</h1>
<ul>
    <li>List item one</li>
    <li>List item two</li>
</ul>
<h2><a href="http://www.cs.luther.edu">Luther CS </a><h2>
</body>
</html>
```

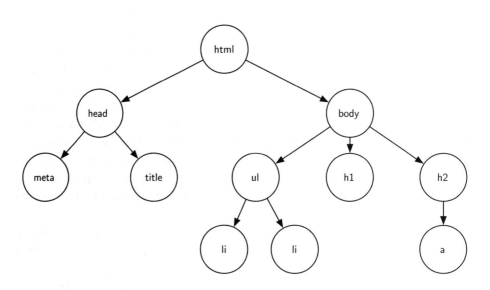

Figure 5.3: A Tree Corresponding to the Markup Elements of a Webpage

5.3 Vocabulary and Definitions

Now that we have looked at examples of trees, we will formally define a tree and its components.

Node A node is a fundamental part of a tree. It can have a name, which we call the "key." A node may also have additional information. We call this additional information the "payload." While the payload information is not central to many tree algorithms, it is often critical in applications that make use of trees.

Edge An edge is another fundamental part of a tree. An edge connects two nodes to show that there is a relationship between them. Every node (except the root) is connected by exactly one incoming edge from another node. Each node may have several outgoing edges.

Root The root of the tree is the only node in the tree that has no incoming edges. In Figure 5.2, / is the root of the tree.

Path A path is an ordered list of nodes that are connected by edges. For example, Mammal→Carnivora→Felidae→Felis→Domestica is a path.

Children The set of nodes c that have incoming edges from the same node to are said to be the children of that node. In Figure 5.2, nodes log/, spool/, and yp/ are the children of node var/.

Parent A node is the parent of all the nodes it connects to with outgoing edges. In Figure 5.2 the node var/ is the parent of nodes log/, spool/, and yp/.

sibling Nodes in the tree that are children of the same parent are said to be siblings. The nodes etc/ and usr/ are siblings in the filesystem tree.

subtree A subtree is a set of nodes and edges comprised of a parent and all the descendants of that parent.

leaf node A leaf node is a node that has no children. For example, Human and Chimpanzee are leaf nodes in Figure 5.1.

Level The level of a node n is the number of edges on the path from the root node to n. For example, the level of the Felis node in Figure 5.1 is five. By definition, the level of the root node is zero.

Height The height of a tree is equal to the maximum level of any node in the tree. The height of the tree in Figure 5.2 is two.

With the basic vocabulary now defined, we can move on to a formal definition of a tree. In fact, we will provide two definitions of a tree. One definition involves nodes and edges. The second definition, which will prove to be very useful, is a recursive definition.

Definition 1: A tree consists of a set of nodes and a set of edges that connect pairs of nodes. A tree has the following properties:

- One node of the tree is designated as the root node.

- Every node n, except the root node, is connected by an edge from exactly one other node p, where p is the parent of n.

- A unique path traverses from the root to each node.

- If each node in the tree has a maximum of two children, we say that the tree is a **binary tree**.

Figure 5.4 illustrates a tree that fits definition one. The arrowheads on the edges indicate the direction of the connection.

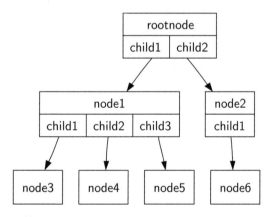

Figure 5.4: A Tree Consisting of a Set of Nodes and Edges

Definition Two: A tree is either empty or consists of a root and zero or more subtrees, each of which is also a tree. The root of each subtree is connected to the root of the parent tree by an edge. Figure 5.5 illustrates this recursive definition of a tree. Using the recursive definition of a tree, we know that the tree in Figure 5.5 has at least four nodes, since each of the

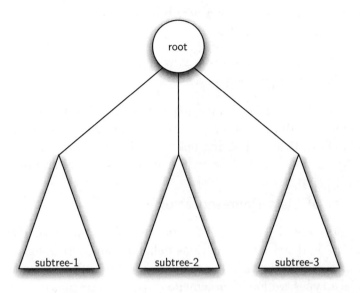

Figure 5.5: A Recursive Definition of a Tree

triangles representing a subtree must have a root. It may have many more
nodes than that, but we do not know unless we look deeper into the tree.

5.4 Implementation

Keeping in mind the definitions from the previous section, we can use the
following functions to create and manipulate a binary tree:

- `BinaryTree()` creates a new instance of a binary tree.

- `getLeftChild()` returns the binary tree corresponding to the left child
  of the current node.

- `getRightChild()` returns the binary tree corresponding to the right
  child of the current node.

- `setRootVal(val)` stores the object in parameter `val` in the current
  node.

- `getRootVal()` returns the object stored in the current node.

- `insertLeft(val)` creates a new binary tree and installs it as the left child of the current node.

- `insertRight(val)` creates a new binary tree and installs it as the right child of the current node.

The key decision in implementing a tree is choosing a good internal storage technique. Python allows us two very interesting possibilities, so we will examine both before choosing one. The first technique we will call "list of lists," the second technique we will call "nodes and references."

5.4.1   List of Lists Representation

In a tree represented by a list of lists, we will begin with Python's list data structure and write the functions defined above. Although writing the interface as a set of operations on a list is a bit different from the other abstract data types we have implemented, it is interesting to do so because it provides us with a simple recursive data structure that we can look at and examine directly. In a list of lists tree, we will store the value of the root node as the first element of the list. The second element of the list will itself be a list that represents the left subtree. The third element of the list will be another list that represents the right subtree. To illustrate this storage technique, let's look at an example. Figure 5.6 shows a simple tree and the corresponding list implementation.

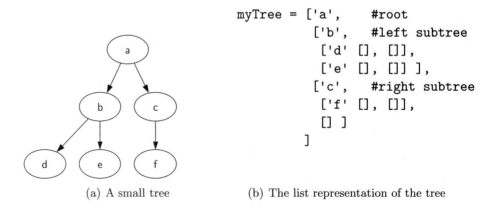

(a) A small tree   (b) The list representation of the tree

Figure 5.6: Representing a Tree As a List of Lists

Notice that we can access subtrees of the list using standard list slices. The root of the tree is `myTree[0]`, the left subtree of the root is `myTree[1]`, and the right subtree is `myTree[2]`. The following Python session illustrates creating a simple tree using a list. Once the tree is constructed, we can access the root and the left and right subtrees. One very nice property of this list of lists approach is that the structure of a list representing a subtree adheres to the structure defined for a tree; the structure itself is recursive! A subtree that has a root value and two empty lists is a leaf node. Another nice feature of the list of lists approach is that it generalizes to a tree that has many subtrees. In the case where the tree is more than a binary tree, another subtree is just another list.

```
>>> myTree = ['a', ['b', ['d',[],[]], ['e',[],[]] ], \
                  ['c', ['f',[],[]], [] ] ]
>>> myTree
['a', ['b', ['d',[],[]], ['e',[],[]]],
    ['c', ['f',[],[]], []]]
>>> myTree[1]
['b', ['d',[],[]], ['e',[],[]]]
>>> myTree[0]
'a'
>>> myTree[2]
['c', ['f'], []]
```

Let's formalize this definition of the tree data structure by providing some functions that make it easy for us to use lists as trees. Note that we are not going to define a binary tree class. The functions we will write will just help us manipulate a standard list as though we are working with a tree.

```
def BinaryTree(r):
    return [r, [], []]
```

Listing 5.1: List Functions

The `BinaryTree` function simply constructs a list with a root node and two empty sublists for the children. To add a left subtree to the root of a tree, we need to insert a new list into the second position of the root list. We must be careful. If the list already has something in the second position, we need to keep track of it and push it down the tree as the left child of the list we are adding. Listing 5.2 shows the Python code for inserting a left child.

```
1 | def insertLeft(root,newBranch):
2 |     t = root.pop(1)
3 |     if len(t) > 1:
4 |         root.insert(1,[newBranch,t,[]])
5 |     else:
6 |         root.insert(1,[newBranch, [], []])
7 |     return root
```

Listing 5.2: Insert a Left Subtree

Notice that to insert a left child, we first obtain the (possibly empty) list that corresponds to the current left child. We then add the new left child, installing the old left child as the left child of the new one. This allows us to splice a new node into the tree at any position. The code for `insertRight` is similar to `insertLeft` and is shown in Listing 5.3.

```
1 | def insertRight(root,newBranch):
2 |     t = root.pop(2)
3 |     if len(t) > 1:
4 |         root.insert(2,[newBranch,[],t])
5 |     else:
6 |         root.insert(2,[newBranch,[],[]])
7 |     return root
```

Listing 5.3: Insert a Right Subtree

To round out this set of tree-making functions, let's write a couple of access functions for getting and setting the root value, as well as getting the left or right subtrees.

The Python session in Figure 5.7 exercises the tree functions we have just written. You should type in this code and try it out for yourself. One of the exercises asks you to draw the tree structure resulting from this set of calls.

5.4.2   Nodes and References

Our second method to represent a tree uses nodes and references. In this case we will define a class that has attributes for the root value, as well as the left and right subtrees. Since this representation more closely follows the object-oriented programming paradigm, we will continue to use this

```
1  def getRootVal(root):
2      return root[0]
3
4  def setRootVal(root,newVal):
5      root[0] = newVal
6
7  def getLeftChild(root):
8      return root[1]
9
10 def getRightChild(root):
11     return root[2]
```

Listing 5.4: Access Functions for Parts of the Tree

representation for the remainder of the chapter.

Using nodes and references, we might think of the tree as being structured like the one shown in Figure 5.8.

We will start out with a simple class definition for the nodes and references approach as shown in Listing 5.5. The important thing to remember about this representation is that the attributes left and right will become references to other instances of the BinaryTree class. For example, when we insert a new left child into the tree we create another instance of BinaryTree and modify self.left in the root to reference the new tree.

```
1  class BinaryTree:
2      def __init__(self,rootObj):
3          self.key = rootObj
4          self.left = None
5          self.right = None
```

Listing 5.5: A Simple Class Definition

Notice that in Listing 5.5, the constructor function expects to get some kind of object to store in the root. Just like you can store any object you like in a list, the root object of a tree can be a reference to any object. For our early examples, we will store the name of the node as the root value. Using nodes and references to represent the tree in Figure 5.8, we would create six instances of the BinaryTree class.

Next let's look at the functions we need to build the tree beyond the root node. To add a left child to the tree, we will create a new binary tree

```
>>> r = BinaryTree(3)
>>> insertLeft(r,4)
[3, [4,[],[]],[]]
>>> insertLeft(r,5)
[3, [5, [4,[],[]],[]],[]]
>>> insertRight(r,6)
[3, [5, [4,[],[]],[]],[6, [], []]]
>>> insertRight(r,7)
[3, [5, [4,[],[]],[]],[7, [6, [], []]]]
>>> l = getLeftChild(r)
>>> l
[5, [4],[]]
>>> setRootVal(l,9)
>>> r
[3, [9, [4,[],[]],[]],[7, [6, [], []]]]
>>> insertLeft(l,11)
[9, [11, [4],[]],[]]
>>> r
[3, [11, [9, [4,[],[]],[]],[]], [7, [6, [], []]]]
>>>
```

Figure 5.7: A Python Session to Illustrate Basic Tree Functions

object and set the **left** attribute of the root to refer to this new object.
The code for **insertLeft** is shown in Listing 5.6.

```
1    def insertLeft(self,newNode):
2        if self.left == None:
3            self.left = BinaryTree(newNode)
4        else:
5            t = BinaryTree(newNode)
6            t.left = self.left
7            self.left = t
```

Listing 5.6: Insert a New Left Child

We must consider two cases for insertion. The first case is characterized
by a node with no existing left child. When there is no left child, simply

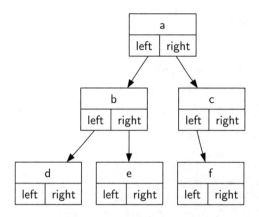

Figure 5.8: A Simple Tree Using a Nodes and References Approach

add a node to the tree. The second case is characterized by a node with an existing right child. In the second case, we insert a node and push the existing child down one level in the tree. The second case is handled by the `else` statement on line 4 of Listing 5.6.

The code for `insertRight` must consider a symmetric set of cases. There will either be no right child, or we must insert the node between the root and an existing right child. The insertion code is shown in Listing 5.7.

```
1    def insertRight(self,newNode):
2        if self.right == None:
3            self.right = BinaryTree(newNode)
4        else:
5            t = BinaryTree(newNode)
6            t.right = self.right
7            self.right = t
```

Listing 5.7: Code to Insert a Right Child

To round out the definition for a simple binary tree data structure, we will write access functions for the left and right children, as well as the root values.

Now that we have all the pieces to create and manipulate a binary tree, let's use them to check on the structure a bit more. Let's make a simple tree with node a as the root, and add nodes b and c as children. The following Python session creates the tree and looks at the some of the values stored

```
1     def getRootVal(self):
2         return self.key
3
4     def setRootVal(self,obj):
5         self.key = obj
6
7     def getLeftChild(self):
8         return self.left
9
10    def getRightChild(self):
11        return self.right
```

Listing 5.8: Access Methods for the Binary Tree Class

in key, left, and right. Notice that both the left and right children of the root are themselves distinct instances of the **BinaryTree** class. As we said in our original recursive definition for a tree, this allows us to treat any child of a binary tree as a binary tree itself.

```
cray:Examples> Python -i binaryTree.py
>>> r = BinaryTree('a')
>>> r.getRootVal()
'a'
>>> print r.getLeftChild()
None
>>> r.insertLeft('b')
>>> print r.getLeftChild()
<__main__.BinaryTree instance at 0x6b238>
>>> print r.getLeftChild().getRootVal()
b
>>> r.insertRight('c')
>>> print r.getRightChild()
<__main__.BinaryTree instance at 0x6b9e0>
>>> print r.getRightChild().getRootVal()
c
>>> r.getRightChild().setRootVal('hello')
>>> print r.getRightChild().getRootVal()
hello
>>>
```

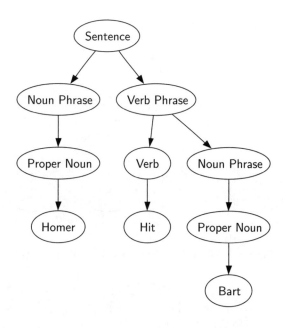

Figure 5.9: A Parse Tree for a Simple Sentence

5.5 | Binary Tree Applications

5.5.1 | Parse Tree

With the implementation of our tree data structure complete, we now look at an example of how a tree can be used to solve some real problems. In this section we will look at parse trees. Parse trees can be used to represent real-world constructions like sentences (see Figure 5.9), or mathematical expressions.

Figure 5.9 shows the hierarchical structure of a simple sentence. Representing a sentence as a tree structure allows us to work with the individual parts of the sentence by using subtrees.

We can also represent a mathematical expression such as $((7+3)*(5-2))$ as a parse tree, as shown in Figure 5.10. We have already looked at fully parenthesized expressions, so what do we know about this expression? We know that multiplication has a higher precedence than either addition or subtraction. Because of the parentheses, we know that before we can do the multiplication we must evaluate the parenthesized addition and subtraction expressions. The hierarchy of the tree helps us understand the order of evaluation for the whole expression. Before we can evaluate the top-level

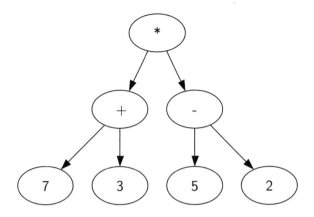

Figure 5.10: Parse Tree for $((7+3)*(5-2))$

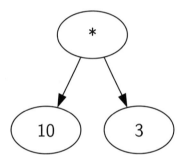

Figure 5.11: A simplified parse tree for $((7+3)*(5-2))$

multiplication, we must evaluate the addition and the subtraction in the subtrees. The addition, which is the left subtree, evaluates to 10. The subtraction, which is the right subtree, evaluates to 3. Using the hierarchical structure of trees, we can simply replace an entire subtree with one node once we have evaluated the expressions in the children. Applying this replacement procedure gives us the simplified tree shown in Figure 5.11.

In the rest of this section we are going to examine parse trees in more detail. In particular we will look at

- How to build a parse tree from a fully parenthesized mathematical expression.

- How to evaluate the expression stored in a parse tree.

- How to recover the original mathematical expression from a parse tree.

The first step in building a parse tree is to break up the expression string into a list of tokens. There are four different kinds of tokens to consider: left parentheses, right parentheses, operators, and operands. We know that whenever we read a left parenthesis we are starting a new expression, and hence we should create a new tree to correspond to that expression. Conversely, whenever we read a right parenthesis, we have finished an expression. We also know that operands are going to be leaf nodes and children of their operators. Finally, we know that every operator is going to have both a left and a right child.

Using the information from above we can define four rules as follows:

1. If the current token is a '(', add a new node as the left child of the current node, and descend to the left child.

2. If the current token is in the list ['+','-','/','*'], set the root value of the current node to the operator represented by the current token. Add a new node as the right child of the current node and descend to the right child.

3. If the current token is a number, set the root value of the current node to the number and return to the parent.

4. If the current token is a ')', go to the parent of the current node.

Before writing the Python code, let's look at an example of the rules outlined above in action. We will use the expression $(3 + (4 * 5))$. We will parse this expression into the following list of character tokens ['(', '3', '+', '(', '4', '*', '5' ,')',')']. Initially we will start out with a parse tree that consists of an empty root node. Figure 5.12 illustrates the structure and contents of the parse tree, as each new token is processed.

Using Figure 5.12, let's walk through the example step by step:

a) Create an empty tree.

b) Read (as the first token. By rule 1, create a new node as the left child of the root. Make the current node this new child.

c) Read 3 as the next token. By rule 3, set the root value of the current node to 3 and go back up the tree to the parent.

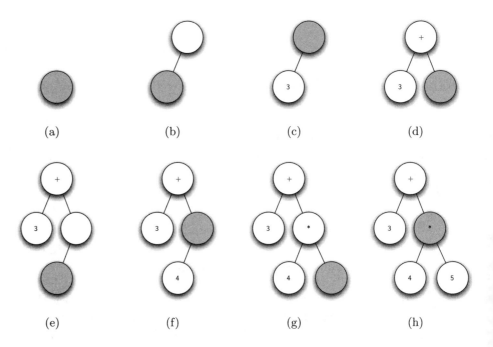

Figure 5.12: Tracing Parse Tree Construction

d) Read + as the next token. By rule 2, set the root value of the current node to + and add a new node as the right child. The new right child becomes the current node.

e) Read a (as the next token. By rule 1, create a new node as the left child of the current node. The new left child becomes the current node.

f) Read a 4 as the next token. By rule 3, set the value of the current node to 4. Make the parent of 4 the current node.

g) Read * as the next token. By rule 2, set the root value of the current node to * and create a new right child. The new right child becomes the current node.

h) Read 5 as the next token. By rule 3, set the root value of the current node to 5. Make the parent of 5 the current node.

i) Read) as the next token. By rule 4 we make the parent of * the current node.

j) Read) as the next token. By rule 4 we make the parent of + the current node. At this point there is no parent for + so we are done.

From the example above, it is clear that we need to keep track of the current node as well as the parent of the current node. The tree interface provides us with a way to get children of a node, through the `getLeftChild` and `getRightChild` methods, but how can we keep track of the parent? A simple solution to keeping track of parents as we traverse the tree is to use a stack. Whenever we want to descend to a child of the current node, we first push the current node on the stack. When we want to return to the parent of the current node, we pop the parent off the stack.

Using the rules described above, along with the `Stack` and `BinaryTree` operations, we are now ready to write a Python function to create a parse tree. The code for our parse tree builder is presented in Listing 5.9.

```python
def buildParseTree(fpexp):
    fplist = fpexp.split()
    pStack = Stack()
    eTree = BinaryTree('')
    pStack.push(eTree)
    currentTree = eTree
    for i in fplist:
        if i == '(':
            currentTree.insertLeft('')
            pStack.push(currentTree)
            currentTree = currentTree.getLeftChild()
        elif i not in '+-*/)':
            currentTree.setRootVal(eval(i))
            parent = pStack.pop()
            currentTree = parent
        elif i in '+-*/':
            currentTree.setRootVal(i)
            currentTree.insertRight('')
            pStack.push(currentTree)
            currentTree = currentTree.getRightChild()
        elif i == ')':
            currentTree = pStack.pop()
        else:
            print "error:  I don't recognize " + i
    return eTree
```

Listing 5.9: Code to Create a Parse Tree

The four rules for building a parse tree are coded as the first four clauses
of the if statement on lines 8, 12, 16, and 21 of Listing 5.9. In each case you
can see that the code implements the rule, as described above, with a few
calls to the BinaryTree or Stack methods. The only error checking we do
in this function is in the else clause, where we print an error message if we
get a token from the list that we do not recognize. Now that we have built
a parse tree, what can we do with it? As a first example, we will write a
function to evaluate the parse tree, returning the numerical result. To write
this function, we will make use of the hierarchical nature of the tree. Look
back at Figure 5.10. Recall that we can replace the original tree with the
simplified tree shown in Figure 5.11. This suggests that we can write an
algorithm that evaluates a parse tree by recursively evaluating each subtree.

As we have done with past recursive algorithms, we will begin the design
for the recursive evaluation function by identifying the base case. A natural
base case for recursive algorithms that operate on trees is to check for a
leaf node. In a parse tree, the leaf nodes will always be operands. Since
numerical objects like integers and floating points require no further interpretation, the evaluate function can simply return the value stored in the
leaf node. The recursive step that moves the function toward the base case
is to call evaluate on both the left and the right children of the current
node. The recursive call effectively moves us down the tree, toward a leaf
node. To put the results of the two recursive calls together, we can simply
apply the operator stored in the parent node to the results returned from
evaluating both children. In the example from Figure 5.11 we see that the
two children of the root evaluate to themselves, namely 10 and 3. Applying
the multiplication operator gives us a final result of 30.

The code for a recursive evaluate function is shown in Listing 5.10.
First, we obtain references to the left and the right children of the current
node. If both the left and right children evaluate to None, then we know that
the current node is really a leaf node. This check is on line 7. If the current
node is not a leaf node, look up the operator in the current node and apply
it to the results from recursively evaluating the left and right children.

To make the evaluation easy, we use a dictionary with the keys '+',
'-', '*', and '/'. The values stored in the dictionary are functions from
Python's operator module. The operator module provides us with the functional versions of many commonly used operators. When we look up an
operator in the dictionary, the corresponding function object is retrieved.
Since the retrieved object is a function, we can call it in the usual way
function(parameter1,parameter2). So the lookup opers['+'](2,2) is
equivalent to operator.add(2,2).

Finally, we will trace the evaluate function on the parse tree we created
in Figure 5.12. When we first call evaluate, we pass the root of the entire

```
1    def evaluate(parseTree):
2        opers = {'+':operator.add, '-':operator.sub,
3                 '*':operator.mul, '/':operator.div}
4        leftC = parseTree.getLeftChild()
5        rightC = parseTree.getRightChild()
6
7        if leftC and rightC:
8            fn = opers[parseTree.getRootVal()]
9            return fn(evaluate(leftC),evaluate(rightC))
10       else:
11           return parseTree.getRootVal()
```

Listing 5.10: A Recursive Function to Evaluate a Binary Parse Tree

tree as the parameter `parseTree`. Then we obtain references to the left and right children to make sure they exist. The recursive call takes place on line 9. We begin by looking up the operator in the root of the tree, which is `'+'`. The `'+'` operator maps to the `operator.add` function call, which takes two parameters. As usual for a Python function call, the first thing Python does is to evaluate the parameters that are passed to the function. In this case both parameters are recursive function calls to our `evaluate` function. Using left-to-right evaluation, the first recursive call goes to the left. In the first recursive call the `evaluate` function is given the left subtree. We find that the node has no left or right children, so we are in a leaf node. When we are in a leaf node we just return the value stored in the leaf node as the result of the evaluation. In this case we return the integer 3.

At this point we have one parameter evaluated for our top-level call to `operator.add`. But we are not done yet. Continuing the left-to-right evaluation of the parameters, we now make a recursive call to evaluate the right child of the root. We find that the node has both a left and a right child so we look up the operator stored in this node, `'*'`, and call this function using the left and right children as the parameters. At this point you can see that both recursive calls will be to leaf nodes, which will evaluate to the integers four and five respectively. With the two parameters evaluated, we return the result of `operator.mul(4,5)`. At this point we have evaluated the operands for the top level `'+'` operator and all that is left to do is finish the call to `operator.add(3,20)`. The result of the evaluation of the entire expression tree for $(3 + (4 * 5))$ is 23.

5.5.2 Tree Traversals

Now that we have examined the basic functionality of our tree data structure, it is time to look at some additional usage patterns for trees. These usage patterns can be divided into the three ways that we access the nodes of the tree. There are three commonly used patterns to visit all the nodes in a tree. The difference between these methods is the order in which each node is visited. We call this visitation of the nodes a "traversal." The three traversals we will look at are the **preorder**, **inorder**, and **postorder**. Let's start out by defining these three traversals more carefully, then look at some examples where these patterns are useful.

preorder In a preorder traversal, we visit the root node first, then recursively do a preorder traversal of the left subtree, followed by a recursive preorder traversal of the right subtree.

inorder In an inorder traversal, we recursively do an inorder traversal on the left subtree, visit the root node, and finally do a recursive inorder traversal of the right subtree.

postorder In a postorder traversal, we recursively do a postorder traversal of the left subtree and the right subtree followed by a visit to the root node.

Let's look at some examples that illustrate each of these three kinds of traversals. First let's look at the preorder traversal. As an example of a tree to traverse, we will represent this book as a tree. The book is the root of the tree, and each chapter is a child of the root. Each section within a chapter is a child of the chapter, and each subsection is a child of its section, and so on. Figure 5.13 shows a limited version of a book with only two chapters. Note that the traversal algorithm works for trees with any number of children, but we will stick with binary trees for now.

Suppose that you wanted to read this book from front to back. The preorder traversal gives you exactly that ordering. Starting at the root of the tree (the Book node) we will follow the preorder traversal instructions. We recursively call `preorder` on the left child, in this case Chapter1. We again recursively call `preorder` on the left child to get to Section 1.1. Since Section 1.1 has no children, we do not make any additional recursive calls. When we are finished with Section 1.1, we move up the tree to Chapter 1. At this point we still need to visit the right subtree of Chapter 1, which is Section 1.2. As before we visit the left subtree, which brings us to Section

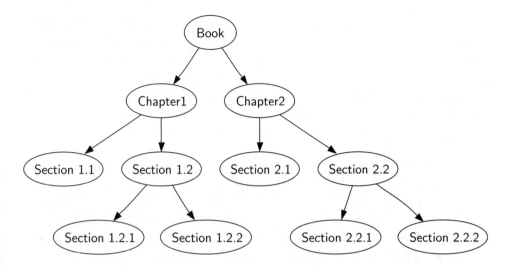

Figure 5.13: Representing a Book As a Tree

1.2.1, then we visit the node for Section 1.2.2. With Section 1.2 finished, we return to Chapter 1. Then we return to the Book node and follow the same procedure for Chapter 2.

The code for writing tree traversals is surprisingly elegant, largely because the traversals are written recursively. Listing 5.12 shows the Python code for a preorder traversal of a binary tree.

You may wonder, what is the best way to write an algorithm like preorder traversal? Should it be a function that simply uses a tree as a data structure, or should it be a method of the tree data structure itself? Listing 5.11 shows a version of the preorder traversal written as an external function that takes a binary tree as a parameter. The external function is particularly elegant because our base case is simply to check if the tree exists. If the tree parameter is None, then the function returns without taking any action.

```
1  def preorder(tree):
2      if tree:
3          print tree.getRootVal()
4          preorder(tree.getLeftChild())
5          preorder(tree.getRightChild())
```

Listing 5.11: External Function Implementing Preorder Traversal of a Tree

We can also implement **preorder** as a method of the **BinaryTree** class. The code for implementing **preorder** as an internal method is shown in Listing 5.12. Notice what happens when we move the code from internal to external. In general, we just replace **tree** with **self**. However, we also need to modify the base case. The internal method must check for the existence of the left and the right children *before* making the recursive call to **preorder**.

```
def preorder(self):
    print self.key
    if self.left:
        self.left.preorder()
    if self.right:
        self.right.preorder()
```

Listing 5.12: Preorder Traversal Implemented as a Method of `BinaryTree`

Which of these two ways to implement **preorder** is best? The answer is that implementing **preorder** as an external function is probably better in this case. The reason is that you very rarely want to just traverse the tree. In most cases you are going to want to accomplish something else while using one of the basic traversal patterns. In fact, we will see in the next example that the **postorder** traversal pattern follows very closely with the code we wrote earlier to evaluate a parse tree. Therefore we will write the rest of the traversals as external functions.

The algorithm for the **postorder** traversal, in Listing 5.13 is nearly identical to **preorder**, except that we move the call to print to the end of the function.

```
def postorder(tree):
    if tree != None:
        postorder(tree.getLeftChild())
        postorder(tree.getRightChild())
        print tree.getRootVal()
```

Listing 5.13: Postorder Traversal Algorithm

We have already seen a common use for the postorder traversal, namely evaluating a parse tree. Look back at Listing 5.10 again. What we are doing is evaluating the left subtree, evaluating the right subtree, and combining them in the root through the function call to an operator. Assume that our binary tree is going to store only expression tree data. Let's rewrite the evaluation function, but model it even more closely on the `postorder` code in Listing 5.13.

```
def postordereval(tree):
    opers = {'+':operator.add, '-':operator.sub,
             '*':operator.mul, '/':operator.div}
    res1 = None
    res2 = None
    if tree:
        res1 = postordereval(tree.getLeftChild())
        res2 = postordereval(tree.getRightChild())
        if res1 and res2:
            return opers[tree.getRootVal()](res1,res2)
        else:
            return tree.getRootVal()
```

Listing 5.14: Postorder Evaluation Algorithm

Notice that the form in Listing 5.14 is the same as the form in Listing 5.13, except that instead of printing the key at the end of the function, we return it. This allows us to save the values returned from the recursive calls in lines 7 and 8. We then use these saved values along with the operator on line 10.

The final traversal we will look at in this section is the inorder traversal. In the inorder traversal we visit the left subtree, followed by the root, and finally the right subtree. Listing 5.15 shows our code for the inorder traversal. Notice that in all three of the traversal functions we are simply changing the position of the `print` statement with respect to the two recursive function calls.

```
def inorder(tree):
    if tree != None:
        inorder(tree.getLeftChild())
        print tree.getRootVal()
        inorder(tree.getRightChild())
```

Listing 5.15: Inorder Traversal Algorithm

If we perform a simple inorder traversal of a parse tree we get our original expression back, without any parentheses. Let's modify the basic inorder algorithm to allow us to recover the fully parenthesized version of the expression. The only modifications we will make to the basic template are as follows: print a left parenthesis *before* the recursive call to the left subtree, and print a right parenthesis *after* the recursive call to the right subtree. The modified code is shown in Listing 5.16.

```
1  def printexp(tree):
2      sVal = ""
3      if tree:
4          sVal = '(' + printexp(tree.getLeftChild())
5          sVal = sVal + str(tree.getRootVal())
6          sVal = sVal + printexp(tree.getRightChild())+')'
7      return sVal
```

Listing 5.16: Modified Inorder Traversal to Print Fully Parenthesized Expression

The following Python session shows the `printexp` and `postordereval` methods in action.

```
>>> x = BinaryTree('*')
>>> x.insertLeft('+')
>>> l = x.getLeftChild()
>>> l.insertLeft(4)
>>> l.insertRight(5)
>>> x.insertRight(7)
>>>
>>> print printexp(x)
(((4) + (5)) * (7))
>>>
>>> import operator
>>> print postordereval(x)
63
>>>
```

Notice that the `printexp` function as we have implemented it puts parentheses around each number. While not incorrect, the parentheses are clearly not needed. In the exercises at the end of this chapter you are asked to modify the `printexp` function to remove this set of parentheses.

5.6   Binary Search Trees

In Chapter 4 we saw two different ways to get key-value pairs in a collection. We call those collections **map** structures. The two implementations of a map structure we discussed were binary search on a list and hash tables. In this section we will study **binary search trees** as yet another way to map from a key to a value. In this case we are not interested in the exact placement of items in the tree, but we are interested in using the binary tree structure to provide for efficient searching.

5.6.1 Search Tree Operations

Before we look at the implementation, let's look at the interface provided by a binary search tree. You will notice that this interface is nearly identical to the Python dictionary!

- `BinaryTree()` Create a new, empty binary tree.

- `put(key,val)` Add a new key-value pair to the tree.

- `get(key)` Given a key, return the value stored in the tree or `None` otherwise.

- `delete_key(key)` Delete the key-value pair from the tree.

- `length()` Return the number of key-value pairs stored in the tree.

- `has_key(key)` Return `True` if the given key is in the dictionary.

- `operators` We can use the above methods to overload the [] operators for both assignment and lookup. In addition, we can use `has_key` to override the `in` operator.

5.6.2 Search Tree Implementation

A binary search tree relies on the property that keys that are less than the parent are found in the left subtree, and keys that are greater than the parent are found in the right subtree. We will call this the **bst property**. As we implement the interface functions described above, the bst property will guide our implementation. Figure 5.14 illustrates this property of a binary search tree, showing the keys without any payload information. Notice that the property holds for each parent and child. All of the keys in the left subtree are less than the key in the root. All of the keys in the right subtree are greater than the root.

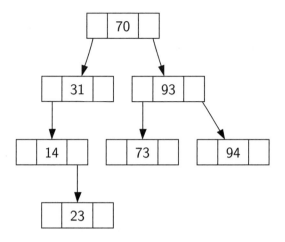

Figure 5.14: A Simple Binary Search Tree

Now that you know what a binary search tree is, we will look at how a binary search tree is constructed. The search tree in Figure 5.14 represents the nodes that exist after we have inserted the following keys in the order shown: 70, 31, 93, 94, 14, 23, 73. Since 70 was the first key inserted into the tree, it is the root. Next, 31 is less than 70, so it becomes the left child of 70. Next, 93 is greater than 70, so it becomes the right child of 70. Now we have two levels of the tree filled, so the next key is going to be the left or right child of either 31 or 93. Since 94 is greater than 70 and 93, it becomes the right child of 93. Similarly 14 is less than 70 and 31, so it becomes the left child of 31. 23 is also less than 31, so it must be in the left subtree of 31. However, it is greater than 14, so it becomes the right child of 14.

To implement the binary search tree, we will use the nodes and references approach similar to the one we used in the expression tree example. However, because we must be able create and work with a binary search tree that is empty, our implementation will use two classes. The first class we will call **BinarySearch** tree, and the second class we will call **TreeNode**. The **BinarySearchTree** class has a reference to the **TreeNode** that is the root of the binary search tree. In most cases the methods defined in the outer class simply check to see if the tree is empty. If there are nodes in the tree, the request is just passed on to the **TreeNode** at the root of the tree. In the case where the tree is empty or we want to delete the key at the root of the tree, we must take special action. The code for the **BinarySearchTree** class is shown in Listing 5.17.

```
1   class BinarySearchTree:
2       def __init__(self):
3           self.root = None
4           self.size = 0
5
6       def put(self,key,val):
7           if self.root:
8               self.root.put(key,val)
9           else:
10              self.root = TreeNode(key,val)
11          self.size = self.size + 1
12
13      def __setitem__(self,k,v):
14          self.put(k,v)
15
16      def get(self,key):
17          if self.root:
18              return self.root.get(key)
19          else:
20              return None
21
22      def __getitem__(self,key):
23          return self.get(key)
24
25      def has_key(self,key):
26          if self.root.get(key):
27              return True
28          else:
29              return False
30
31      def length(self):
32          return self.size
33
34      def __len__(self):
35          return self.size
36
37      def delete_key(self,key):
38          if self.size > 1:
39              self.root.delete_key(key)
40              self.size = self.size-1
41          elif self.root.key == key:
42              self.root = None
43              self.size = self.size - 1
44          else:
45              print 'error, bad key'
```

Listing 5.17: The Binary Search Tree Outer Class

```
1  class TreeNode:
2      def __init__(self,key,val,parent=None,
3                                left=None,right=None):
4          self.key = key
5          self.payload = val
6          self.leftChild = left
7          self.rightChild = right
8          self.parent = parent
```

Listing 5.18: Constructor for a TreeNode

All the really interesting work is done by the `TreeNode`, so we will focus our attention on the design and implementation of this class. The constructor for a `TreeNode` is shown in Listing 5.18. One big difference between the `TreeNode` class and the `BinaryTree` class from Section 5.4.1 is that we will explicitly keep track of the parent as an attribute of each node. You will see why this is important when we discuss the implementation for the `delete_key` method. Another interesting aspect of the implementation of `TreeNode` in Listing 5.18 is that we use Python's optional parameters. Optional parameters make it easy for us to create a `TreeNode` under several different circumstances. Sometimes we will want to construct a new `TreeNode` that already has both a `parent` and a `child`. With an existing parent and child, we can pass parent and child as parameters. At other times we will just create a `TreeNode` with the key value pair, and we will not pass any parameters for `parent` or `child`. In this case, the default value on the optional parameters are used.

Now that we have the constructor, let's write the put method that will allow us to build our binary search tree. The `put` method will do the following:

- Starting at the root of the tree, search the binary tree comparing the new key to the key in the current node. If the new key is less than the current node, search the left subtree. If the new key is greater than the current node, search the right subtree.

- When there is no left (or right) child to search, we have found the position in the tree where the new node should be installed.

- To add a node to the tree, create a new `BinarySearchTree` object and insert the object at the point discovered in the previous step.

Listing 5.19 shows the Python code for inserting a new node in the tree. The put function is written recursively following the steps outlined above. Notice that when a new child is inserted into the tree, the current node is passed to the new tree as the parent, using self.

```python
def put(self,key,val):
    if key < self.key:
        if self.leftChild:
            self.leftChild.put(key,val)
        else:
            self.leftChild = TreeNode(key,val,self)
    else:
        if self.rightChild:
            self.rightChild.put(key,val)
        else:
            self.rightChild = TreeNode(key,val,self)
```

Listing 5.19: Insert a New Node in a Binary Search Tree

With the put method defined, we can easily overload the [] operator for assignment by having the __setitem__ method call the put method. This allows us to write Python statements like myZipTree['Plymouth'] = 55446, just like a Python dictionary.

```python
def __setitem__(self,k,v):
    self.put(k,v)
```

Listing 5.20: Overloading __setitem__

Figure 5.15 illustrates the process for inserting a new node into a binary search tree. The lightly shaded nodes indicate the nodes that were visited during the insertion process.

Once the tree is constructed, the next task is to implement the retrieval of a value for a given key. The get method is even easier than the put method because it only needs to recursively search the tree until it gets to a non-matching leaf node or finds a matching key. When a matching key is found, the value stored in the payload of the node is returned.

Listing 5.21 shows the code for both get and __getitem__. The search code in the get method uses the same logic for choosing the left or right child as the put method. Once again, we can write a Python statement that

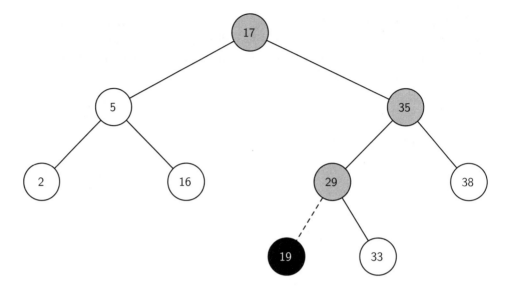

Figure 5.15: Inserting a Node with Key $= 19$

looks just like we are accessing a dictionary, when in fact we are using a binary search tree, for example `z = myZipTree['Fargo']`.

Using `get`, we can implement both `has_key` as well as `__contains__`, by simply calling `get` and returning `True` if it returns a value, or `False` if it returns `None`. Recall that `__contains__` overloads the `in` operator, and allows us to write statements such as:

```
if 'Northfield' in myZipTree:
    print "oom ya ya"
```

Now let's look at the `length` method, which we will also use to overload the `len` operator. The `length` method must return the number of nodes in the tree. There are a couple of ways we could solve this problem. First, we could write a method that traverses all the nodes in the tree and counts the nodes as it visits each one. Any of the traversal algorithms we wrote in section 5.5.2 could be modified to do this. However, that is a lot of work to do each time we want to know how big our tree has become. An easier solution is to store the length of the tree in the root. Each time we add a node to a tree, we increment the counter in the root. Of course since our tree is defined recursively, this means that each node knows the size of the subtree rooted at that node. By trading off a bit of storage, the `length` method is now simple. We leave it as an exercise to add one line to

```
1  def get(self,key):
2      if key == self.key:
3          return self.payload
4      elif key < self.key:
5          if self.leftChild:
6              return self.leftChild.get(key)
7          else:
8              return None
9      elif key > self.key:
10         if self.rightChild:
11             return self.rightChild.get(key)
12         else:
13             return None
14     else:
15         print 'error: this line should never be executed'
16
17 def __getitem__(self,key):
18     return self.get(key)
```

Listing 5.21: Find the Value Stored with a Key

__init__, and put(key,val) to keep track of the size attribute.

```
1      def length(self):
2          return self.size
3
4      def __len__(self):
5          return self.size
```

Listing 5.22: A Simple length Method

Finally, we turn our attention to the most challenging method in the binary search tree, the deletion of a key. When we delete a key from a tree, there are three cases that we must consider:

1. The node to be deleted has no children (see Figure 5.16).

2. The node to be deleted has only one child (see Figure 5.17).

3. The node to be deleted has two children (see Figure 5.18).

The first case is straightforward. If the node has no children all we need to do is delete the node and remove the reference to this node in the parent. The code for this case is shown in Listing 5.23.

```
if not (self.leftChild or self.rightChild):
    print "removing a node with no children"
    if self == self.parent.leftChild:
        self.parent.leftChild = None
    else:
        self.parent.rightChild = None
```

Listing 5.23: Case 1: Deleting a Node with No Children

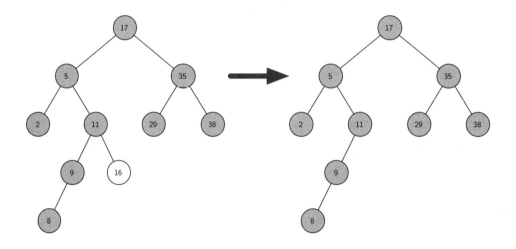

Figure 5.16: Deleting Node 16, a Node Without Children

The second case is only slightly more complicated. If a node has only a single child, then we can simply promote the child to take the place of its parent. The code for this case is shown in Listing 5.24.

The third case is the most difficult case to handle. If a node has two children, then it is unlikely that we can simply promote one of them to take the node's place. We can, however, search the tree for a node that can be used to replace the one scheduled for deletion. What we need is a node that will preserve the binary search tree relationships for both of the existing left and right subtrees. The node that will do this is the node that has the next-largest key in the tree. We call this node the **successor**, and we will look at a way to find the successor shortly. The successor is guaranteed to

```
1  elif (self.leftChild or self.rightChild) \
2        and (not (self.leftChild and self.rightChild)):
3      print "removing a node with one child"
4      if self.leftChild:
5          if self == self.parent.leftChild:
6              self.parent.leftChild = self.leftChild
7          else:
8              self.parent.rightChild = self.leftChild
9      else:
10         if self == self.parent.leftChild:
11             self.parent.leftChild = self.rightChild
12         else:
13             self.parent.rightChild = self.rightChild
```

Listing 5.24: Case 2: Deleting a Node with One Child

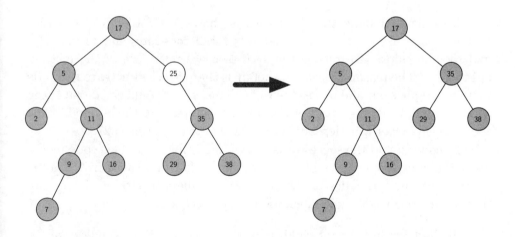

Figure 5.17: Deleting Node 25, a Node That Has a Single Child

have zero or one children, so we know how to remove it using cases one or two. Once the node has been removed, we simply put it in the tree in place of the node to be deleted.

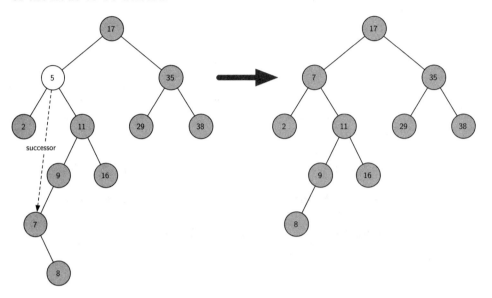

Figure 5.18: Deleting Node 5, a Node with Two Children

The code to handle the third case is shown in Listing 5.25. Notice that we make use of the helper methods `findSuccessor` and `findMin` to find the successor. To remove the successor, we make use of the method `spliceOut`. The reason we use `spliceOut` is that it goes directly to the node we want to splice out and makes the right changes. We could call `delete_key` recursively, but then we would waste time re-searching for the key node. The code for the helper function `spliceOut` is shown in Listing 5.27.

The code to find the successor is shown in Listing 5.26. This code makes use of the same properties of binary search trees that cause an inorder traversal to print out the nodes in the tree from smallest to largest. There are three cases to consider when looking for the successor:

1. If the node has a right child, then the successor is the smallest key in the right subtree.

2. If the node has no right child and is the immediate left child of its parent, then the parent is the successor.

3. If the node is the immediate right child of its parent, and itself has

```
1  else:
2      succ = self.findSuccessor()
3      succ.spliceOut()
4      if self == self.parent.leftChild:
5          self.parent.leftChild = succ
6      else:
7          self.parent.rightChild = succ
8      succ.leftChild = self.leftChild
9      succ.rightChild = self.rightChild
```

Listing 5.25: Case 3: Delete a Node with Two Children

no right child, then the successor to this node is the successor of its parent, excluding this node.

The first condition is the only one that matters for us when deleting a node from a binary search tree. However, the `findSuccessor` method has other uses that we will explore in the exercises at the end of this chapter. The `findMin` method is called to find the minimum key in a subtree. You should convince yourself that the minimum valued key in any binary search tree is the left most child of the tree. Therefore the `findMin` method simply follows the `leftChild` references in each node of the subtree until it reaches a node that does not have a left child. The complete listing for `delete_key` is given in Listing 5.28.

We need to look at one last interface method for the binary search tree. Suppose that we would like to simply iterate over all the keys in the tree in order. This is definitely something we have done with dictionaries, so why not trees? You already know how to traverse a binary tree in order, using the `inorder` traversal algorithm. However, writing an iterator requires a bit more work, since an iterator should return only one node each time the iterator is called.

Python provides us with a very powerful function to use when creating an iterator. The function is called `yield`. `yield` is similar to `return` in that it returns a value to the caller. However, `yield` also takes the additional step of freezing the state of the function so that the next time the function is called it continues executing from the exact point it left off earlier. The code for an `inorder` iterator of a binary tree is shown in Listing 5.29. Look at this code carefully; at first glance you might think that the code is not recursive. However, remember that `__iter__` overrides the `for x in` operation for iteration, so it really is recursive!

```
1     def findSuccessor(self):
2         succ = None
3         if self.rightChild:
4             succ = self.rightChild.findMin()
5         else:
6             if self.parent.leftChild == self:
7                 succ = self.parent
8             else:
9                 self.parent.rightChild = None
10                succ = self.parent.findSuccessor()
11                self.parent.rightChild = self
12        return succ
13
14    def findMin(self):
15        n = self
16        while n.leftChild:
17            n = n.leftChild
18        print 'found min, key = ', n.key
19        return n
```

Listing 5.26: Finding the Successor

```
1   def spliceOut(self):
2       if (not self.leftChild and not self.rightChild):
3           if self == self.parent.leftChild:
4               self.parent.leftChild = None
5           else:
6               self.parent.rightchild = None
7       elif (self.leftChild or self.rightChild):
8           if self.leftChild:
9               if self == self.parent.leftChild:
10                  self.parent.leftChild = self.leftChild
11              else:
12                  self.parent.rightChild = self.leftChild
13          else:
14              if self == self.parent.leftChild:
15                  self.parent.leftChild = self.rightChild
16              else:
17                  self.parent.rightChild = self.rightChild
```

Listing 5.27: Helper Method to Splice Out a Node

```
 1  def delete_key(self,key):
 2      if self.key == key:    # do the removal
 3          if not (self.leftChild or self.rightChild):
 4              if self == self.parent.leftChild:
 5                  self.parent.leftChild = None
 6              else:
 7                  self.parent.rightChild = None
 8          elif (self.leftChild or self.rightChild) and \
 9                (not (self.leftChild and self.rightChild)):
10              if self.leftChild:
11                  if self == self.parent.leftChild:
12                      self.parent.leftChild = self.leftChild
13                  else:
14                      self.parent.rightChild = self.leftChild
15              else:
16                  if self == self.parent.leftChild:
17                      self.parent.leftChild = self.rightChild
18                  else:
19                      self.parent.rightChild = self.rightChild
20          else:  # replace self with successor
21              succ = self.findSuccessor()
22              succ.spliceOut()
23              if self == self.parent.leftChild:
24                  self.parent.leftChild = succ
25              else:
26                  self.parent.rightChild = succ
27              succ.leftChild = self.leftChild
28              succ.rightChild = self.rightChild
29      else: # continue looking
30          if key < self.key:
31              if self.leftChild:
32                  self.leftChild.delete_key(key)
33              else:
34                  print "Trying to remove a non-existant node"
35          else:
36              if self.rightChild:
37                  self.rightChild.delete_key(key)
38              else:
39                  print "Trying to remove a non-existant node"
```

Listing 5.28: Code for Deleting a Key

```
1    def __iter__(self):
2        if self:
3            if self.leftChild:
4                for elem in self.leftChild:
5                    yield elem
6            yield self.key
7            if self.rightChild:
8                for elem in self.rightChild:
9                    yield elem
```

Listing 5.29: An Iterator for a Binary Search Tree

5.6.3 Search Tree Analysis

With the implementation of a binary search tree now complete, we will do a quick analysis of the interface calls.

Let's first look at the put method. The limiting factor on its performance is the height of the binary tree. Recall from section 5.3 that the height of a tree is the number of edges between the root and the deepest leaf node. The height is the limiting factor because when we are searching for the appropriate place to insert a node into the tree, we will need to do at most one comparison at each level of the tree.

How high is a binary tree likely to be? The answer to this question depends on how the keys are added to the tree. If the keys are added in a random order, the height of the tree is going to be $\log_2 n$ where n is the number of nodes in the tree. In this case the tree has roughly the same number of nodes in the left subtree as the right subtree. We call such a tree "balanced." In a balanced binary tree, the worst-case performance of put is $O(\log_2 n)$.

Unfortunately it is possible to construct a search tree that has height n simply by inserting the keys in sorted order! An example of such a tree is shown in Figure 5.19. In this case the performance of the put method is $O(n)$.

There are improvements to the binary search tree that ensure the tree remains balanced. These improved trees are called "AVL" and "red-black trees." You will most likely study one of the two in your advanced data structures course.

Now that you understand that the performance of the put method is limited by the height of the tree, you can probably guess that other methods, get, has_key, and delete_key, are limited as well. Since get searches the

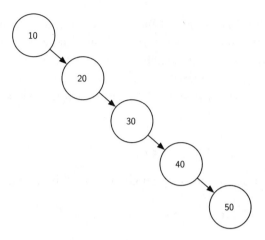

Figure 5.19: A Skewed Binary Search Tree

tree to find the key, in the worst case the tree is searched all the way to the bottom and no key is found. At first glance `delete_key` might seem more complicated, since it may need to search for the successor before the deletion operation can complete. But remember that the worst-case scenario to find the successor is also just the height of the tree.

5.7 Priority Queues with Binary Heaps

In Chapter 2 you learned about the first in first out data structure called a queue. One important variation of a queue is called a **priority queue**. A priority queue acts like a queue in that you dequeue an item by removing it from the front. However, in a priority queue the logical order of items inside a queue is determined by their priority. The highest priority items are at the front of the queue and the lowest priority items are at the back. Thus when you enqueue an item on a priority queue, the new item may move all the way to the front. We will see that the priority queue is a useful data structure for some of the graph algorithms we will study in the next chapter.

You can probably think of a couple of easy ways to implement a priority queue using sorting functions and lists. However, inserting into a list is $O(n)$ and sorting a list is $O(n \log n)$. We can do better. The classic way to implement a priority queue is using a data structure called a **binary heap**. A binary heap will allow us both enqueue and dequeue items in $O(\log n)$.

The binary heap is interesting to study because when we diagram the heap it looks a lot like a tree, but when we implement it we use only a single list as an internal representation. The binary heap has two common variations: the **min heap**, in which the smallest key is always at the front, and the **max heap**, in which the largest key value is always at the front. In this section we will implement the min heap. We leave a max heap implementation as an exercise.

5.7.1 Binary Heap Operations

The basic operations we will implement for our binary heap are as follows:

- `BinaryHeap()` creates a new binary heap.

- `insert(k)` adds a new item to the heap.

- `findMin()` returns the item with the minimum key value, leaving item in the heap.

- `delMin()` returns the item with the minimum key value, removing the item from the heap.

- `isEmpty()` returns true if the heap is empty, false otherwise.

- `size()` returns the number of items in the heap.

- `buidHeap(list)` builds a new heap from a list of keys.

- `decreaseKey(k)` finds a key in the heap and updates its key value to a new lower value.

The following Python session demonstrates the use of some of the binary heap methods.

```
>>> bh = BinaryHeap()
>>> bh.insert(5)
>>> bh.insert(7)
>>> bh.insert(3)
>>> bh.insert(11)
>>> print bh.delMin()
3
>>> print bh.delMin()
5
>>> print bh.delMin()
```

```
7
>>> print bh.delMin()
11
```

5.7.2 | Binary Heap Implementation

5.7.2.1 | The Structure Property

In order to make our heap work efficiently, we will take advantage of the logarithmic nature of the tree to represent our heap. You learned in section 5.6.3 that in order to guarantee logarithmic performance, we must keep our tree balanced. To keep the tree balanced we will create a **complete binary tree**. A complete binary tree is a tree in which each level has all of its nodes. The exception to this is the bottom level of the tree, which we fill in from left to right. Figure 5.20 shows an example of a complete binary tree.

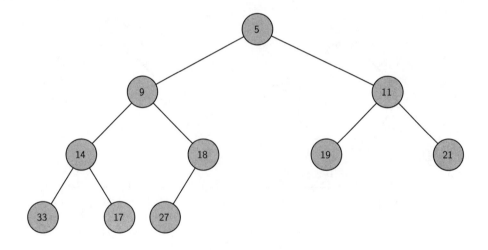

Figure 5.20: A Complete Binary Tree

Another interesting property of a complete tree is that we can represent it using a single list. We do not need to use nodes and references or even lists of lists. Because the tree is complete, the left child of a parent (at position p) is the node that is found in position $2p$ in the list. Similarly, the right child of the parent is at position $2p+1$ in the list. To find the parent of any node in the tree, we can simply use Python's integer division. Given that a node is at position n in the list, the parent is at position $n/2$. Figure 5.21

illustrates a complete binary tree and also gives the list representation of the tree. The list representation of the tree, along with the full structure property, allows us to efficiently traverse a complete binary tree using only a few simple mathematical operations. We will see that this also leads to an efficient implementation of our binary heap.

5.7.2.2   The Heap Order Property

The method that we will use to store items in a heap relies on maintaining the heap order property. The **heap order property** is as follows: In a heap, for every node x with parent p, the key in p is smaller than or equal to the key in x. Figure 5.21 also illustrates a complete binary tree that has the heap order property.

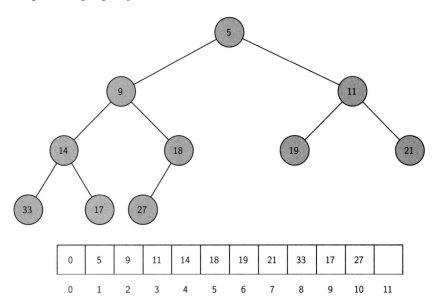

0	5	9	11	14	18	19	21	33	17	27	
0	1	2	3	4	5	6	7	8	9	10	11

Figure 5.21: A Complete Binary Tree, Along with its List Representation

5.7.2.3   Heap Operations

We will begin our implementation of a binary heap with the constructor. Since the entire binary heap can be represented by a single list, all the constructor will do is initialize the list and an attribute `currentSize` to keep track of the current size of the heap. Listing 5.30 shows the Python code for the constructor.

```
1    def __init__(self):
2        self.heapList = [0]
3        self.currentSize = 0
```

Listing 5.30: Create a New Binary Heap

The next method we will implement is **insert**. The easiest, and most efficient, way to add an item to a list is to simply append the item to the end of the list. The good news about appending is that it guarantees that we will maintain the complete tree property. The bad news about appending is that we will very likely violate the heap structure property. However, it is possible to write a method that will allow us to regain the heap structure property by comparing the newly added item with its parent. If the newly added item is less than its parent, then we can swap the item with its parent. Figure 5.22 shows the series of swaps needed to percolate the newly added item up to its proper position in the tree.

Notice that when we percolate an item up, we are restoring the heap property between the newly added item and the parent. We are also preserving the heap property for any siblings. Of course, if the newly added item is very small, we may still need to swap it up another level. In fact, we may need to keep swapping until we get to the top of the tree. Listing 5.31 shows the **percUp** method, which percolates a new item as far up in the tree as it needs to go to maintain the heap property.

We are now ready to write the **insert** method. The Python code for insert is shown in Listing 5.32. Most of the work in the insert method is really done by **percUp**. Once a new item is appended to the tree, **percUp** takes over and positions the new item properly.

```
1    def percUp(self,i):
2        while i > 0:
3            if self.heapList[i] < self.heapList[i/2]:
4                tmp = self.heapList[i/2]
5                self.heapList[i/2] = self.heapList[i]
6                self.heapList[i] = tmp
7            i = i/2
```

Listing 5.31: The percUp Method

With the **insert** method properly defined, we can now look at the **delMin** method. Since the heap property requires that the root of the tree

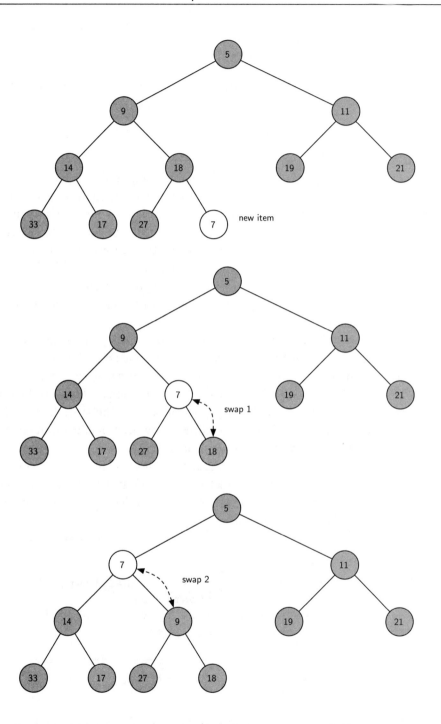

Figure 5.22: Percolate the New Node up to its Proper Position

```
1     def insert(self,k):
2         self.heapList.append(k)
3         self.currentSize = self.currentSize + 1
4         self.percUp(self.currentSize)
```

Listing 5.32: Adding a New Item to the Binary Heap

be the smallest item in the tree, finding the minimum item is easy. The hard part of `delMin` is restoring full compliance with the heap structure and heap order properties after the root has been removed. We can restore our heap in two steps. First, we will restore the root item by taking the last item in the list and moving it to the root position. Moving the last item maintains our heap structure property. However, we have probably destroyed the heap order property of our binary heap. Second, we will restore the heap order property by pushing the new root node down the tree to its proper position. Figure 5.23 shows the series of swaps needed to move the new root node to its proper position in the heap.

In order to maintain the heap order property, all we need to do is swap the root with its smallest child less than the root. After the initial swap, we may repeat the swapping process with a node and its children until the node is swapped into a position on the tree where it is already less than both children. The code for percolating a node down the tree is found in the `percDown` and `minChild` methods in Listing 5.33.

The code for the `delmin` operation is in Listing 5.34. Note that once again the hard work is handled by a helper function, in this case `percDown`.

To finish our discussion of binary heaps, we will look at a method to build an entire heap from a list of keys. The first method you might think of may be like the following. Given a list of keys, you could easily build a heap by inserting each key one at a time. Since you are starting with a list of one item, the list is sorted and you could use binary search to find the right position to insert the next key at a cost of approximately $O(\log n)$ operations. However, remember that inserting an item in the middle of the list may require $O(n)$ operations to shift the rest of the list over to make room for the new key. Therefore, to insert n keys into the heap would require a total of $O(n \log n)$ operations. However, if we start with an entire list then we can build the whole heap in $O(n)$ operations. Listing 5.35 shows the code to build the entire heap.

Look at what happens when we build a heap starting from the list [9, 5, 6, 2, 3]. Figure 5.24 shows the position of each item in the `heapArray`

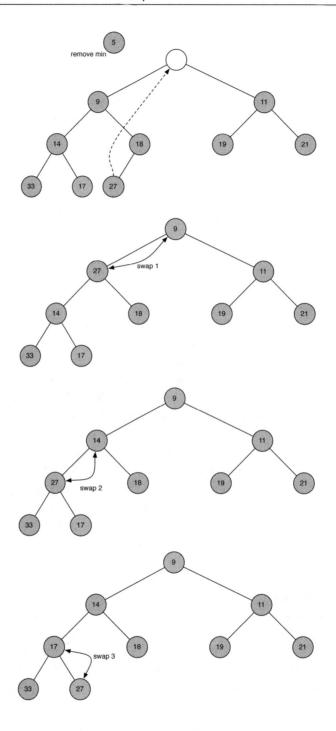

Figure 5.23: Percolating the Root Node down the Tree

```
 1  def percDown(self,i):
 2      while (i * 2) <= self.currentSize:
 3          mc = self.minChild(i)
 4          if self.heapList[i] > self.heapList[mc]:
 5              tmp = self.heapList[i]
 6              self.heapList[i] = self.heapList[mc]
 7              self.heapList[mc] = tmp
 8          i = mc
 9
10
11
12
13
14
15  def minChild(self,i):
16          if i*2 + 1 > self.currentSize:
17              return i*2
18          else:
19              if self.heapList[i*2] < self.heapList[i*2+1]:
20                  return i*2
21              else:
22                  return i*2+1
```

Listing 5.33: The percDown Method

```
 1  def delMin(self):
 2      retval = self.heapList[1]
 3      self.heapList[1] = self.heapList[self.currentSize]
 4      self.currentSize = self.currentSize - 1
 5      self.heapList.pop()
 6      self.percDown(1)
 7      return retval
```

Listing 5.34: Deleting the Minimum Item from the Binary Heap

```
1  def buildHeap(self,alist):
2      i = len(alist) / 2
3      self.currentSize = len(alist)
4      self.heapList = [0] + alist[:]
5      while (i > 0):
6          self.percDown(i)
7          i = i - 1
```

Listing 5.35: Building a New Heap from a List of Items

each time through the `while` loop on line 5. Notice that the first time through the loop, 5 and 2 swap places as 5 is percolated down. Then, in the next iteration, 9 is swapped with 2, and then again with 3. When `i=0` the list obeys the heap order property.

$$i = 2 \quad [0, 9, 5, 6, 2, 3]$$
$$i = 1 \quad [0, 9, 2, 6, 5, 3]$$
$$i = 0 \quad [0, 2, 3, 6, 5, 9]$$

Figure 5.24: Building a Heap from the List [9, 5, 6, 2, 3]

The assertion that we can build the heap in $O(n)$ may seem a bit mysterious at first, and a proof is beyond the scope of this book. However, the key to understanding that you can build the heap in $O(n)$ is to remember that the $\log n$ factor is derived from the height of the tree. For most of the work in `buildHeap`, the tree is shorter than $\log n$.

Using the fact that you can build a heap from a list in $O(n)$ time, you will construct a sorting algorithm that uses a heap and sorts a list in $O(n \log n))$ as an exercise at the end of this chapter.

5.8 Summary

In this chapter we have looked at the tree data structure. The tree data structure enables us to write many interesting algorithms. In this chapter we have looked at algorithms that use trees to do the following:

- A binary tree for parsing and evaluating expressions.

- A binary tree for implementing a dictionary.

- A binary tree to implement a min heap.

- A min heap used to implement a priority queue.

5.9 Key Terms

Successor	Binary heap	Binary search tree
Binary tree	Child / Children	Complete binary tree
Edge	Heap order property	Height
inorder	Leaf node	Level
Map	Min/Max heap	Node
Parent	Path	postorder
preorder	Priority queue	Root
Sibling	Subtree	Tree

5.10 Discussion Questions

1. Draw the tree structure resulting from the following set of tree function calls:

```
>>> r = makeTree(3)
>>> insertLeft(r,4)
[3, [4]]
>>> insertLeft(r,5)
[3, [5, [4]]]
>>> insertRight(r,6)
[3, [5, [4]], [6]]
>>> insertRight(r,7)
[3, [5, [4]], [7, [], [6]]]
>>> setRootVal(l,9)
>>> insertLeft(l,11)
[9, [11, [4]]]
```

2. Trace the algorithm for creating an expression tree for the expression $(4 * 8)/6 - 3$.

3. Consider the following list of integers: [1,2,3,4,5,6,7,8,9,10]. Show the binary search tree resulting from inserting the integers in the list.

4. Consider the following list of integers: [10,9,8,7,6,5,4,3,2,1]. Show the binary search tree resulting from inserting the integers in the list.

5. Generate a random list of integers. Show the binary heap tree resulting from inserting the integers on the list one at a time.

6. Using the list from the previous question Show the binary heap tree resulting from using the list as a parameter to the buildHeap method. Show both the tree and list form.

7. Draw the binary search tree that results from inserting the following keys in the order given: 68,88,61,89,94,50,4,76,66, and 82.

8. Generate a random list of integers. Draw the binary search tree resulting from inserting the integers on the list.

9. Consider the following list of integers: [1,2,3,4,5,6,7,8,9,10]. Show the binary heap resulting from inserting the integers one at a time.

10. Consider the following list of integers: [10,9,8,7,6,5,4,3,2,1]. Show the binary heap resulting from inserting the integers one at a time.

11. Consider the two different methods we used for implementing a binary tree. Why must we check before the call to preorder when implementing as a method, whereas we could check inside the call when implementing as a function?

12. Show the function calls needed to build the following binary tree.

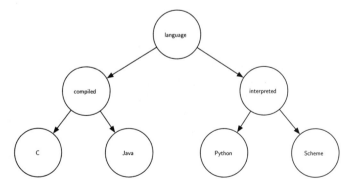

5.11 Programming Exercises

1. Extend the `buildParseTree` function to handle mathematical expressions that do not have spaces between every character.

2. Modify the `buildParseTree` and `evaluate` functions to handle boolean statements (and, or, and not). Remember that "not" is a unary operator, so this will complicate your code somewhat.

3. Using the `findSuccessor` method, write a non-recursive inorder traversal for a binary search tree.

4. Modify the code for a binary search tree to make it threaded. Write a non-recursive inorder traversal method for the threaded binary search tree. A threaded binary tree maintains a reference from each node to its successor.

5. Create a binary heap with a limited heap size. In other words, the heap only keeps track of the **n** most important items. If the heap grows in size to more than **n** items the least important item is dropped.

6. Clean up the `printexp` function so that it does not include an 'extra' set of parentheses around each number.

7. Using the `buildHeap` method, write a sorting function that can sort a list in $O(n \log n)$ time.

8. Write a function that takes a parse tree for a mathematical expression and calculates the derivative of the expression with respect to some variable.

9. Implement a binary heap as a max heap.

10. Using the `BinaryHeap` class, implement a new class called `PriorityQueue`. Your `PriorityQueue` class should implement the constructor, plus the `enqueue` and `dequeue` methods.

Chapter 6   Graphs

6.1   Objectives

- To learn what a graph is and how it is used.

- To implement the graph abstract data type using multiple internal representations.

- To see how graphs can be used to solve a wide variety of problems

In this chapter we will study graphs. Graphs are a more general structure than the trees we studied in the last chapter; in fact you can think of a tree as a special kind of graph. Graphs can be used to represent many interesting things about our world, including systems of roads, airline flights from city to city, how the Internet is connected, or even the sequence of classes you must take to complete a major in computer science. We will see in this chapter that once we have a good representation for a problem, we can use some standard graph algorithms to solve what otherwise might seem to be a very difficult problem.

While it is relatively easy for humans to look at a map and understand the relationships between different places, a computer has no such knowledge. However, we can also think of a map as a graph. When we do so we can have our computer do interesting things for us. If you have ever used one of the Internet map sites, you know that a computer can find the shortest, quickest, or easiest path from one place to another.

As a student of computer science you may wonder about the classes you must take in order to get a major. A graph is good way to represent the prerequisites and other interdependencies among classes. Figure 6.1 shows another graph that represents the classes and the order in which the classes must be taken to complete a major in computer science at Luther College.

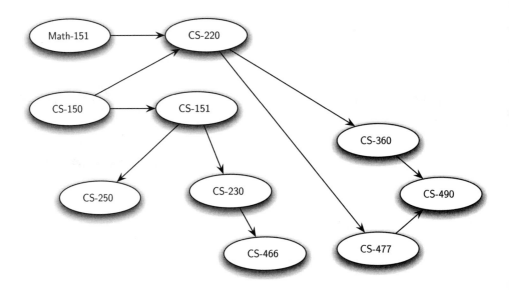

Figure 6.1: Prerequisites for a Computer Science Major

6.2   Vocabulary and Definitions

Now that we have looked at some examples of graphs, we will more formally define a graph and its components. We already know some of these terms from our discussion of trees.

Vertex A vertex (also called a "node") is a fundamental part of a graph. It can have a name, which we will call the "key." A vertex may also have additional information. We will call this additional information the "payload".

Edge An edge (also called an "arc") is another fundamental part of a graph. An edge connects two vertices to show that there is a relationship between them. Edges may be one-way or two-way. If the edges in a graph are all one-way, we say that the graph is a **directed graph**, or a **digraph**. The class prerequisites graph shown above is clearly a digraph since you must take some classes before others.

Weight Edges may be weighted to show that there is a cost to go from one vertex to another. For example in a graph of roads that connect one city to another, the weight on the edge might represent the distance between the two cities.

With those definitions in hand we can formally define a graph. A graph $G = (V, E)$, where V is a set of vertices and E is a set of edges. Each edge is a tuple (v, w) where $w, v \in V$. We can add a third component to the edge tuple to represent a weight. A subgraph s is a set of edges e and vertices v such that $e \subset E$ and $v \subset V$.

Figure 6.2 shows another example of a simple weighted digraph. Formally we can represent this graph as the set of six vertices:

$$V = \{V0, V1, V2, V3, V4, V5\}$$

and the set of nine edges:

$$E = \left\{ \begin{array}{l} (v0, v1, 5), (v1, v2, 4), (v2, v3, 9), (v3, v4, 7), (v4, v0, 1), \\ (v0, v5, 2), (v5, v4, 8), (v3, v5, 3), (v5, v2, 1) \end{array} \right\}$$

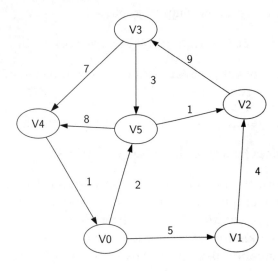

Figure 6.2: A Simple Example of a Directed Graph

The example graph in Figure 6.2 helps illustrate two other key graph terms:

Path A path in a graph is a sequence of vertices that are connected by edges. Formally we would define a path as $w_1, w_2, ..., w_n$ such that

$(w_i, w_{i+1}) \in E$ for all $1 \le i \le n$. The unweighted path length is the number of edges in the path, specifically $n - 1$. The weighted path length is the sum of the weights of all the edges in the path. For example in Figure 6.2 the path from $V3$ to $V1$ is the sequence of vertices $(V3, V4, V0, V1)$. The edges are $\{(v3, v4, 7), (v4, v0, 1), (v0, v1, 5)\}$.

Cycle A cycle in a directed graph is a path that starts and ends at the same vertex. For example, in Figure 6.2 the path $(V5, V2, V3, V5)$ is a cycle. A graph with no cycles is called an **acyclic graph**. A directed graph with no cycles is called a **directed acyclic graph** or a **DAG**. We will see that we can solve several important problems if the problem can be represented as a DAG.

6.3   Representation

The interface to a graph should support the following operations:

- `Graph()` creates a new, empty graph.

- `addVertex(vert)` adds an instance of `Vertex` to the graph.

- `addEdge(fromVert, toVert)` Adds a new, directed edge to the graph that connects two vertices.

- `getVertex(vertKey)` finds the vertex in the graph named `vertKey`.

- `getVertices()` returns the list of all vertices in the graph.

Beginning with the formal definition for a graph there are several ways we can represent a graph in Python. We will see that there are trade-offs in using different representations to implement the interface described above. There are two well-known representations for a graph, the **adjacency matrix** and the **adjacency list**. We will explain both of these representations, and then implement one as a Python class.

6.3.1   An Adjacency Matrix

One of the easiest ways to represent a graph is by using a two-dimensional matrix. In this matrix representation, each of the rows and columns represent a vertex in the graph. The value that is stored in the cell at the intersection of row v and column w indicates that there is an edge from vertex v to vertex w. When an two vertices are connected by an edge, we say that they are **adjacent**. Figure 6.3 illustrates the adjacency matrix for the graph in Figure 6.2. A value in a cell represents the weight of the edge from vertex v to vertex w.

	V0	V1	V2	V3	V4	V5
V0		5				2
V1			4			
V2				9		
V3					7	3
V4	1					
V5			1		8	

Figure 6.3: An Adjacency Matrix Representation for a Graph

The advantage of the adjacency matrix is that it is simple, and for small graphs it is easy to see which nodes are connected to other nodes. However, notice that most of the cells in the matrix are empty. Because most of the cells are empty we say that this matrix is "sparse." A matrix is not a very efficient way to store sparse data. In fact, in Python you must go out of your way to even create a matrix structure like the one in Figure 6.3.

The adjacency matrix is a good representation for a graph when the number of edges is large. But what do we mean by large? How many edges would be needed to fill the matrix? Since there is one row and one column for every vertex in the graph, the number of edges required to fill the matrix is $|V|^2$. A matrix is full when every vertex is connected to every other vertex. There are few real problems that approach this sort of connectivity. The problems we will look at in this chapter all involve graphs that are sparsely connected.

6.3.2 An Adjacency List

A more space-efficient way to represent a sparsely connected graph is to use an adjacency list. In an adjacency list representation we keep a master list of all the vertices in the graph and then each vertex in the graph maintains a list of the other vertices that it is connected to. Figure 6.4 illustrates the adjacency list representation for the graph in Figure 6.2.

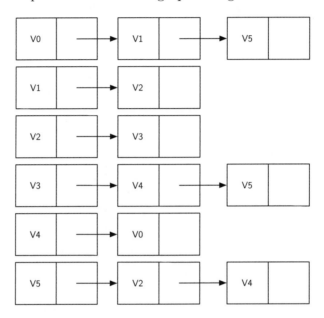

Figure 6.4: An Adjacency List Representation of a Graph

The advantage of the adjacency list representation is that it allows us to compactly represent a sparse graph. The adjacency list representation also allows us to easily find all the links that are directly connected to a particular vertex.

6.3.3 Implementation

It is easy to implement the adjacency list in Python, using dictionaries and lists. In our implementation of the graph abstract data type we will create two classes, `Graph`, which has the interface defined above, and `Vertex`, which will represent each vertex in the graph. In Figure 6.4, you can think of the leftmost column as a dictionary of vertices, where the identifier for each vertex is the key in the dictionary. The value stored in the dictionary is a **Vertex** object. Each vertex is responsible for maintaining its own list of other vertices it is connected to. Listing 6.1 shows the code for the **Vertex** class.

You will notice that the **Vertex** class contains several additional attributes. We will see in the following sections that color, discovery time, finish time, distance, and predecessor all play important roles in different algorithms. For now, the key attributes are a vertex's id, and the adj attribute, which is a list of the other connected vertex objects.

The **Graph** class, shown in Listing 6.2, contains a dictionary of vertices. **Graph** also provides methods for adding vertices to a graph and connecting one vertex to another. In addition, we have implemented the __iter__ method to make it easy to iterate over all the vertices in a particular graph.

Using the **Graph** and **Vertex** classes just defined, the following Python session creates the graph in Figure 6.2. First we create six vertices numbered 0 through 5. Then we display the vertex dictionary. Notice that for each key 0 through 5 we have created an instance of a **Vertex**. Next, we add the edges that connect the vertices together. Finally, a nested loop verifies that each edge in the graph is properly stored. You should check the output of the edge list at the end of this session against Figure 6.2.

```
>>> g = Graph()
>>> for i in range(6):
...     g.addVertex(i)
...
>>> g.vertList
{0: <adjGraph.Vertex instance at 0x41e18>,
 1: <adjGraph.Vertex instance at 0x7f2b0>,
 2: <adjGraph.Vertex instance at 0x7f288>,
 3: <adjGraph.Vertex instance at 0x7f350>,
 4: <adjGraph.Vertex instance at 0x7f328>,
 5: <adjGraph.Vertex instance at 0x7f300>}
>>> g.addEdge(0,1)
>>> g.addEdge(0,5)
>>> g.addEdge(1,2)
>>> g.addEdge(2,3)
>>> g.addEdge(3,4)
>>> g.addEdge(3,5)
>>> g.addEdge(4,0)
>>> g.addEdge(5,4)
>>> g.addEdge(5,2)
>>> for v in g:
```

```python
class Vertex:
    def __init__(self,num):
        self.id = num
        self.adj = []
        self.color = 'white'
        self.dist = sys.maxint
        self.pred = None
        self.disc = 0
        self.fin = 0
        self.cost = {}

    def addNeighbor(self,nbr,cost=0):
        self.adj.append(nbr)
        self.cost[nbr] = cost

    def __str__(self):
        return str(self.id) + ":color " + self.color + \
                ":dist " + str(self.dist) + \
                ":pred [" + str(self.pred)+ "]\n"

    def getCost(self,nbr):
        return self.cost[nbr]
    def setCost(self,nbr,cost):
        self.cost[nbr] = cost
    def setColor(self,color):
        self.color = color
    def setDistance(self,d):
        self.dist = d
    def setPred(self,p):
        self.pred = p
    def setDiscovery(self,dtime):
        self.disc = dtime
    def setFinish(self,ftime):
        self.fin = ftime
    def getFinish(self):
        return self.fin
    def getDiscovery(self):
        return self.disc
    def getPred(self):
        return self.pred
    def getDistance(self):
        return self.dist
    def getColor(self):
        return self.color
    def getAdj(self):
        return self.adj
    def getId(self):
        return self.id
```

Listing 6.1: The Vertex Class

```
1  class Graph:
2     def __init__(self):
3        self.vertList = {}
4        self.numVertices = 0
5
6     def addVertex(self,key):
7        self.numVertices = self.numVertices + 1
8        newVertex = Vertex(key)
9        self.vertList[key] = newVertex
10       return newVertex
11
12    def getVertex(self,n):
13       if self.vertList.has_key(n):
14          return self.vertList[n]
15       else:
16          return None
17
18    def has_key(self,n):
19       return self.vertList.has_key(n)
20
21    def addEdge(self,f,t,c=0):
22       if not self.vertList.has_key(f):
23          nv = self.addVertex(f)
24       if not self.vertList.has_key(t):
25          nv = self.addVertex(t)
26       self.vertList[f].addNeighbor(self.vertList[t],c)
27
28    def getVertices(self):
29       return self.vertList.values()
30
31    def __iter__(self):
32       return self.vertList.itervalues()
```

Listing 6.2: The Graph Class

```
...     for w in v.getAdj():
...         print "(",v,",",w,")"
...
( 0 , 1 )
( 0 , 5 )
( 1 , 2 )
( 2 , 3 )
( 3 , 4 )
( 3 , 5 )
( 4 , 0 )
( 5 , 4 )
( 5 , 2 )
```

6.4 Graph Algorithms

6.4.1 A Breadth First Search

6.4.1.1 The Word Ladder Problem

To begin our study of graph algorithms let's consider the following puzzle called a word ladder. Transform the word "FOOL" into the word "SAGE". In a word ladder puzzle you must make the change occur gradually by changing one letter at a time. At each step you must transform one word into another word, you are not allowed to transform a word into a non-word. The word ladder puzzle was invented in 1878 by Lewis Carroll, the author of *Alice in Wonderland*.

FOOL

POOL

POLL

POLE

PALE

SALE

SAGE

Table 6.1: Word ladder transformation

There are many variations of the word ladder puzzle, for example you might be given a particular number of steps in which to accomplish the transformation. In this section we are interested in figuring out the smallest number of transformations needed to turn the starting word into the ending word.

Not surprisingly, since this chapter is on graphs, we can solve this problem using a graph algorithm. Here is an outline of where we are going:

- Represent the relationships between the words as a graph.

- Use the graph algorithm known as breadth first search to find an efficient path from the starting word to the ending word.

Our first problem is to figure out how to turn a dictionary full of words into a graph. What we would like is to have an edge from one word to another if the two words are only different by a single letter. If we can create such a graph, then any path from one word to another is a solution to the word ladder puzzle. Figure 6.5 shows a small graph of some words that solve the FOOL to SAGE word ladder problem. Notice that the graph is an undirected graph and that the edges are unweighted.

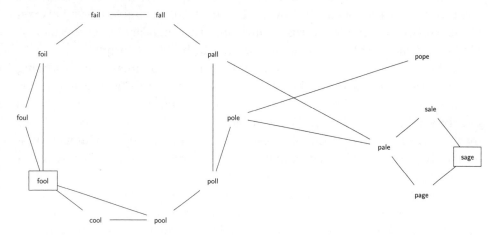

Figure 6.5: A Small Word Ladder Graph

We could use several different approaches to create the graph we need to solve this problem. Let's start with the assumption that we have a list of words that are all the same length. As a starting point, we can create a vertex in the graph for every word in the list. To figure out how to connect the words, we could compare each word in the list with every other. When we compare we are looking to see how many letters are different. If the two

words in question are different by only one letter, we can create an edge
between them in the graph. For a small set of words that approach would
work fine; however let's suppose we have a list of 5,700 words. Roughly
speaking, comparing one word to every other word on the list is an $O(n^2)$
algorithm. For 5,700 words, n^2 is more than 32 million comparisons.

We can do much better by using the following approach. Suppose that
we have a huge number of buckets, each of them with a five-letter word on
the outside, except that one of the letters in the label has been replaced by
an underscore. For example we might have a bucket labeled "_rave." As we
process each word in our list we compare the word with each bucket, using
the '_' as a wildcard, so both "crave" and "brave" would match "_rave."
Every time we find a matching bucket, we put our word in that bucket.
Once we have all the words in the appropriate buckets we know that all the
words in the bucket must be connected.

In Python, we can implement the scheme we have just described by using
a dictionary. The labels on the buckets we have just described are the keys
in our dictionary. The value stored for that key is a list of words. Once we
have the dictionary built we can create the graph. We start our graph by
creating a vertex for each word in the graph. Then we create edges between
all the vertices we find for words found under the same key in the dictionary.
Listing 6.3 shows the Python code required to build the graph.

Since this is our first real world-graph problem, you might be wondering
how sparse is the graph? The list of five-letter words we have for this
problem is 5,757 words long. If we were to use an adjacency matrix, the
matrix would have 5,757*5,757 = 33,143,049 cells. The graph constructed
by the `buildGraph` function has exactly 28,810 edges, so the matrix would
have only 0.086% of the cells filled! That is a very sparse matrix indeed.

With the graph constructed we can now turn our attention to the algorithm we will use to solve the shortest ladder problem. The graph algorithm
we are going to use is called the "breadth first search" algorithm. **Breadth
first search (BFS)** is one of the easiest algorithms for searching a graph.
It also serves as a prototype for several other important graph algorithms
that we will study later.

Given a graph G and a starting vertex s, a breadth first search proceeds
by exploring edges in the graph to find all the vertices in G for which there
is a path from s. The remarkable thing about a breadth first search is that it
finds *all* the vertices that are a distance k from s before it finds *any* vertices
that are a distance $k + 1$. One good way to visualize what the breadth first
search algorithm does is to imagine that it is building a tree, one level of
the tree at a time. A breadth first search adds all children of the starting

```
 1  def buildGraph():
 2      d = {}
 3      g = Graph()
 4      wfile = file('words.dat')
 5      # create buckets of words that differ by one letter.
 6      for line in wfile:
 7          word = line[0:5]
 8          for i in range(5):
 9              bucket = word[0:i] + '_' + word[i+1:5]
10              if d.has_key(bucket):
11                  d[bucket].append(word)
12              else:
13                  d[bucket] = [word]
14      # add vertices and edges for words in the same bucket.
15      for i in d.keys():
16          for j in d[i]:
17              for k in d[i]:
18                  if j != k:
19                      g.addEdge(j,k)
20      return g
```

Listing 6.3: Building a Graph of Words for the Word Ladder Problem

vertex before it begins to discover any of the grandchildren.

To keep track of its progress, BFS colors each of the vertices white, gray, or black. All the vertices are initialized to "white" when they are constructed. A white vertex is an undiscovered vertex. When a vertex is initially discovered it is colored gray, and when BFS has completely explored a vertex it is colored black. This means that once a vertex is colored black, it has no white vertices adjacent to it. A gray node, on the other hand, may have some white vertices adjacent to it, indicating that there are still additional vertices to explore.

The breadth first search algorithm shown in Listing 6.4 uses the adjacency list graph representation we developed earlier in Listings 6.1 and 6.2. In addition it uses a Queue, a crucial point as we will see, to decide which vertex to explore next.

BFS begins at the starting vertex s and colors s gray to show that it is currently being explored. Two other values, the distance and the predecessor, are initialized to 0 and none respectively for the starting vertex. Finally, s is placed on a Queue. The next step is to begin to systematically explore vertices at the front of the queue. We explore each new node at the front of the queue by iterating over its adjacency list. As each node on the adjacency list is examined its color is checked. If it is white, the vertex is unexplored, and four things happen:

1. The new, unexplored vertex v, is colored gray.

2. The predecessor of v is set to the current node w

3. The distance to v is set to the distance to w + 1

4. v is added to the end of a queue. Adding v to the end of the queue effectively schedules this node for further exploration, but not until all the other vertices on the adjacency list of w have been explored.

```
1  def bfs(g,vertKey):
2      s = g.getVertex(vertKey)
3      s.setDistance(0)
4      s.setPred(None)
5      s.setColor('gray')
6      Q = Queue()
7      Q.enqueue(s)
8      while (Q.size() > 0):
9          w = Q.dequeue()
10         for v in w.getAdj():
11             if (v.getColor() == 'white'):
12                 v.setColor('gray')
13                 v.setDistance( w.getDistance() + 1 )
14                 v.setPred(w)
15                 Q.enqueue(v)
16         w.setColor('black')
```

Listing 6.4: Breadth First Search

Let's look at how the `bfs` function would construct the breadth first tree corresponding to the graph in Figure 6.5. Starting from fool we take all nodes that are adjacent to fool and add them to the tree. The adjacent nodes include pool, foil, foul, and cool. Each of these nodes are added to the queue of new nodes to expand. Figure 6.6 shows the state of the in-progress tree along with the queue after this step.

In the next step `bfs` removes the next node (pool) from the front of the queue and repeats the process for all of its adjacent nodes. However, when `bfs` examines the node cool, it finds that the color of cool has already been

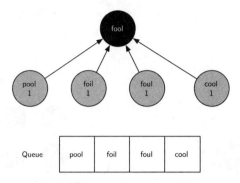

Figure 6.6: Fist Step in the Breadth First Search

changed to gray. This indicates that there is a shorter path to cool and that cool is already on the queue for further expansion. The only new node added to the queue while examining pool is poll. The new state of the tree and queue is shown in Figure 6.7.

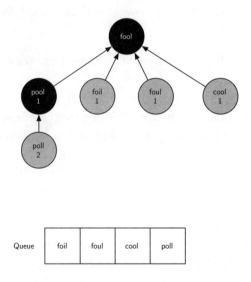

Figure 6.7: The Second Step in the Breadth First Search

The next vertex on the queue is foil. The only new node that foil can add to the tree is fail. As **bfs** continues to process the queue, neither of the next two nodes add anything new to the queue or the tree. Figure 6.8(a)

shows the tree and the queue after expanding all the vertices on the second
level of the tree.

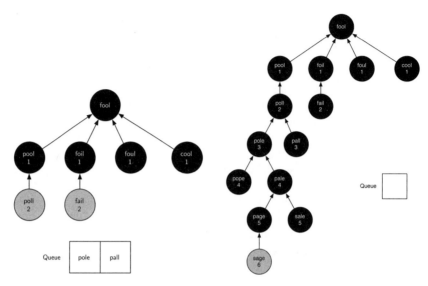

(a) Breadth First Search Tree After Com-   (b) Final Breadth First Search Tree
pleting One Level

Figure 6.8: Constructing the Breadth First Search Tree

You should continue to work through the algorithm on your own so that
you are comfortable with how it works. Figure 6.8(b) shows the final breadth
first search tree after all the vertices in Figure 6.5 have been expanded. The
amazing thing about the breadth first search solution is that we have not
only solved the FOOL–SAGE problem we started out with, but we have
solved many other problems along the way. We can start at any vertex in
the breadth first search tree and follow the predecessor arrows back to the
root to find the shortest word ladder from any word back to fool.

The breadth first search algorithm is an excellent tool. You can use a
breadth first search to help you under the following conditions:

- You can represent your problem in terms of an unweighted graph.

- The solution to your problem is to find the shortest path between two
  nodes in the graph.

6.4.2 Depth First Search

6.4.2.1 The Knights Tour Problem

Another classic problem that we can use to illustrate a second common graph algorithm is called the "knights tour." The knights tour puzzle is played on a chess board with a single chess piece, the knight. The object of the puzzle is to find a sequence of moves that allow the knight to visit every square on the board exactly once. One such sequence is called a "tour." The knights tour puzzle has fascinated chess players, mathematicians and computer scientists alike for many years. The upper bound on the number of possible legal tours for an eight-by-eight chessboard is known to be 1.305×10^{35}, however there are even more possible dead ends. Clearly this is a problem that requires some real brains, some real computing power, or both.

Although researchers have studied many different algorithms to solve the knights tour problem, a graph search is one of the easiest to understand and program. Once again we will solve the problem using two main steps:

- Represent the legal moves of a knight on a chessboard as a graph.

- Use a graph algorithm to find a path through the graph of length *rows* × *columns* where every vertex on the path is visited exactly once.

To represent the knights tour problem as a graph we will use the following two ideas: Each square on the chessboard can be represented as a node in the graph. Each legal move by the knight can be represented as an edge in the graph. Figure 6.9 illustrates the legal moves by a knight and the corresponding edges in a graph.

To build the full graph for an n-by-n board we can use the Python function shown in Listing 6.5. The `knightGraph` function makes one pass over the entire board. At each square on the board the `knightGraph` function calls a helper, `genLegalMoves`, to create a list of legal moves for that position on the board. All legal moves are then converted into edges in the graph. Another helper function `posToNodeId` converts a location on the board in terms of a row and a column into a linear vertex number similar to the vertex numbers shown in Figure 6.9.

The `genLegalMoves` function takes the position of the knight on the board and generates each of the eight possible moves. The `legalCoord` helper function makes sure that a particular move that is generated is still on the board.

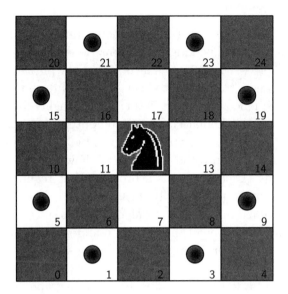 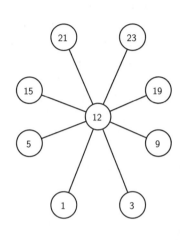

Figure 6.9: Legal Moves for a Knight on Square 12, and the Corresponding Graph

```
1  def knightGraph(bdSize):
2      ktGraph = Graph()
3      # Build the graph
4      for row in range(bdSize):
5          for col in range(bdSize):
6              nodeId = posToNodeId(row,col,bdSize)
7              newPositions = genLegalMoves(row,col,bdSize)
8              for e in newPositions:
9                  nid = posToNodeId(e[0],e[1])
10                 ktGraph.addEdge(nodeId,nid)
11     return ktGraph
```

Listing 6.5: Create a Graph Corresponding to All Legal Knight Moves

```
1  def genLegalMoves(x,y,bdSize):
2      newMoves = []
3      moveOffsets = [(-1,-2),(-1,2),(-2,-1),(-2,1),
4                     ( 1,-2),( 1,2),( 2,-1),( 2,1)]:
5      for i in moveOffsets:
6          newX = x + i[0]
7          newY = y + i[1]
8          if legalCoord(newX,bdSize) and \
9                          legalCoord(newY,bdSize):
10             newMoves.append((newX,newY))
11     return newMoves
12
13 def legalCoord(x,bdSize):
14     if x >= 0 and x < bdSize:
15         return True
16     else:
17         return False
```

Listing 6.6: Generate a List of Legal Moves for a Chess Board Position

Figure 6.10 shows the complete graph of possible moves on an eight-by-eight board. There are exactly 336 edges in the graph. Notice that the vertices corresponding to the edges of the board have fewer connections (legal moves) than the vertices in the middle of the board. Once again we can see how sparse the graph is. If the graph was fully connected there would be 4,096 edges. Since there are only 336 edges, the adjacency matrix would be only 8.2 percent full.

The search algorithm we will use to solve the knights tour problem is called **depth first search(DFS)** . Whereas the breadth first search algorithm discussed in the previous section builds a search tree one level at a time, a depth first search creates a search tree by exploring one branch of the tree as deeply as possible. In this section we will look at two algorithms that implement a depth first search. The first algorithm we will look at directly solves the knights tour problem by explicitly forbidding a node to be visited more than once. The second implementation is more general, but allows nodes to be visited more than once as the tree is constructed. The second version is used in subsequent sections to develop additional graph algorithms.

The depth first exploration of the graph is exactly what we need in order to find a path that is exactly 64 nodes in length. We will see that when the

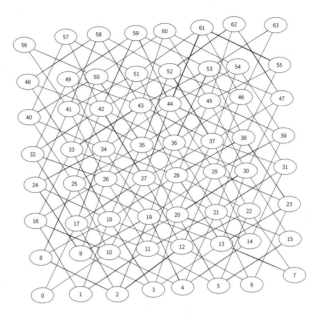

Figure 6.10: All Legal Moves for a Knight on an 8×8 Chessboard

depth first search algorithm finds a dead end (a place in the graph where there are no more moves possible) it backs up the tree to the next deepest vertex that allows it to make a legal move.

The `knightTour` function takes three parameters: n, the current depth in the search tree; `path`, an array of vertices visited up to this point; and u, the vertex in the graph we wish to explore. The `knightTour` function is recursive. When the `knightTour` function is called, it first checks the base case condition. If we have a path that is 64 vertices in length, we return from `knightTour` with a status of `True`, indicating that we have found a successful tour. If the path is not long enough we continue to explore one level deeper by choosing a new vertex to explore and calling `knightTour` recursively for that vertex.

DFS also uses colors to keep track of which vertices in the graph have been visited. Unvisited vertices are colored white, and visited vertices are colored gray. If all neighbors of a particular vertex have been explored and we have not yet reached our goal length of 64 vertices, we have reached a dead end. When we reach a dead end we must backtrack. Backtracking happens when we return from `knightTour` with a status of `False`. In the breadth first search we used a queue to keep track of which vertex to visit next. In a depth first search we are implicitly using a stack to help us with our backtracking. When we return from a call to knightTour with a status of False, in line 10, we remain inside the while loop and look at the next vertex in nbrList.

```
1  def knightTour(n,path,u,limit):
2          u.setColor('gray')
3          path.append(u)
4          if n < limit:
5              nbrList = orderByAvail(u)
6              i = 0
7              done = False
8              while i < len(nbrList) and not done:
9                  if nbrList[i].getColor() == 'white':
10                     done = knightTour(n+1,
11                                       path,
12                                       nbrList[i],
13                                       limit)
14                 if not done:  # prepare to backtrack
15                     path.remove(u)
16                     u.setColor('white')
17          else:
18              done = True
19          return done
```

Listing 6.7: Depth First Search Algorithm for Knights Tour

Let's look at a simple example of knightTour in action. You can refer to Figure 6.11 to follow the steps of the search. For this example we will assume that the function orderByAvail in line 5 of Listing 6.7 orders the nodes in alphabetical order. We begin by calling knightTour(0,path,A,6)

knightTour starts with node A. The nodes adjacent to A are B and D. Since B is before D alphabetically, DFS selects B to expand next as shown in Figure 6.11(b). Exploring B happens when knightTour is called recursively. B is adjacent to C and D, so knightTour elects to explore C next. However, as you can see in Figure 6.11(c) node C is a dead end with no adjacent white nodes. At this point we change the color of node C back to white. The call to knightTour returns a value of False. The return from the recursive call effectively backtracks the search to vertex B (see Figure 6.11(d)). The next vertex on the list to explore is vertex D, so knightTour makes a recursive call moving to node D.

From vertex D on, `knightTour` can continue to make recursive calls until we get to node C again. However, this time when we get to node C the test `n < limit` fails so we know that we have exhausted all the nodes in the graph. At this point we can return `True` to indicate that we have made a successful tour of the graph. When we return the list, `path` has the values [A,B,D,E,F,C], which is the the order we need to traverse the graph to visit each node exactly once.

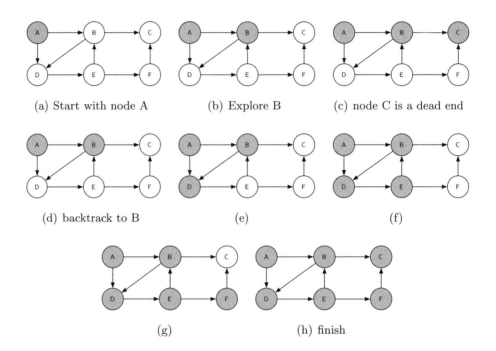

(a) Start with node A   (b) Explore B   (c) node C is a dead end

(d) backtrack to B   (e)   (f)

(g)   (h) finish

Figure 6.11: Finding a Path Through a Graph with `knightTour`

Figure 6.12 shows you what a complete tour around an eight-by-eight board looks like. There are many possible tours; some are symmetric. With some modification you can make circular tours that start and end at the same square.

There is one last interesting topic regarding the knights tour problem, then we will move on to the general version of the depth first search. The topic is performance. In particular, `knightTour` is very sensitive to the method you use to select the next vertex to visit. You might want to try simply using the nodes in whatever order they appear on the adjacency list. However, using this order can produce some interesting results. For example, on a five-by-five board you can produce a path in about 1.5 seconds on a

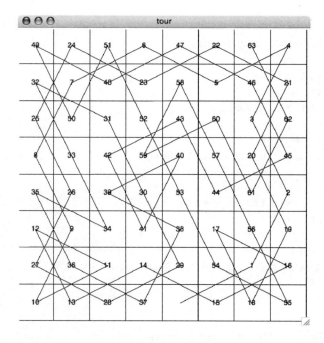

Figure 6.12: A Complete Tour of the Board

reasonably fast computer. But what happens if you try an eight-by-eight board? In this case, depending on the speed of your computer, you may have to wait up to a half hour to get the results!

Luckily there is a way to speed up the eight-by-eight case so that it runs in under one second. In listing 6.8 we show the code that speeds up the knightTour. The critical line in the orderByAvail function is 10. This line ensures that we select the vertex to go next that has the fewest available moves. You might think this is really counter productive; why not select the node that has the most available moves? You can try that approach easily by running the program yourself and inserting the line resList.reverse() right after the sort.

The problem with using the vertex with the most available moves as your next vertex on the path is that it tends to have the knight visit the middle squares early on in the tour. When this happens it is easy for the knight to get stranded on one side of the board where it cannot reach unvisited squares on the other side of the board. On the other hand, visiting the squares with the fewest available moves first pushes the knight to visit the squares around the edges of the board first. This ensures that the knight

will visit the hard-to-reach corners early and can use the middle squares to
hop across the board only when necessary.

```
def orderByAvail(n):
    resList = []
    for v in n.getAdj():
        if v.getColor() == 'white':
            c = 0
            for w in v.getAdj():
                if w.getColor() == 'white':
                    c = c + 1
            resList.append((c,v))
    resList.sort()
    return [y[1] for y in resList]
```

Listing 6.8: Selecting the Next Vertex to Visit Is Critical

6.4.2.2 General Depth First Search

The knights tour is a special case of a depth first search where the goal
is to create the deepest depth first tree, without any branches. The more
general depth first search is actually easier. Its goal is to search as deeply as
possible, connecting as many nodes in the graph as possible and branching
where necessary.

It is even possible that a depth first search will create more than one
tree. It is possible for a depth first search to create a group of trees (called a
depth first forest). As with the breadth first search our depth first search
makes use of predecessor links to construct the forest. In addition the depth
first search will make use of the discovery and finish times. As we will see
after looking at the algorithm, the discovery and finish times of the nodes
provide some interesting properties we can use in later algorithms.

The code for our depth first search is shown in Listing 6.9. Look carefully
at the code for breadth first search and compare it to the depth first search.
What you should notice is that the dfsvisit algorithm is almost identical
to bfs except that dfsvisit uses a stack instead of a queue. The reason is
to make sure that all nodes in the graph are considered and that no vertices
are left out of the depth first forest. This is different from bfs, where we
were interested only in considering nodes for which there was a path leading
back to the start. In our next two algorithms we will see why keeping track
of the whole forest is important.

```
1   def dfs(theGraph):
2       for u in theGraph:
3           u.setColor('white')
4           u.setPred(-1)
5       time = 0
6       for u in theGraph:
7           if u.getColor() == 'white':
8               dfsvisit(u)
9
10  def dfsvisit(s):
11      s.setDistance(0)
12      s.setPred(None)
13      S = Stack()
14      S.push(s)
15      while (S.size() > 0):
16          w = S.pop()
17          w.setColor('gray')
18          for v in w.getAdj():""
19              if (v.getColor() == 'white'):
20                  v.setDistance( w.getDistance() + 1 )
21                  v.setPred(w)
22                  S.push(v)
23          w.setColor('black')
```

Listing 6.9: General Depth First Search

Figure 6.13 illustrates the depth first search algorithm in action for a small graph. In Figure 6.13 the dotted lines indicate edges that are checked, but the node at the other end of the edge has already been added to the depth first tree.

The starting and finishing times for each node display a property called the **parenthesis property**. This property means that all the children of a particular node in the depth first tree have a later discovery time and an earlier finish time than their parent. Figure 6.14 shows the tree constructed by the depth first search algorithm.

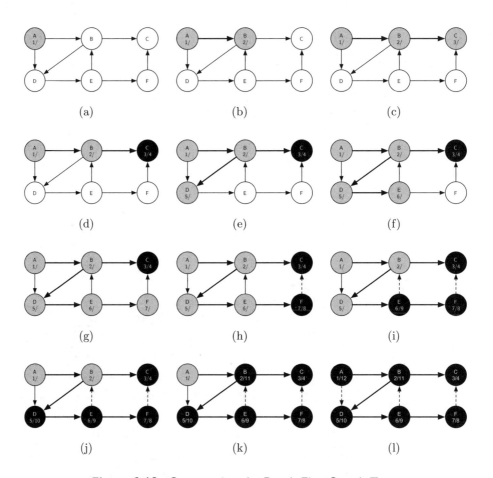

Figure 6.13: Constructing the Depth First Search Tree

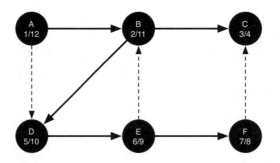

Figure 6.14: The Resulting Depth First Search Tree

6.4.3 Topological Sorting

To demonstrate that computer scientists can turn just about anything into a graph problem, let's consider the difficult problem of stirring up a batch of pancakes. The recipe is really quite simple, 1 egg, 1 cup of pancake mix, 1 tablespoon oil, and $\frac{3}{4}$ cup of milk. To make pancakes you must heat the griddle, mix all the ingredients together and spoon the mix onto a hot griddle. When the pancakes start to bubble you turn them over and let them cook until they are golden brown on the bottom. Before you eat your pancakes you are going to want to heat up some syrup. Figure 6.15 illustrates this process as a graph.

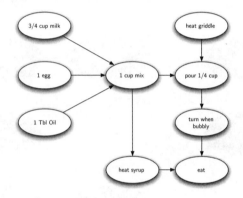

Figure 6.15: The Steps for Making Pancakes

The difficult thing about making pancakes is knowing what to do first. As you can see from Figure 6.15 you might start by heating the griddle or by adding any of the ingredients to the pancake mix. To help us decide the precise order in which we should do each of the steps required to make our pancakes we turn to a graph algorithm called the **topological sort**.

A topological sort takes a directed acyclic graph and produces a linear ordering of all its vertices such that if the graph G contains an edge (v, w) then the vertex v comes before the vertex w in the ordering. Directed acyclic graphs are used in many applications to indicate the precedence of events. Making pancakes is just one example; other examples include software project schedules, precedence charts for optimizing database queries, and multiplying matrices.

The topological sort is a simple but useful adaptation of a depth first search. The algorithm for the topological sort is as follows:

1. Call `dfs(g)` for some graph `g`. The main reason we want to call depth first search is to compute the finish times for each of the vertices.

2. Store the vertices in a list in decreasing order of finish time.

3. Return the ordered list as the result of the topological sort.

Figure 6.16 shows the depth first forest constructed by `dfs` on the pancake-making graph shown in Figure 6.15.

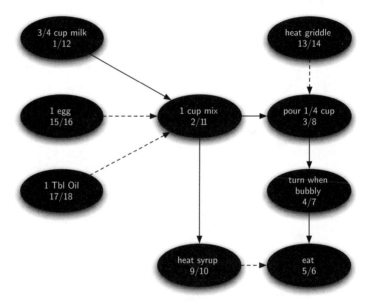

Figure 6.16: Result of Depth First Search on the Pancake Graph

Finally, Figure 6.17 shows the results of applying the topological sort algorithm to our graph. Now all the ambiguity has been removed and we know exactly the order in which to perform the pancake making steps.

Figure 6.17: Result of Topological Sort on Directed Acyclic Graph

6.4.4 Strongly Connected Components

For the remainder of this chapter we will turn our attention to some extremely large graphs. The graphs we will use to study some additional algorithms are the graphs produced by the connections between hosts in the Internet and the links between web pages. We will begin with web pages.

Search engines like Google and Yahoo! exploit the fact that the pages in the web form a very large directed graph. To transform the World Wide Web into a graph, we will treat a page as a vertex, and the hyperlinks on the page as edges connecting one vertex to another. Figure 6.18 shows a very small part of the graph produced by following the links from one page to the next, beginning at Luther College's Computer Science home page. Of course this graph could be huge, so we have limited it to web sites that are no more than 10 links away from the CS home page.

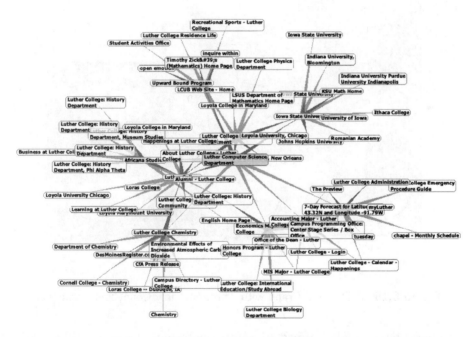

Figure 6.18: The Graph Produced by Links
from the Luther Computer Science Home Page

If you study the graph in Figure 6.18 you might make some interesting observations. First you might notice that many of the other web sites on the graph are other Luther College web sites. Second, you might notice that

there are several links to other colleges in Iowa. Third, you might notice
that there are several links to other liberal arts colleges. You might conclude
from this that there is some underlying structure to the web that clusters
together web sites that are similar on some level.

One graph algorithm that can help find clusters of highly interconnected
vertices in a graph is called the strongly connected components algorithm
(**SCC**). We formally define a **strongly connected component**, C, of a
graph G, as the largest subset of vertices $C \subset V$ such that for every pair
of vertices $v, w \in C$ we have a path from v to w and a path from w to v.
Figure 6.19 shows a simple graph with three strongly connected components.
The strongly connected components are identified by the different shaded
areas.

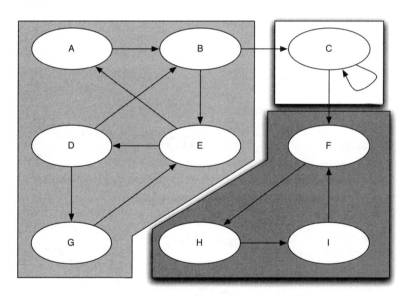

Figure 6.19: A Directed Graph with Three Strongly Connected Components

Once the strongly connected components have been identified we can
show a simplified view of the graph by combining all the vertices in one
strongly connected component into a single larger vertex. The simplified
version of the graph in Figure 6.19 is shown in Figure 6.20.

Once again we will see that we can create a very powerful and efficient
algorithm by making use of a depth first search. Before we tackle the main
SCC algorithm we must look at one other definition. The transposition of

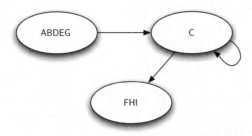

Figure 6.20: The Reduced Graph

a graph G is defined as the graph G^T where all the edges in the graph have been reversed. Figure 6.21 shows a simple graph and its transposition.

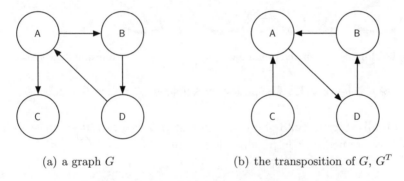

(a) a graph G (b) the transposition of G, G^T

Figure 6.21: A Graph G and Its Transpose G^T

Look at Figure 6.21 again. Notice that the graph in Figure 6.21(a) has two strongly connected components. Now look at the 6.21(b). Notice that it has the same two strongly connected components.

We can now describe the algorithm to compute the strongly connected components for a graph.

1. Call `dfs` for the graph G to compute the finish times for each vertex.

2. Compute G^T.

3. Call `dfs` for the graph G^T but in the main loop of DFS explore each vertex in decreasing order of finish time.

4. Each tree in the forest computed in step 3 is a strongly connected component. Output the vertex ids for each vertex in each tree in the forest to identify the component.

Lets trace the operation of the steps described above on the example graph in Figure 6.19. Figure 6.22(a) shows the starting and finishing times computed for the original graph. Figure 6.22(b) shows the starting and finishing times for the transposed graph.

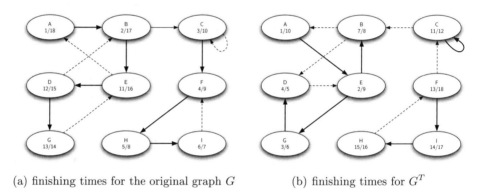

(a) finishing times for the original graph G (b) finishing times for G^T

Figure 6.22: Computing the Strongly Connected Components

Finally Figure 6.23 shows the forest of trees produced in step 3 of the strongly connected component algorithm.

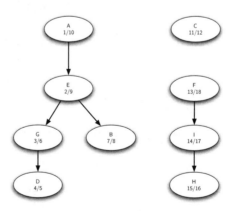

Figure 6.23: The Strongly Connected Components as a Forest of Trees

6.4.5   Shortest Path Problems

When you surf the web, send an email, or log in to a laboratory computer from another location on campus a lot of work is going on behind the scenes to get the information on your computer transferred to another computer. The in-depth study of how information flows from one computer to another over the Internet is the primary topic for a class in computer networking. However, we will talk about how the Internet works just enough to understand another very important graph algorithm.

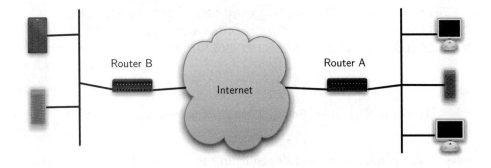

Figure 6.24: Overview of Connectivity in the Internet

Figure 6.24 shows you a high-level overview of how communication on the Internet works. When you request a web page from a server using your browser, the request must travel over your local area network and out onto the Internet through a router. The request travels over the Internet and eventually arrives at a router for the local area network where the server is located. The web page you requested then travels back through the same routers to get to your browser. Inside the cloud labelled "Internet" in Figure 6.24 are additional routers. The job of all of these routers is to work together to get your information from place to place. You can see there are many routers for yourself if your computer supports the **traceroute** command. Figure 6.25 shows the output of the **traceroute** command which illustrates that there are thirteen routers between the web server at Luther College and the mail server at the University of Minnesota.

Each router on the Internet is connected to one or more other routers. So if you run the **traceroute** command at different times of the day, you are likely to see that your information flows through different routers at different times. This is because there is a cost associated with each connection

```
 1   192.203.196.1
 2   hilda.luther.edu (216.159.75.1)
 3   ICN-Luther-Ether.icn.state.ia.us (207.165.237.137)
 4   ICN-ISP-1.icn.state.ia.us (209.56.255.1)
 5   p3-0.hsa1.chi1.bbnplanet.net (4.24.202.13)
 6   ae-1-54.bbr2.Chicago1.Level3.net (4.68.101.97)
 7   so-3-0-0.mpls2.Minneapolis1.Level3.net (64.159.4.214)
 8   ge-3-0.hsa2.Minneapolis1.Level3.net (4.68.112.18)
 9   p1-0.minnesota.bbnplanet.net (4.24.226.74)
10   TelecomB-BR-01-V4002.ggnet.umn.edu (192.42.152.37)
11   TelecomB-BN-01-Vlan-3000.ggnet.umn.edu (128.101.58.1)
12   TelecomB-CN-01-Vlan-710.ggnet.umn.edu (128.101.80.158)
13   baldrick.cs.umn.edu (128.101.80.129)(N!)   88.631 ms (N!)
```

Figure 6.25: Routers from One Host to the Next over the Internet

between a pair of routers that depends on the volume of traffic, the time of day, and many other factors. By this time it will not surprise you to learn that we can represent the network of routers as a graph with weighted edges.

Figure 6.26 shows a small example of a weighted graph that represents the interconnection of routers in the Internet. The problem that we want to solve is to find the cheapest path along which to route any given message. This problem should sound familiar because it is similar to the problem we solved using a breadth first search.

The algorithm we are going to use to determine the shortest path is called "Dijkstra's algorithm". Dijkstra's algorithm is an iterative algorithm that provides us with the shortest path from one particular starting node to all other nodes in the graph. Again this is similar to the results of a breadth first search.

To keep track of the total cost from the start node to each destination we will make use of a global dictionary D. At any time during the running of Dijkstra's algorithm D will contain the current cost of the least cost path from the start to the destination. The algorithm iterates once for every vertex in the graph; however the order that we iterate over the vertices is controlled by a priority queue.

The code for Dijkstra's algorithm is shown in Listing 6.10 When the algorithm finishes the distances are set correctly as are the predecessor links for each vertex in the graph.

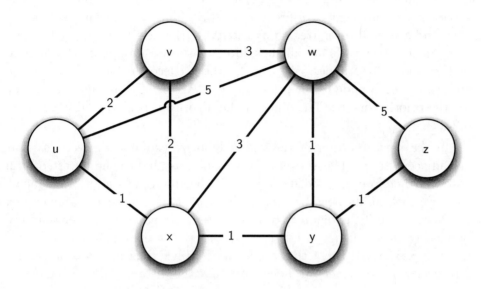

Figure 6.26: Connections and Weights Between Routers in the Internet

```
1   def dijkstra(G,start):
2       PQ = PriorityQueue()
3       start.setDistance(0)
4       PQ.buildHeap([(v.getDistance(),v) for v in G])
5       while not PQ.isEmpty():
6           w = PQ.delMin()
7           for v in w.getAdj():
8               newDist = w.getDistance() + w.getCost(v)
9               if newDist < v.getDistance():
10                  v.setDistance( newDist )
11                  v.setPred(w)
12                  PQ.decreaseKey(v,newDist)
```

Listing 6.10: Dijkstra's Algorithm

Let's walk through an application of Dijkstra's algorithm one vertex at a time using Figure 6.27 as our guide. We begin with the vertex u. The three vertices adjacent to u are v, w, and x. Since the initial distances to v, w, and x are all initialized to `sys.maxint`, the new costs to get to them through the start node are all their direct costs. So we update the costs to each of these three nodes. We also set the predecessor for each node to u and we add each node to the priority queue. We use the distance as the key for the priority queue. The state of the algorithm is shown in figure part 6.27(a).

In the next iteration of the `while` loop we examine the vertices that are adjacent to x. The vertex x is next because it has the lowest overall cost and therefore bubbled its way to the beginning of the priority queue. At x we look at its neighbors u, v, w and y. For each neighboring vertex we check to see if the distance to that vertex through x is smaller than the previously known distance. Obviously this is the case for y since its distance was `sys.maxint`. It is not the case for u or v since their distances are 0 and 2 respectively. However, we now learn that the distance to w is smaller if we go through x than from u directly to w. Since that is the case we update w with a new distance and change the predecessor for w from u to x. See Figure 6.27(b) for the state of all the vertices.

The next step is to look at the vertices neighboring v. This step results in no changes to the graph, so we move on to node y. At node y we discover that it is cheaper to get to both w and z, so we adjust the distances and predecessor links accordingly. Finally we check nodes w and z. However, no additional changes are found and so the priority queue is empty and Dijkstra's algorithm exits.

It is important to note that Dijkstra's algorithm works only when the weights are all positive. You should convince yourself that if you introduced a negative weight on one of the edges to the graph in Figure 6.26 that the algorithm would never exit.

Finally, we note that to route messages through the Internet, other algorithms are used for finding the shortest path. One of the problems with using Dijkstra's algorithm on the Internet is that you must have a complete representation of the graph in order for the algorithm to run. The implication of this is that every router has a complete map of all the routers in the Internet. In practice this is not the case and other variations of the algorithm allow each router to discover the graph as they go. One such algorithm that you may want to read about is called the "distance vector" routing algorithm.

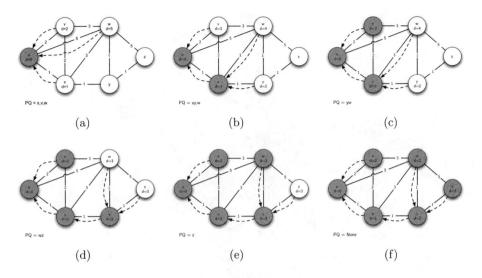

Figure 6.27: Tracing Dijkstra's Algorithm

6.4.6 Spanning Trees

For our last graph algorithm let's consider a problem that online game designers and Internet radio providers face. The problem is that they want to efficiently transfer a piece of information to anyone and everyone who may be listening. This is important in gaming so that all the players know the very latest position of every other player. This is important for Internet radio so that all the listeners that are tuned in are getting all the data they need to reconstruct the song they are listening to. Figure 6.28 illustrates the broadcast problem.

There are some brute force solutions to this problem, so let's look at them first to help understand the broadcast problem better. This will also help you appreciate the solution that we will propose when we are done. To begin, the broadcast host has some information that the listeners all need to receive. The simplest solution is for the broadcasting host to keep a list of all of the listeners and send individual messages to each. In Figure 6.28 we show a small network with a broadcaster and some listeners. Using this first approach, four copies of every message would be sent. Assuming that the least cost path is used, lets see how many times each router would handle the same message.

All messages from the broadcaster go through router A, so A sees all four copies of every message. Router C sees only one copy of each message

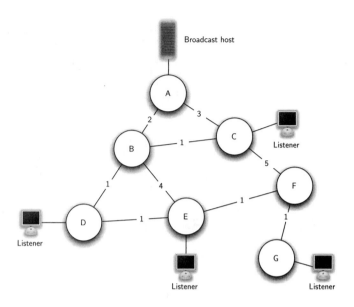

Figure 6.28: The Broadcast Problem

for its listener. However, routers B and D would see three copies of every message since routers B and D are on the cheapest path for listeners 1, 2, and 3. When you consider that the broadcast host must send hundreds of messages each second for a radio broadcast, that is a lot of extra traffic.

A brute force solution is for the broadcast host to send a single copy of the broadcast message and let the routers sort things out. In this case, the easiest solution is a strategy called **uncontrolled flooding**. The flooding strategy works as follows. Each message starts with a time to live (**ttl**) value set to some number greater than or equal to the number of edges between the broadcast host and its most distant listener. Each router gets a copy of the message and passes the message on to *all* of its neighboring routers. When the message is passed on the **ttl** is decreased. Each router continues to send copies of the message to all its neighbors until the **ttl** value reaches 0. It is easy to convince yourself that uncontrolled flooding generates many more unnecessary messages than our first strategy.

The solution to this problem lies in the construction of a minimum weight **spanning tree**. Formally we define the minimum spanning tree T for a graph $G = (V, E)$ as follows. T is an acyclic subset of E that connects all the vertices in V. The sum of the weights of the edges in T is minimized.

Figure 6.29 shows a simplified version of the broadcast graph and high-lights the edges that form a minimum spanning tree for the graph. Now to solve our broadcast problem, the broadcast host simply sends a single copy of the broadcast message into the network. Each router forwards the message to any neighbor that is part of the spanning tree, excluding the neighbor that just sent it the message. In this example A forwards the message to B. B forwards the message to D and C. D forwards the message to E, which forwards it to F, which forwards it to G. No router sees more than one copy of any message, and all the listeners that are interested see a copy of the message.

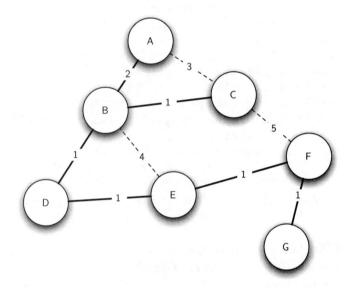

Figure 6.29: Minimum Spanning Tree for the Broadcast Graph

The algorithm we will use to solve this problem is called Prim's algorithm. Prim's algorithm belongs to a family of algorithms called the "greedy algorithms" because at each step we will choose the cheapest next step. Our last step is to develop Prim's algorithm.

The basic idea in constructing a spanning tree is as follows:

1. While T is not yet a spanning tree

    (a) Find an edge that is safe to add to the tree
    (b) Add the new edge to T

The trick is in the step that directs us to "find an edge that is safe." We define a safe edge as any edge that connects a vertex that is in the spanning tree to a vertex that is not in the spanning tree. This ensures that the tree will always remain a tree and therefore have no cycles.

The Python code to implement Prim's algorithm is shown in Listing 6.11. Prim's algorithm is similar to Dijkstra's algorithm in that they both use a priority queue to select the next vertex to add to the growing graph.

```
 1  def prim(G,start):
 2      PQ = PriorityQueue()
 3      for v in G:
 4          v.setDistance(sys.maxint)
 5          v.setPred(None)
 6      start.setDistance(0)
 7      PQ.buildHeap([(v.getDistance(),v) for v in G])
 8      while not PQ.isEmpty():
 9          u = PQ.delMin()
10          for v in u.getAdj():
11              if v in PQ and u.getCost(v) < v.getDistance():
12                  v.setPred(u)
13                  v.setDistance(u.getCost(v))
14                  PQ.decreaseKey((u.getCost(v)))
```

Listing 6.11: Prim's Minimum Spanning Tree Algorithm

Figure 6.30 shows the algorithm in operation on our sample tree. We begin with the starting vertex as A. The distances to all the other vertices are initialized to infinity. Looking at the neighbors of A we can update distances to two of the additional vertices B and C because the distances to B and C through A are less than infinite. This moves B and C to the front of the priority queue. Update the predecessor links for B and C by setting them to point to A. It is important to note that we have not formally added B or C to the spanning tree yet. A node is not considered to be part of the spanning tree until it is removed from the priority queue.

Since B has the smallest distance we look at B next. Examining B's neighbors we see that D and E can be updated. Both D and E get new distance values and their predecessor links are updated. Moving on to the next node in the priority queue we find C. The only node C is adjacent to that is still in the priority queue is F, thus we can update the distance to F and adjust F's position in the priority queue.

Now we examine the vertices adjacent to node D. We find that we can update E and reduce the distance to E from 6 to 4. When we do this we change the predecessor link on E to point back to D, thus preparing it to be grafted into the spanning tree but in a different location. The rest of the algorithm proceeds as you would expect, adding each new node to the tree.

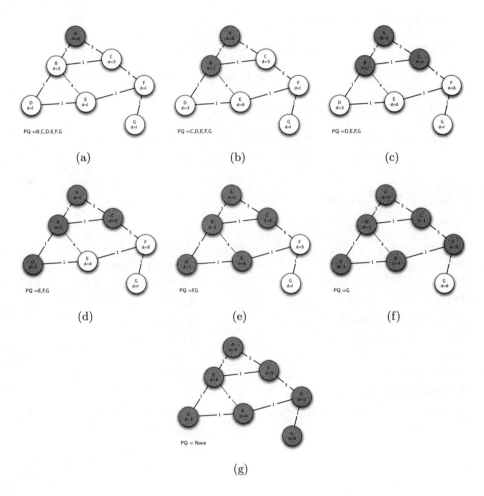

Figure 6.30: Tracing Prim's Algorithm

6.5 Summary

In this chapter we have looked at the graph data structure. The graph data structure enables us to solve many problems provided we can transform the original problem into something that can be represented by a graph. In particular, we have seen that graphs are useful to solve problems in the following general areas.

- Breadth first search for finding the unweighted shortest path.

- Dijkstra's algorithm for weighted shortest path.

- Depth first search for graph exploration.

- Strongly connected components for simplifying a graph.

- Topological sort for ordering tasks.

- Minimum weight spanning trees for broadcasting messages.

6.6   Key Terms

Adjacency list	Adjacency matrix
Adjacent	Breadth first search (BFS)
cycle	Cyclic graph
DAG	Depth first forest
Depth first search (DFS)	Digraph
Directed acyclic graph (DAG)	Directed graph
Edge cost	Edge
Parenthesis Property	Path
Shortest path	Spanning tree
Strongly Connected Components (SCC)	Topological Sort
Uncontrolled flooding	Vertex
Weight	

6.7 Discussion Questions

1. Draw the graph corresponding to the following adjacency matrix.

	A	B	C	D	E	F
A		7	5			1
B	2			7	3	
C		2				8
D	1				2	4
E	6			5		
F		1			8	

2. Draw the graph corresponding to the following list of edges.

from	to	cost
1	2	10
1	3	15
1	6	5
2	3	7
3	4	7
3	6	10
4	5	7
6	4	5
5	6	13

3. Ignoring the weights, perform a breadth first search on the graph from question 1.

4. Show each step in applying Dijkstra's algorithm to the graph in question 2.

5. Using Prim's algorithm, find the minimum weight spanning tree for the graph in question 1.

6. Draw a dependency graph illustrating the steps needed to send an email. Perform a topological sort on your graph.

6.8 Programming Exercises

1. Modify the depth first search function to produce a topological sort.

2. Modify the depth first search to produce strongly connected components.

3. Write the `transpose` method for the `Graph` class.

4. Write a program to solve the following problem: You have two jugs, a 4-gallon and a 3-gallon. Neither of the jugs has markings on them. There is a pump that can be used to fill the jugs with water. How can you get exactly two gallons of water in the 4 gallon jug?

5. Generalize the problem above so that the parameters to your solution include the sizes of each jug and the final amount of water to be left in the larger jug.

6. Write a program that solves the following problem: Three missionaries and three cannibals come to a river and find a boat that holds two people. Everyone must get across the river to continue on the journey. However, if the cannibals ever outnumber the missionaries on either bank, the missionaries will be eaten. Find a series of crossings that will get everyone safely to the other side of the river.

Chapter 7   Advanced Topics

―――――――――――――――――

7.1   Objectives

- To further explore and expand a number of the ideas presented earlier.

- To be able to implement a linked list.

- To understand dynamic programming as it relates to recursion.

- To understand the expected behavior of a skip list as an alternative implementation for dictionaries.

- To understand OctTrees and their use in image processing.

- To understand string-matching as a graph problem.

7.2   Lists Revisited: Linked Lists

Throughout the earlier chapters of this text, we have used Python lists to implement a number of the abstract data types presented. The list is a powerful, yet simple, collection mechanism that provides the programmer with a wide variety of operations. However, not all programming languages include a list collection. In these cases, the notion of a list must be implemented by the programmer.

A **list** is a collection of items where each item holds a relative position with respect to the others. More specifically, we will refer to this type of list as an unordered list. We can consider the list as having a first item, a second item, a third item, and so on. We can also refer to the beginning of the list (the first item) or the end of the list (the last item). For simplicity we will assume that lists cannot contain duplicate items.

For example, the collection of integers 54, 26, 93, 17, 77, and 31 might represent a simple unordered list of exam scores. Note that we have written them as comma-delimited values, a common way of showing the list structure. Of course, Python would show this list as [54, 26, 93, 17, 77, 31].

7.2.1   The List Abstract Data Type

The unordered list abstract data type is defined by the following structure and operations. The structure of an unordered list, as described above, is a collection of items where each item holds a relative position with respect to the others. The unordered list operations are given below.

- `List()` creates a new list that is empty. It needs no parameters and returns an empty list.

- `add(item)` adds a new item to the list. It needs the item and returns nothing. Assume the item is not already in the list.

- `remove(item)` removes the item from the list. It needs the item and modifies the list. Assume the item is present in the list.

- `search(item)` searches for the item in the list. It needs the item and returns a boolean value.

- `isEmpty()` tests to see whether the list is empty. It needs no parameters and returns a boolean value.

- `length()` returns the number of items in the list. It needs no parameters and returns an integer.

We will also consider a variation of the unordered list known as an ordered list. For example, if the list of integers shown above were an ordered list (ascending order), then it could be written as 17, 26, 31, 54, 77, and 93. Since 17 is the smallest item, it occupies the first position in the list. Likewise, since 93 is the largest, it occupies the last position.

The structure of an ordered list is a collection of items where each item holds a relative position that is based upon some underlying characteristic of the item. The ordering is typically either ascending or descending. The ordered list operations are the same as those of the unordered list. In fact, the only difference is that the `add` operation (often called `insert` for reasons that will become obvious as we explore the implementation) needs to make sure that new items are added to the list in the proper position to maintain the underlying order. For consistency, we will call the operation **add** in both lists.

7.2.2 Implementing a List in Python: Linked Lists

We will base our implementation of the list on two ideas. The first, something you may have already noticed in the abstract data type definitions above, is that the relationship between unordered and ordered lists is hierarchical. An ordered list IS-A unordered list (see Figure 7.1) so we will likely want to use inheritance to implement these two classes. Since the operation names for both lists will be the same, this will require that we simply override those methods whose behavior must change.

Figure 7.1: Hierarchical Relationship Between Unordered and Ordered Lists

The second idea is based on the node and link technique that we used to implement binary trees. We will refer to this notion as a **linked list**. In order to implement a list, we need to be sure that we can maintain the relative positioning of the items. However, there is no requirement that we maintain that positioning in contiguous memory. For example, consider the collection of items shown in Figure 7.2. It appears that these values have been placed randomly. However, if we can maintain some explicit information in each item, namely the location of the next item (see Figure 7.3), then the relative position of each item can be expressed by simply following the link from one item to the next.

It is important to note that the location of the first item of the list must be explicitly specified. Once we know where the first item is, it can tell us where the second is, and so on. This external reference is often referred to as the **head** of the list. Similarly, the last item needs to know that there is no next item.

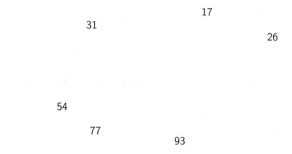

Figure 7.2: Items Not Constrained in Their Physical Placement

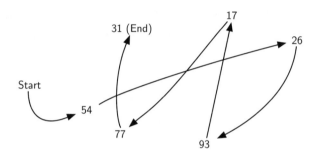

Figure 7.3: Relative Positions Maintained by Explicit Links.

7.2.2.1   The Node Class

The basic building block for the linked list implementation is the **node**. Each node object must hold at least two pieces of information. First, the node must contain the list item itself. We will call this the **data field** of the node. In addition, each node must hold a reference to the next node. Listing 7.1 shows the Python implementation. To construct a node, you need to supply the initial data value for the node. Evaluating the assignment statement below will yield a node object containing the value 93 (see Figure 7.4). You should note that we will typically represent a node object as shown in Figure 7.5. The Node class also includes the usual methods to access and modify the data and the next reference.

```
>>> temp = Node(93)
>>> temp.getData()
93
```

The special Python reference value None will play an important role in the Node class and later in the linked list itself. A reference to None will denote the fact that there is no next node. Note in the constructor that a node is initially created with **next** set to None. Since this is sometimes referred to as "grounding the node," we will use the standard ground symbol to denote a reference that is referring to None. It is always a good idea to explicitly assign None to your initial next reference values.

```python
class Node:
    def __init__(self,initdata):
        self.data = initdata
        self.next = None

    def getData(self):
        return self.data

    def getNext(self):
        return self.next

    def setData(self,newdata):
        self.data = newdata

    def setNext(self,newnext):
        self.next = newnext
```

Listing 7.1: A Node Class

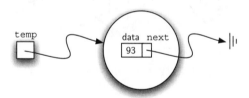

Figure 7.4: A Node Object Contains the Item and a Reference to the Next Node

Figure 7.5: A Typical Representation for a Node

7.2.2.2 The `List` Class

As we suggested above, the unordered list will be built from a collection of nodes, each linked to the next by explicit references. As long as we know where to find the first node (containing the first item), each item after that can be found by successively following the next links. With this in mind, the `UnorderedList` class must maintain a reference to the first node. Listing 7.2 shows the constructor. Note that each list object will maintain a single reference to the head of the list.

Initially when we construct a list, there are no items. The assignment statement

```
>>> mylist = UnorderedList()
```

creates the linked list representation shown in Figure 7.6. As we discussed in the `Node` class, the special reference `None` will again be used to state that the head of the list does not refer to anything. Eventually, the example list given earlier will be represented by a linked list as shown in Figure 7.7. The head of the list refers to the first node which contains the first item of the list. In turn, that node holds a reference to the next node (the next item) and so on. It is very important to note that the list class itself does not contain any node objects. Instead it contains a single reference to only the first node in the linked structure.

Figure 7.6: An Empty List

Figure 7.7: A Linked List of Integers

The `isEmpty` method, shown in Listing 7.3, simply checks to see if the head of the list is a reference to `None`. The boolean expression `self.head == None` will only be true if there are no nodes in the linked list. Since a new list is empty, the constructor and the check for empty must be consistent

```
1  class UnorderedList:
2      def __init__(self):
3          self.head = None
```

Listing 7.2: The UnorderedList Class Constructor

with one another. This shows the advantage to using the reference **None** to denote the "end" of the linked structure. In Python, **None** can be compared to any reference. Two references are equal if they both refer to the same object. We will use this often in our remaining methods.

```
1  def isEmpty(self):
2      return self.head == None
```

Listing 7.3: The isEmpty Method

So, how do we get items into our list? We need to implement the **add** method. However, before we can do that, we need to address the important question of where in the linked list to place the new item. Since this list is unordered, the specific location of the new item with respect to the other items already in the list is not important. The new item can go anywhere. With that in mind, it makes sense to place the new item in the easiest location possible.

Recall that the linked list structure provides us with only one entry point, the head of the list. All of the other nodes can only be reached by accessing the first node and then following **next** links. This means that the easiest place to add the new node is right at the head, or beginning, of the list. In other words, we will make the new item the first item of the list and the existing items will need to be linked to this new first item so that they follow.

The linked list shown in Figure 7.7 was built by calling the **add** method a number of times.

```
>>> mylist.add(31)
>>> mylist.add(77)
>>> mylist.add(17)
>>> mylist.add(93)
>>> mylist.add(26)
>>> mylist.add(54)
```

Note that since 31 is the first item added to the list, it will eventually be the last node on the linked list as every other item is added ahead of it. Also, since 54 is the last item added, it will become the data value in the first node of the linked list.

The **add** method is shown in Listing 7.4. Each item of the list must reside in a node object. Line 2 creates a new node and places the item as its data. Now we must complete the process by linking the new node into the existing structure. This requires two steps as shown in Figure 7.8. Step 1 (line 3) changes the **next** reference of the new node to refer to the old first node of the list. Now that the rest of the list has been properly attached to the new node, we can modify the head of the list to refer to the new node. The assignment statement in line 4 sets the head of the list.

The order of the two steps described above is very important. What happens if the order of line 3 and line 4 is reversed? If the modification of the head of the list happens first, the result can be seen in Figure 7.9. Since the head was the only external reference to the list nodes, all of the original nodes are lost and can no longer be accessed.

```
1  def add(self,item):
2      temp = Node(item)
3      temp.setNext(self.head)
4      self.head = temp
```

Listing 7.4: The add Method

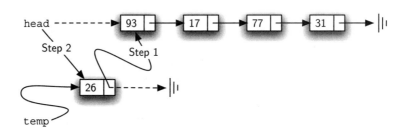

Figure 7.8: Adding a New Node is a Two-Step Process

The remaining methods, **length**, **search**, and **remove**, are all based on a technique known as **linked list traversal**. Traversal refers to the process of systematically visiting each node. To do this we use an external reference that starts at the first node in the list. As we visit each node, we move the reference to the next node by "traversing" the next reference.

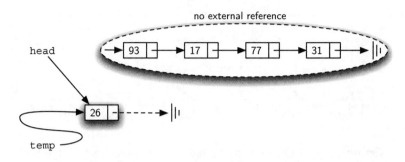

Figure 7.9: Result of Reversing the Order of the Two Steps

To implement the `length` method, we need to traverse the linked list and keep a count of the number of nodes that occurred. Listing 7.5 shows the Python code for counting the number of nodes in the list. The external reference is called `current` and is initialized to the head of the list in line 2. At the start of the process we have not seen any nodes so the count is set to 0. Lines 4–6 actually implement the traversal. As long as the current reference has not seen the end of the list (`None`), we move current along to the next node via the assignment statement in line 6. Again, the ability to compare a reference to `None` is very useful. Every time current moves to a new node, we add 1 to `count`. Finally, `count` gets returned after the iteration stops. Figure 7.10 shows this process as it proceeds down the list.

```
1  def length(self):
2      current = self.head
3      count = 0
4      while current != None:
5          count = count + 1
6          current = current.getNext()
7
8      return count
```

Listing 7.5: The `length` Method

Searching for a value in a linked list implementation of an unordered list also uses the traversal technique. As we visit each node in the linked list we will ask whether the data stored there matches the item we are looking for. In this case, however, we may not have to traverse all the way to the end of the list. In fact, if we do get to the end of the list, that means that the item we are looking for must not be present. Also, if we do find the item, there is no need to continue.

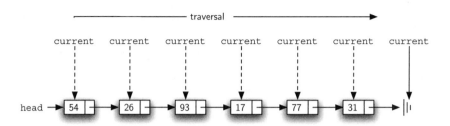

Figure 7.10: Traversing the Linked List from the Head to the End

Listing 7.6 shows the implementation for the **search** method. As in the **length** method, the traversal is initialized to start at the head of the list (line 2). We also use a boolean variable called **found** to remember whether we have located the item we are searching for. Since we have not found the item at the start of the traversal, **found** can be set to **False** (line 3). The iteration in line 4 takes into account both conditions discussed above. As long as there are more nodes to visit and we have not found the item we are looking for, we continue to check the next node. The question in line 5 asks whether the data item is present in the current node. If so, **found** can be set to **True**.

```
1  def search(self,item):
2      current = self.head
3      found = False
4      while current != None and not found:
5          if current.getData() == item:
6              found = True
7          else:
8              current = current.getNext()
9
10     return found
```

Listing 7.6: The search Method

As an example, consider invoking the **search** method looking for the item 17.

```
>>> mylist.search(17)
True
>>>
```

Since 17 is in the list, the traversal process needs to move only to the node containing 17. At that point, the variable **found** is set to **True** and the **while** condition will fail, leading to the return value seen above. This process can be seen in Figure 7.11.

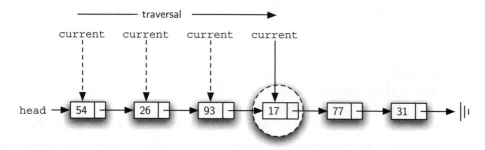

Figure 7.11: Successful Search for the Value 17

The **remove** method requires two logical steps. First, we need to traverse the list looking for the item we want to remove. Once we find the item (recall that we assume it is present), we must remove it. The first step is very similar to **search**. Starting with an external reference set to the head of the list, we traverse the links until we discover the item we are looking for. Since we assume that item is present, we know that the iteration will stop before **current** gets to **None**. This means that we can simply use the boolean **found** in the condition.

When **found** becomes **True**, **current** will be a reference to the node containing the item to be removed. But how do we remove it? One possibility would be to replace the value of the item with some marker that suggests that the item is no longer present. The problem with this approach is the number of nodes will no longer match the number of items. It would be much better to remove the item by removing the entire node.

In order to remove the node containing the item, we need to modify the link in the previous node so that it refers to the node that comes after **current**. Unfortunately, there is no way to go backward in the linked list. Since **current** refers to the node ahead of the node where we would like to make the change, it is too late to make the necessary modification.

The solution to this dilemma is to use two external references as we traverse down the linked list. **current** will behave just as it did before, marking the current location of the traverse. The new reference, which we will call **previous**, will always travel one node behind **current**. That way, when **current** stops at the node to be removed, **previous** will be referring to the proper place in the linked list for the modification.

Listing 7.7 shows the complete **remove** method. Lines 2–3 assign initial values to the two references. Note that **current** starts out at the list head as in the other traversal examples. **previous**, however, is assumed to always travel one node behind current. For this reason, **previous** starts out with a value of None since there is no node before the head (see Figure 7.12). The boolean variable **found** will again be used to control the iteration.

In lines 6–7 we ask whether the item stored in the current node is the item we wish to remove. If so, **found** can be set to **True**. If we do not find the item, **previous** and **current** must both be moved one node ahead. Again, the order of these two statements is crucial. **previous** must first be moved one node ahead to the location of **current**. At that point, **current** can be moved. This process is often referred to as "inch-worming" as **previous** must catch up to **current** before **current** moves ahead. Figure 7.13 shows the movement of **previous** and **current** as they progress down the list looking for the node containing the value 17.

```python
1  def remove(self,item):
2      current = self.head
3      previous = None
4      found = False
5      while not found:
6          if current.getData() == item:
7              found = True
8          else:
9              previous = current
10             current = current.getNext()
11
12     if previous == None:
13         self.head = current.getNext()
14     else:
15         previous.setNext(current.getNext())
```

Listing 7.7: The **remove** Method

Once the searching step of the **remove** has been completed, we need to remove the node from the linked list. Figure 7.14 shows the link that must be modified. However, there is a special case that needs to be addressed. If the item to be removed happens to be the first item in the list, then **current** will reference the first node in the linked list. This also means that **previous** will be None. We said earlier that **previous** would be referring to the node whose next reference needs to be modified in order to complete

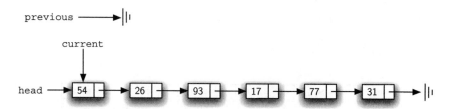

Figure 7.12: Initial Values for the previous and current References

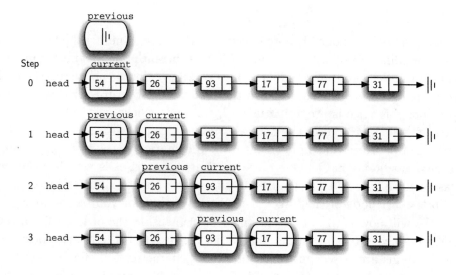

Figure 7.13: previous and current Move Down the List

the remove. In this case, it is not **previous** but rather the head of the list that needs to be changed (see Figure 7.15).

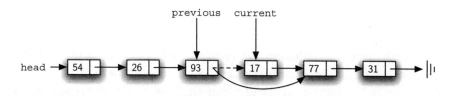

Figure 7.14: Removing an Item from the Middle of the List

Line 12 allows us to check whether we are dealing with the special case described above. If **previous** did not move, it will still have the value **None**

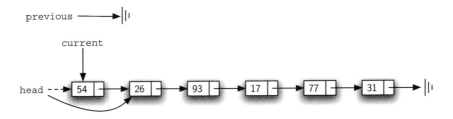

Figure 7.15: Removing the First Node from the List

when the boolean `found` becomes `True`. In that case (line 13) the head of the list is modified to refer to the node after the current node, in effect removing the first node from the linked list. However, if previous is not `None`, the node to be removed is somewhere down the linked list structure. In this case the previous reference is providing us with the node whose next reference must be changed. Line 15 uses the `setNext` method from `previous` to accomplish the removal. Note that in both cases the destination of the reference change is `current.getNext()`. One question that often arises is whether the two cases shown here will also handle the situation where the item to be removed is in the last node of the linked list. We leave that for you to consider.

We will now turn our attention to implementing the ordered list as described above. Recall that an ordered list requires that the relative positions of the items are based on some underlying characteristic. The ordered list of integers given above (17, 26, 31, 54, 77, and 93) can be represented by a linked structure as shown in Figure 7.16. Again, the node and link structure is ideal for representing the relative positioning of the items.

Figure 7.16: An Ordered Linked List

To implement the `OrderedList` class, we will inherit the basic structure and behavior from the `UnorderedList` class. Since there is no additional data required, we can simply call upon the parent (`UnorderedList`) constructor to set up the `head` reference. Once again, an empty list will be denoted by a `head` reference to `None`.

The `isEmpty` and `length` methods do not need to change at all since they deal only with the number of nodes in the list without regard to the actual item values. Likewise, the `remove` method will work just fine since we

```
1   class OrderedList(UnorderedList):
2       def __init__(self):
3           UnorderedList.__init__(self)
```

Listing 7.8: OrderedList Inherits from UnorderedList

still need to find the item and then link around the node to remove it. The two remaining methods, search and add, will require some modification.

The search of an unordered linked list required that we traverse the nodes one at a time until we either find the item we are looking for or run out of nodes (None). It turns out that the same approach would actually work with the ordered list and in fact in the case where we find the item it is exactly what we need. However, in the case where the item is not in the list, we can take advantage of the ordering to stop the search as soon as possible.

For example, Figure 7.17 shows the ordered linked list as a search is looking for the value 45. As we traverse, starting at the head of the list, we first compare against 17. Since 17 is not the item we are looking for, we move to the next node, in this case 26. Again, this is not what we want, so we move on to 31 and then on to 54. Now, at this point, something is different. Since 54 is not the item we are looking for, our former strategy would be to move forward. However, due to the fact that this is an ordered list, that will not be necessary. Once the value in the node becomes greater than the item we are searching for, the search can stop and return False. There is no way the item could exist further out in the linked list.

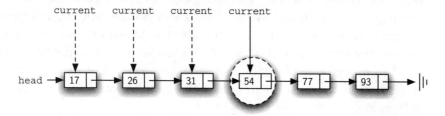

Figure 7.17: Searching an Ordered Linked List

Listing 7.9 shows the complete search method. It is easy to incorporate the new condition discussed above by adding another boolean variable, stop, and initializing it to False (line 4). While stop is False (not stop) we can continue to look forward in the list (line 5). If any node is ever discovered that contains data greater than the item we are looking for, we will set stop to True (lines 9–10). The remaining lines are identical to the unordered list search.

```
1  def search(self,item):
2      current = self.head
3      found = False
4      stop = False
5      while current != None and not found and not stop:
6          if current.getData() == item:
7              found = True
8          else:
9              if current.getData() > item:
10                 stop = True
11             else:
12                 current = current.getNext()
13
14     return found
```

Listing 7.9: The Modified search Method for the Ordered List

The most significant method modification will take place in add. Recall that for unordered lists, the add method could simply place a new node at the head of the list. It was the easiest point of access. Unfortunately, this will no longer work with ordered lists. It is now necessary that we discover the specific place where a new item belongs in the existing ordered list.

Assume we have the ordered list consisting of 17, 26, 54, 77, and 93 and we want to add the value 31. The add method must decide that the new item belongs between 26 and 54. Figure 7.18 shows the setup that we need. As we explained earlier, we need to traverse the linked list looking for the place where the new node will be added. We know we have found that place when either we run out of nodes (current becomes None) or the value of the current node becomes greater than the item we wish to add. In our example, seeing the value 54 causes us to stop.

As we saw with unordered lists, it is necessary to have an additional reference, again called previous, since current will not provide access to the node that must be modified. Listing 7.10 shows the complete add method. Lines 2–3 set up the two external references and lines 9–10 again allow previous to follow one node behind current every time through the iteration. The condition (line 5) allows the iteration to continue as long as there are more nodes and the value in the current node is not larger than the item. In either case, when the iteration fails, we have found the location for the

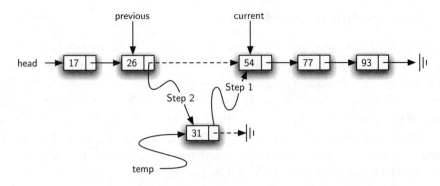

Figure 7.18: Adding an Item to an Ordered Linked List

new node.

The remainder of the method completes the two-step process shown in Figure 7.18. Once a new node has been created for the item, the only remaining question is whether the new node will be added at the beginning of the linked list or some place in the middle. Again, previous == None (line 13) can be used to provide the answer.

```python
def add(self,item):
    current = self.head
    previous = None
    stop = False
    while current != None and not stop:
        if current.getData() > item:
            stop = True
        else:
            previous = current
            current = current.getNext()

    temp = Node(item)
    if previous == None:
        temp.setNext(self.head)
        self.head = temp
    else:
        temp.setNext(current)
        previous.setNext(temp)
```

Listing 7.10: The Modified add Method for the Ordered List

$\boxed{7.2.2.3}$ **Analysis of Linked Lists**

To analyze the complexity of the linked list operations, we need to consider whether they require traversal. Consider a linked list that has n nodes. The isEmpty method is $O(1)$ since it requires one step to check the head reference for None. length, on the other hand, will always require n steps since there is no way to know how many nodes are in the linked list without traversing from head to end. Therefore, length is $O(n)$. search, add, and remove will also require the traversal process. Although on average they may need to traverse only half of the nodes, these methods are all $O(n)$ since in the worst case each will process every node in the list.

$\boxed{7.3}$ Recursion Revisited: Dynamic Programming

Many programs in computer science are written to optimize some value; for example, find the shortest path between two points, find the line that best fits the set of points, or find the smallest set of objects that satisfies some criteria. There are many strategies that computer scientists use to solve these problems. One of the goals of this book is to expose you to several different strategies. **Dynamic programming** is one such strategy for optimization problems.

A classic example of an optimization problem involves making change using the fewest coins. Suppose you are a programmer for a vending machine manufacturer. Your company wants to maximize profits by giving out the fewest possible coins in change for each transaction. Suppose a customer puts in a dollar bill and purchases an item for 37 cents. What is the smallest number of coins you can use to make change? The answer is six coins: two quarters, one dime, and three pennies. How did we arrive at the answer of six coins? We start with the largest coin in our arsenal (a quarter) and use as many of those as possible, then we go to the next lowest coin value and use as many of those as possible. This first approach is called a **greedy method** because we try to solve as big a piece of the problem as possible right away.

The greedy method works fine when we are using U.S. coins, but suppose that your company decides to deploy its vending machines in Lower Elbonia where, in addition to the usual 1, 5, 10, and 25 cent coins they also have a 21 cent coin. In this instance our greedy method fails to find the optimal solution for 63 cents in change. With the addition of the 21 cent coin the greedy method would still find the solution to be six coins. However, the optimal answer is three 21 cent pieces.

Let's look at a method where we could be sure that we would find the optimal answer to the problem. Since this section is about recursion, you may have guessed that we will use a recursive solution. Let's start with identifying the base case. If we are trying to make change for the same amount as the value of one of our coins, the answer is easy, one coin.

If the amount does not match we have several options. What we want is the minimum of a penny plus the number of coins needed to make change for the original amount minus a penny, a nickel plus the number of coins needed to make change for the original amount minus five cents, and so on.

$$min \begin{cases} 1 + numCoins(originalamount - 1) \\ 1 + numCoins(originalamount - 5) \\ 1 + numCoins(originalamount - 10) \\ 1 + numCoins(originalamount - 25) \end{cases}$$

The algorithm for doing what we have just described is shown in Listing 7.11. In line 3 we are checking our base case; that is, we are trying to make change in the exact amount of one of our coins. If we do not have a coin equal to the amount of change, we make recursive calls for each different coin value less than the amount of change we are trying to make. Line 6 shows how we filter the list of coins to those less than the current value of change using a list intention. The recursive call also reduces the total amount of change we need to make by the value of the coin selected. The recursive call is made in line 7. Notice that on that same line we add 1 to our number of coins to account for the fact that we are using a coin. Just adding 1 is the same as if we had made a recursive call asking where we satisfy the base case condition immediately.

```
def recMC(coins,change):
    minCoins = change
    if change in coins:
        return 1
    else:
        for i in [c for c in coins if c <= change]:
            numCoins = 1 + recMC(coins,change-i)
            if numCoins < minCoins:
                minCoins = numCoins
    return minCoins
```

Listing 7.11: Recursive Version of Coin Optimization Problem

The trouble with the algorithm in Listing 7.11 is that it is extremely inefficient. In fact, it takes 67,716,925 recursive calls to find the optimal solution to the 4 coins, 63 cents problem! To understand the fatal flaw in our approach look at Figure 7.19, which illustrates a small fraction of the 377 function calls needed to find the optimal set of coins to make change for 26 cents.

Each node in the graph corresponds to a call to `recMC`. The label on the node indicates the amount of change for which we are computing the number of coins. The label on the arrow indicates the coin that we just used. By following the graph we can see the combination of coins that got us to any point in the graph. The main problem is that we are re-doing too many calculations. For example, the graph shows that the algorithm would recalculate the optimal number of coins to make change for 15 cents three times. Each of these computations to find the optimal number of coins for 15 cents itself takes 52 function calls. Clearly we are wasting a lot of time and effort recalculating old results.

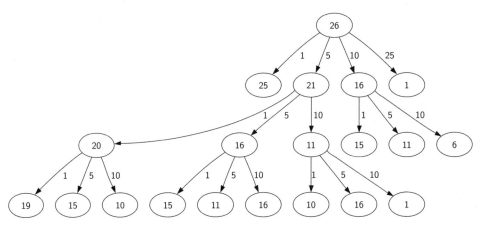

Figure 7.19: Call Tree for Listing 7.11.

The key to cutting down on the amount of work we do is to remember some of the past results so we can avoid recomputing results we already know. A simple solution is to store the results for the minimum number of coins in a table when we find them. Then before we compute a new minimum, we first check the table to see if a result is already known. If there is already a result in the table, we use the value from the table rather than recomputing. Listing 7.12 shows a modified algorithm to incorporate our table lookup scheme.

Notice that in line 6 we have added a test to see if our table contains the

```
1   def recDC(coins,change,res):
2       minCoins = change
3       if change in coins:        base case!
4           res[change] = 1
5           return 1
6       elif res[change] > 0:
7           return res[change]
8       else:
9           for i in [c for c in coins if c <= change]:
10              numCoins = 1 + recDC(coins,change-i,res)
11              if numCoins < minCoins:
12                  minCoins = numCoins
13                  res[change] = minCoins
14      return minCoins
```

Listing 7.12: Recursive Coin Optimization Using Table Lookup

minimum number of coins for a certain amount of change. If it does not, we compute the minimum recursively and store the computed minimum in the table. Using this modified algorithm reduces the number of recursive calls we need to make for the four coin, 63 cent problem to 221 calls!

Although the algorithm in Listing 7.12 is correct it looks and feels like a bit of a hack, and if we look at the result table we can see that there are some holes in the table. In fact the term for what we have done is not dynamic programming but rather we have improved the performance of our program by using a technique known as "memoization," or more commonly called "caching."

A truly dynamic programming algorithm will take a more systematic approach to the problem. Our dynamic programming solution is going to start with making change for one cent and systematically work its way up to the amount of change we require. This guarantees us that at each step of the algorithm we already know the minimum number of coins needed to make change for any smaller amount.

Let's look at how we would fill in a table of minimum coins to use in making change for 11 cents. Figure 7.20 illustrates the process. We start with one cent. The only solution possible is one coin (a penny). The next row shows the minimum for one cent and two cents. Again, the only solution is two pennies. The fifth row is where things get interesting. Now we have two options to consider, five pennies or one nickel. How do we decide which is best? We consult the table and see that the number of coins needed to make change for four cents is four, plus one more penny to make five, equals five coins. Or we can look at zero cents + one more nickel to make five cents equals 1 coin. Since the minimum of one and five is one we store 1 in the table. Fast forward again to the end of the table and consider 11 cents. Figure 7.21 shows the three options that we have to consider:

1. A penny plus the minimum number of coins to make change for $11-1 = 10$ cents (1)

2. A nickel plus the minimum number of coins to make change for $11-5 = 6$ cents (2)

3. A dime plus the minimum number of coins to make change for $11-10 = 1$ cent (1)

Either option 1 or 3 will give us a total of two coins which is the minimum number of coins for 11 cents.

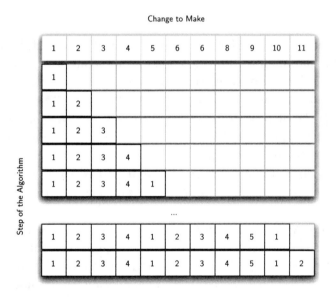

Figure 7.20: Minimum Number of Coins Needed to Make Change

Listing 7.13 is a dynamic programming algorithm to solve our change-making problem. dpMakeChange takes three parameters, a list of valid coin values, the amount of change we want to make, and a list of the minimum number of coins needed to make each value. When the function is done minCoins will contain the solution for all values from 0 to the value of change.

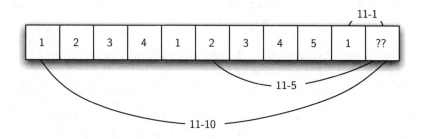

Figure 7.21: Three Options to Consider for the
Minimum Number of Coins for Eleven Cents

```
1  def dpMakeChange(coinList,change,minCoins):
2      for cents in range(change+1):
3          coinCount = cents
4          for j in [c for c in coinList if c <= cents]:
5              if minCoins[cents-j] + 1 < coinCount:
6                  coinCount = minCoins[cents-j]+1
7          minCoins[cents] = coinCount
8      return minCoins[change]
```

Listing 7.13: Dynamic Programming Solution

Note that dpMakeChange is not a recursive function, even though we
started with a recursive solution to this problem. It is important to realize
that just because you can write a recursive solution to a problem does not
mean it is the best or most efficient solution. The bulk of the work in this
function is done by the loop that starts on line 4. In this loop we consider
using all possible coins to make change for the amount specified by cents.
Like we did for the 11 cent example above, we remember the minimum value
and store it in our minCoins list.

Although our making change algorithm does a good job of figuring out
the minimum number of coins, it does not help us make change since we do
not keep track of the coins we use. We can easily extend dpMakeChange to
keep track of the coins used by simply remembering the last coin we add for
each entry in the minCoins table. If we know the last coin added, we can
simply subtract the value of the coin to find a previous entry in the table
that tells us the last coin we added to make that amount. We can keep
tracing back through the table until we get to the beginning. Listing 7.14
shows the dpMakeChange algorithm modified to keep track of the coins used,

along with a function `printCoins` that walks backward through the table
to print out the value of each coin used.

```
 1  def dpMakeChange(coinList,change,minCoins,coinsUsed):
 2      for cents in range(change+1):
 3          coinCount = cents
 4          newCoin = 1
 5          for j in [c for c in coinList if c <= cents]:
 6              if minCoins[cents-j] + 1 < coinCount:
 7                  coinCount = minCoins[cents-j]+1
 8                  newCoin = j
 9          minCoins[cents] = coinCount
10          coinsUsed[cents] = newCoin
11      return minCoins[change]
12
13  def printCoins(coinsUsed,change):
14      coin = change
15      coinDict = {}
16      while coin > 0:
17          thisCoin = coinsUsed[coin]
18          print thisCoin
19          coin = coin - thisCoin
```

Listing 7.14: Modified Dynamic Programming Solution

Finally, here is a sample Python session that shows the algorithm in
action. The first three lines of the session create the list of coins used. The
next two lines create the lists we need to store the results. `coinsUsed` is
a list of the coins used to make change, and `coinCount` is the minimum
number of coins used to make change for the amount corresponding to the
position in the list.

```
>>> cl = [1,5,10,21,25]
>>> coinsUsed = [0]*64
>>> coinCount = [0]*64
>>> dpMakeChange(cl,63,coinCount,coinsUsed)
3
>>> printCoins(coinsUsed,63)
21
21
21
>>> printCoins(coinsUsed,52)
10
```

```
21
21
>>> coinsUsed
[1, 1, 1, 1, 1, 5, 1, 1, 1, 1, 10, 1, 1, 1, 1, 5, 1, 1, 1, 1, 10,
21, 1, 1, 1, 25, 1, 1, 1, 1, 5, 10, 1, 1, 1, 10, 1, 1, 1, 1, 5, 10,
21, 1, 1, 10, 21, 1, 1, 1, 25, 1, 10, 1, 1, 5, 10, 1, 1, 1, 10, 1, 10, 21]
```

Notice that the coins we print out come directly from the `coinsUsed` array. For the first call we start at array position 63 and print 21. Then we take $63 - 21 = 42$ and look at the 42nd element of the list. Once again we find a 21 stored there. Finally, element 21 of the array also contains 21, giving us the three 21 cent pieces.

7.4 Dictionaries Revisited: Skip Lists

One of the most versatile collections available in Python is the **dictionary**. Dictionaries, often referred to as **maps**, store a collection of key-value pairs. The key, which must be unique, is assigned an association with a particular data value. Given a key, it is possible to ask the map for the corresponding, associated data value. The abilities to put a key-value pair into the map and then look up a data value associated with a given key are the fundamental operations that all maps must provide.

For example, Figure 7.22 shows a map containing key-value pairs. In this case, the keys are integers and the values are small, two-character words. From a logical perspective, there is no inherent order or organization within the pairs themselves. However, as the example shows, if a key (93) is provided to the map, the associated value (be) is returned.

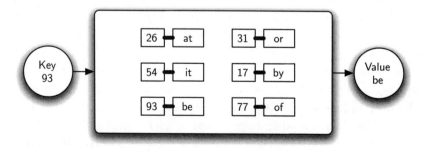

Figure 7.22: An Example Map

7.4.1   The Map Abstract Data Type

The map abstract data type is defined by the following structure and operations. The structure of a map, as described above, is a collection of key-value pairs where values can be accessed via their associated key. The map operations are given below:

- `Map()` creates a new map that is empty. It needs no parameters and returns an empty map.

- `put(key,value)` adds a new key-value pair to the map. It needs the key and the associated value and returns nothing. Assume the key is not already in the map.

- `get(key)` searches for the key in the map and returns the associated value. It needs the key and returns a value.

It should be noted that there are a number of other possible operations that we could add to the map abstract data type. We will explore these in the exercises.

7.4.2   Implementing a Dictionary in Python

We have already seen a number of interesting ways to implement the map idea. In Chapter 3 we considered the hash table as a means of providing map behavior. Given a set of keys and a hash function, we could place the keys in a collection that allowed us to search and retrieve the associated data value. Our analysis showed that this technique could potentially yield a $O(1)$ search. However, performance degraded due to issues such as table size, collisions, and collision resolution strategy.

In Chapter 5 we considered a binary search tree as a way to store such a collection. In this case the keys were placed in the tree such that searching could be done in $O(\log n)$. However, this was only true if the tree was balanced; that is, the left and the right subtrees were all of similar size. Unfortunately, depending on the order of insertion, the keys could end up being skewed to the right or to the left. In this case the search again degrades.

The problem we would like to address here is to come up with an implementation that has the advantages of an efficient search without the drawbacks described above. One such possibility is called a **skip list**. Figure 7.23 shows a possible skip list for the collection of key-value pairs shown above (the reason for saying "possible" will become apparent later). As you can see, a skip list is basically a two-dimensional linked list where the links all go forward (to the right) or down. The **head** of the list can be seen in the upper-left corner. Note that this is the only entry point into the skip list structure.

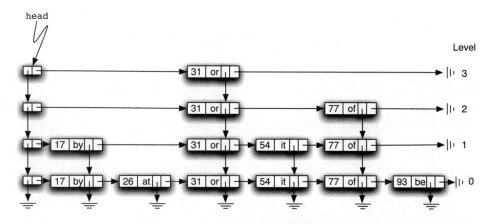

Figure 7.23: An Example Skip List

Before moving on to the details of skip-list processing it will be useful to explain some vocabulary. Figure 7.24 shows that the majority of the skip list structure consists of a collection of data nodes, each of which holds a key and an associated value. In addition, there are two references from each data node. Figure 7.25 shows a detailed view of a single data node.

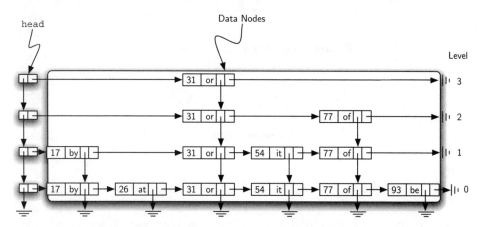

Figure 7.24: The Body of the Skip List Is Made Up of Data Nodes

Figure 7.26 shows two different vertical columns. The leftmost column consists of a linked list of header nodes. Each header node holds two ref-

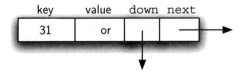

Figure 7.25: A Single Data Node

erences called **down** and **next**. The **next** reference refers to a linked list of data nodes. The **down** reference refers to the next lower header node. A detailed view of a header node can be seen in Figure 7.27.

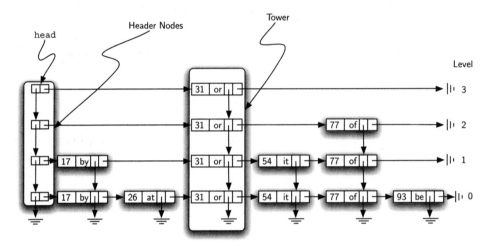

Figure 7.26: Header Nodes and Towers

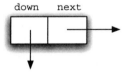

Figure 7.27: Each Header Node Holds Two References

The columns of data nodes are known as **towers**. Towers are linked together by the **down** reference in the data node. We can see that each tower corresponds to a particular key-value pair and towers can have different heights. We will explain how the height of the tower is determined later when we consider how to add data to the skip list.

Finally, Figure 7.28 shows a horizontal collection of nodes. If you look closely, you will notice that each level is actually an ordered linked list of data nodes where the order is maintained by the key. Each linked list is given a name, commonly referred to as its **level**. Levels are named starting with 0 at the lowest row. Level 0 consists of the entire collection of nodes. Every key-value pair must be present in the level-0 linked list. However, as we move up to higher levels, we see that the number of nodes decreases. This is one of the important characteristics of a skip list and will lead to our efficient search. Again, it can be seen that the number of nodes at each level is directly related to the heights of the towers.

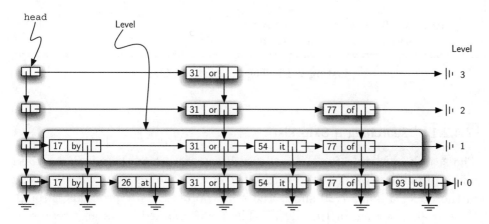

Figure 7.28: Each Horizontal Group of Data Nodes Is a Level

Classes for the two types of nodes described above can easily be constructed in the same fashion as for simple linked lists in the previous section. A header node (see Listing 7.15) consists of two references, **next** and **down**, both of which are initialized to **None** in the constructor. A data node (see Listing 7.16) has four fields, two for the key and value and then two additional for the references **next** and **down**. Again, the references are initialized to **None** and the standard **get** and **set** methods are provided for manipulating nodes.

The constructor for the entire skip list is shown in Listing 7.17. When a skip list is created there are no data and therefore no header nodes. The head of the skip list is set to **None**. As key-value pairs are added to the structure, the list head refers to the first header node which in turn provides access to a linked list of data nodes as well as access to lower levels.

```
1  class HeaderNode:
2      def __init__(self):
3          self.next = None
4          self.down = None
5
6      def getNext(self):
7          return self.next
8
9      def getDown(self):
10         return self.down
11
12     def setNext(self,newnext):
13         self.next = newnext
14
15     def setDown(self,newdown):
16         self.down = newdown
```

Listing 7.15: The HeaderNode Class

7.4.2.1 Searching a Skip List

The search operation for a skip list will require a key. It will find a data node containing that key and return the corresponding value that is stored in the node. Figure 7.29 shows the search process as it proceeds through the skip list looking for the key 77. The nodes marked by "stars" represent those that are considered during the search process.

As we search for 77, we begin at the head of the skip list. The first header node refers to the data node holding 31. Since 31 is less than 77, we move forward. Now since there is no next data node from 31 at that level (level 3), we must drop down to level 2. This time, when we look to the right, we see a data node with the key 77. Our search is successful and the word "of" is returned. It is important to note that our first comparison, data node 31, allowed us to "skip" over 17 and 26. Likewise, from 31 we were able to go directly to 77, bypassing 54.

Listing 7.18 shows the Python implementation of the **search** method. The search starts at the head of the list and searches through nodes until either the key is found or there are no more nodes to check. The two boolean variables, **found** and **stop** (lines 3–4), are used to control for these conditions. The basic idea is to start at the header node of the highest level and begin to look to the right. If no data node is present, the search continues on the next lower level (lines 9–10). On the other hand, if a data

```
1   class DataNode:
2       def __init__(self,key,value):
3           self.key = key
4           self.data = value
5           self.next = None
6           self.down = None
7
8       def getKey(self):
9           return self.key
10
11      def getData(self):
12          return self.data
13
14      def getNext(self):
15          return self.next
16
17      def getDown(self):
18          return self.down
19
20      def setData(self,newdata):
21          self.data = newdata
22
23      def setNext(self,newnext):
24          self.next = newnext
25
26      def setDown(self,newdown):
27          self.down = newdown
```

Listing 7.16: The DataNode Class

```
1   class SkipList:
2       def __init__(self):
3           self.head = None
```

Listing 7.17: The SkipList Constructor

node exists, we compare the keys. If there is a match, we have found a data node with the key we are looking for and we can report **found** as **True** (lines 12–13).

Since each level is an ordered linked list, a key mismatch provides us with very useful information. If the key we are looking for is less than the

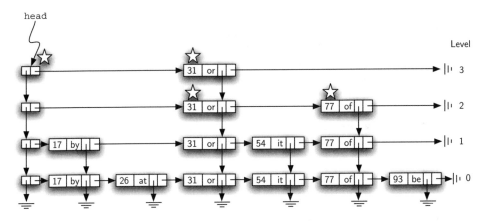

Figure 7.29: Searching for the Key 77

key contained in the data node (line 15), we know that no other data node on that level can contain our key since everything to the right has to be greater. In that case, we drop down one level in that tower (line 16). If no such level exists (we drop to None), we have discovered that the key is not present in our skip list and the boolean variable stop is set to True. On the other hand, as long as there are data nodes on the current level with key values less than the key we are looking for, we continue moving to the next node (line 18).

Once we enter a lower level, we repeat the process of checking to see if there is a next node. Each level lower in the skip list has the potential to provide additional data nodes. If the key is present, it will have to be discovered no later than level 0 since level 0 is the complete ordered linked list. Our hope is that we will find it sooner.

7.4.2.2   Adding Key-Value Pairs to a Skip List

If we are given a skip list, the search method is fairly easy to implement. Our task here is to understand how the skip list structure was built in the first place and how it is possible that the same set of keys, added in the same order, can give us different skip lists.

Adding a new key-value pair to the skip list is essentially a two-step process. First, we search the skip list looking for the position where the key should have been. Remember that we are assuming the key is not already present. Figure 7.30 shows this process as we look to add the key 65 (data value "hi") to the collection. We have used the stars once again to show the

```
1  def search(self,key):
2      current = self.head
3      found = False
4      stop = False
5      while not found and not stop:
6          if current == None:
7              stop = True
8          else:
9              if current.getNext() == None:
10                 current = current.getDown()
11             else:
12                 if current.getNext().getKey() == key:
13                     found = True
14                 else:
15                     if key < current.getNext().getKey():
16                         current = current.getDown()
17                     else:
18                         current = current.getNext()
19      if found:
20          return current.getNext().getData()
21      else:
22          return None
```

Listing 7.18: The search Method.

path of the search process as it proceeds through the skip list.

As we proceed using the same searching strategy as in the previous section, we find that 65 is larger than 31. Since there are no more nodes on level 3, we drop to level 2. Here we find 77, which is larger than 65. Again, we drop, this time to level 1. Now, the next node is 54, which is less than 65. Continuing to the right, we hit 77, which again causes us to drop down until eventually we hit the None at the base of the tower.

The second step in the process is to create a new data node and add it to the level 0 linked list (Figure 7.31). However, if we stop at that point, the best we will ever have is a single linked list of key-value pairs. We also need to build a tower for the new entry and this is where the skip list gets very interesting. How high should the tower be? The height of the tower for the new entry will not be predetermined but instead will be completely probabilistic. In essence, we will "flip a coin" to decide whether to add another level to the tower. Each time the coin comes up heads, we will add one more level to the current tower.

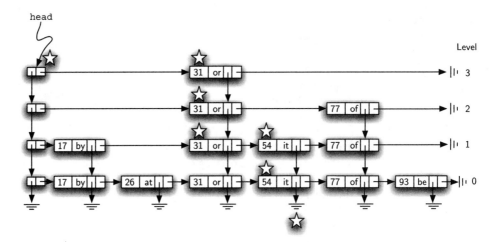

Figure 7.30: Searching for the Key 65

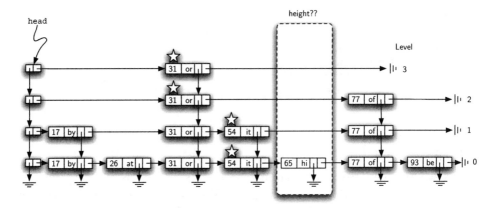

Figure 7.31: Adding the Data Node and Tower for 65

It is easy to use a random number generator to simulate a coin flip. Listing 7.19 shows a method that simply returns either 0 or 1 using the **randrange** function from the Python **random** module. If the value of **flip** returns 1, we will interpret it to be "heads."

Listing 7.20 shows the first part of the **insert** method. You will note immediately in line 2 that we need to check to see if this is the first node being added to the skip list. This is the same question we asked for simple linked lists. If we are adding to the head of the list, a new header node as well as data node must be created. The iteration in lines 7–14 continues as

```
1  from random import randrange
2  def flip():
3      return randrange(2)
```

Listing 7.19: A Method to Flip a Coin

long as the `flip` method returns a 1 (the coin toss returns heads). Each time a new level is added to the tower, a new data node and a new header node are created.

```
1  def insert(self,key,data):
2      if self.head == None:
3          self.head = HeaderNode()
4          temp = DataNode(key,data)
5          self.head.setNext(temp)
6          top = temp
7          while flip() == 1:
8              newhead = HeaderNode()
9              temp = DataNode(key,data)
10             temp.setDown(top)
11             newhead.setNext(temp)
12             newhead.setDown(self.head)
13             self.head = newhead
14             top = temp
15     else:
```

Listing 7.20: The Insert Method: Part 1

In the case of a non-empty skip list (Listing 7.21), we need to search for the insert position as described above. Since we have no way of knowing how many data nodes will be added to the tower, we need to save the insert points for every level that we enter as part of the search process. These insert points will be processed in reverse order, so a stack will work nicely to allow us to back up through the linked lists inserting tower data nodes as necessary. The stars in Figure 7.31 show the insert points that would be stacked in the example. These points represent only those places where we dropped down during the search.

Again, in Listing 7.22, we flip our coin to determine the number of levels for the tower. This time we pop the insert stack to get the next higher insertion point as the tower grows. Only after the stack becomes empty will

```
1     towerStack = Stack()
2     current = self.head
3     stop = False
4     while not stop:
5         if current == None:
6             stop = True
7         else:
8             if current.getNext() == None:
9                 towerStack.push(current)
10                current = current.getDown()
11            else:
12                if current.getNext().getKey() > key:
13                    towerStack.push(current)
14                    current = current.getDown()
15                else:
16                    current = current.getNext()
17
18    lowestLevel = towerStack.pop()
19    temp = DataNode(key,data)
20    temp.setNext(lowestLevel.getNext())
21    lowestLevel.setNext(temp)
22    top = temp
```

Listing 7.21: The Insert Method: Part 2

we need to return to creating new header nodes. We leave the remaining details of the implementation for you to trace.

We should make one final note about the structure of the skip list. We had mentioned earlier that there are many possible skip lists for a set of keys, even if they are inserted in the same order. Now we see why. Depending on the random nature of the coin flip, the height of the towers for any particular key is bound to change each time we build the skip list.

7.4.2.3 Building the Map

Now that we have implemented the skip list behavior allowing us to add data to the list and search for data that is present, we are in a position to finally implement the map abstract data type. As we discussed above, maps must provide two operations, put and get. Listing 7.23 shows that these operations can easily be implemented by constructing an internal skip list collection (line 3) and using the insert and search operations shown in the

```
1    while flip() == 1:
2        if towerStack.isEmpty():
3            newhead = HeaderNode()
4            temp = DataNode(key,data)
5            temp.setDown(top)
6            newhead.setNext(temp)
7            newhead.setDown(self.head)
8            self.head = newhead
9            top = temp
10       else:
11           nextLevel = towerStack.pop()
12           temp = DataNode(key,data)
13           temp.setDown(top)
14           temp.setNext(nextLevel.getNext())
15           nextLevel.setNext(temp)
16           top = temp
```

Listing 7.22: The Insert Method: Part 3

previous two sections.

```
1   class Map:
2       def __init__(self):
3           self.collection=SkipList()
4
5       def put(self,key,value):
6           self.collection.insert(key,value)
7
8       def get(self,key):
9           return self.collection.search(key)
```

Listing 7.23: The Map Class Implemented Using Skip Lists

7.4.2.4   Analysis of a Skip List

If we had simply stored the key-value pairs in an ordered linked list, we know that the search method would be $O(n)$. Can we expect better performance from the skip list? Recall that the skip list is a probabilistic data structure. This means that the analysis will be dependent upon the probability of some event, in this case, the flip of a coin. Although a rigorous analysis of this structure is beyond the scope of this text, we can make a strong informal argument.

Assume that we are building a skip list for n keys. We know that each tower starts off with a height of 1. As we add data nodes to the tower, assuming the probability of getting "heads" is $\frac{1}{2}$, we can say that $\frac{n}{2}$ of the keys have towers of height 2. As we flip the coin again, $\frac{n}{4}$ of the keys have a tower of height 3. This corresponds to the probability of flipping two heads in a row. Continuing this argument shows $\frac{n}{8}$ keys have a tower of height 4 and so on. This means that we expect the height of the tallest tower to be $\log_2(n) + 1$. Using our "Big-O" notation, we would say that the height of the skip list is $O(\log(n))$.

To analyze the `search` method recall that there are two scans that need to be considered as we look for a given key. The first is the down direction. The previous result suggests that in the worst case we will expect to consider $O(\log(n))$ levels to find a key. In addition, we need to include the number of forward links that need to be scanned on each level. We drop down a level when one of two events occurs. Either we find a data node with a key that is greater than the key we are looking for or we find the end of a level. If we are currently looking at some data node, the probability that one of those two events will happen in the next link is $\frac{1}{2}$. This means that after looking at 2 links, we would expect to drop to the next lower level (we expect to get heads after two coin flips). In any case, the number of nodes that we need to look at on any given level is constant. The entire result then becomes $O(\log(n))$. Since inserting a new node is dominated by searching for its location, the `insert` operation will also have $O(\log(n))$ performance.

7.5 Trees Revisited: Quantizing Images

Next to text, digital images are the most common element found on the Internet. However, the Internet would feel much slower if every advertisement sized image required 196,560 bytes of memory. Instead, a banner-ad image requires only 14,246, just 7.2% of what it could take. Where do these numbers come from? How is such a phenomenal savings achieved? The answers to these questions are the topic of this section.

7.5.1 A Quick Review of Digital Images

A digital image is composed of thousands of individual components called **pixels**. The pixels are arranged as a rectangle that forms the image. Each pixel in an image represents a particular color in the image. On a computer, the color of each pixel is determined by a mixture of three primary colors:

red, green, and blue. A simple example of how pixels are arranged to form a picture is shown in Figure 7.32.

Figure 7.32: A Simple Image

In the physical world colors are not discrete quantities. The colors in our physical world have an infinite amount of variation to them. Just as computers must approximate floating point numbers, they also must approximate the colors in an image. The human eye can distinguish between 200 different levels in each of the three primary colors, or a total of about 8 million individual colors. In practice we use one byte (8 bits) of memory for each color component of a pixel. Eight bits gives us 256 different levels for each of the red, green, and blue components, for a total of 16.7 million different possible colors for each pixel. While the huge number of colors allows artists and graphic designers to create wonderfully detailed images, the downside of all of these color possibilities is that image size grows very rapidly. For example a single image from a one-megapixel camera would take 3 megabytes of memory.

In Python we might represent an image using a list of a list of tuples, where the tuples consist of three numbers between 0 and 255, one for each of the red, green, and blue components. In other languages such as C++ and Java an image could be represented as a two-dimensional array. The list of lists representation of the first two rows of the image in Figure 7.32 are shown below:

```
im = [[(255,255,255),(255,255,255),(255,255,255),(12,28,255),
       (12,28,255),(255,255,255),(255,255,255),(255,255,255),],
      [(255,255,255),(255,255,255),(12,28,255),(255,255,255),
```

```
        (255,255,255),(12,28,255),(255,255,255),(255,255,255)],
 ... ]
```

The color white is represented by the tuple (255,255,255). A blueish color is represented by the tuple (12,28,255). You can obtain the color value for any pixel in the image by simply using list indices, for example:

```
>>> im[3][2]
(255, 18, 39)
```

With this representation for an image in mind you can imagine that it would be easy to store an image to a file just by writing a tuple for each pixel. You might start by writing the number of rows and columns in the image and then by writing three integer values per line. In practice the Python Image Library (PIL) provides us with some more powerful image classes. Using the image class we can get and set pixels using `getPixel((col,row))` and `setPixel((col,row),colorTuple)`. Note that the parameters for the image methods are in a the traditional x,y order but many people forget and think in terms of row, column order.

7.5.2   Quantizing an Image

There are many ways of reducing the storage requirements for an image. One of the easiest ways is to simply use fewer colors. Fewer color choices means fewer bits for each red, green, and blue component, which means reduced memory requirements. In fact, one of the most popular image formats used for images on the World Wide Web uses only 256 colors for an image. Using 256 colors reduces the storage requirements from three bytes per pixel to one byte per pixel.

The question you are probably asking yourself right now is, How do I take an image that may have as many as 16 million colors and reduce it to just 256? The answer is a process called **quantization**. To understand the process of quantization let's think about colors as a three-dimensional space. Each color can be represented by a point in space where the red component is the x axis, the green component is the y axis, and the blue component is the z axis. We can think of the space of all possible colors as a $256 \times 256 \times 256$ cube. The colors closest to the vertex at (0,0,0) are going to be black and dark color shades. The colors closest to the vertex at (255,255,255) are bright and close to white. The colors closest to (255,0,0) are red and so forth.

The simplest way way to think about quantizing an image is to imagine taking the $256 \times 256 \times 256$ cube and turning it into an $8 \times 8 \times 8$ cube. The overall size of the cube stays the same, but now many colors in the old cube are represented by a single color in the new cube. Figure 7.33 shows an example of the quantization just described.

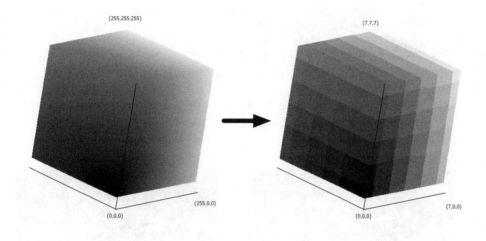

Figure 7.33: Color Quantization

We can turn this simple idea of color quantization into the Python program shown in listing 7.24 The `simpleQuant` algorithm works by mapping the color components for each pixel represented by its full 256 bits to the color at the center of the cube in its area. This is easy to do using integer division in Python. In the `simpleQuant` algorithm there are seven distinct values in the red dimension and six distinct values in the green and blue dimensions.

Figure 7.34 shows a before and after comparison of an original and quantized image. Of course, these are color pictures that have been converted to grayscale for publication. You can download the color images from this book's web page. After you download the images you can run the programs for yourself to see the real difference in full color. Notice how much detail is lost in the quantized picture. The grass has lost nearly all its detail and is uniformly green, and the skin tones have been reduced to two shades of tan.

```python
import sys
import os
import Image
def simpleQuant():
    im = Image.open('bubbles.jpg')
    w,h = im.size
    for row in range(h):
        for col in range(w):
            r,g,b = im.getpixel((col,row))
            r = r / 36 * 36
            g = g / 42 * 42
            b = b / 42 * 42
            im.putpixel((col,row),(r,g,b))
    im.show()
```

Listing 7.24: Simple Quantization Algorithm

(a) Original Image   (b) Image Quantized with simpleQuant

Figure 7.34: Comparison of Original Image with Simple Quantized Image

7.5.3 An Improved Quantization Algorithm Using OctTrees

The problem with the simple method of quantization just described is that the colors in most pictures are not evenly distributed throughout the color cube. Many colors may not appear in the image, and so parts of the cube may go completely unused. Allocating an unused color to the quantized image is a waste. Figure 7.35 shows the distribution of the colors that are used in the example image. Notice how little of the color cube space is actually used.

To make a better quantized image we need to find a way to do a better job of selecting the set of colors we want to use to represent our image.

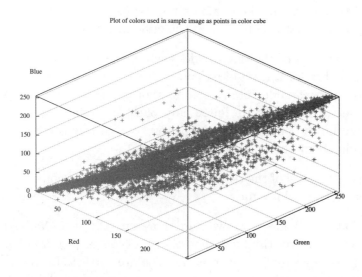

Figure 7.35: Plot of Colors Used in Image as Points in Color Cube

There are several algorithms for dividing the color cube in different ways to allow for the better use of colors. In this section we are going to look at a tree-based solution. The tree solution we will use makes use of an **OctTree**. An OctTree is similar to a binary tree; however, each node in an OctTree has eight children. Here is the interface we will implement for our OctTree abstract data type:

- OctTree() Create a new empty OctTree.

- insert(r,g,b) Add a new node to the OctTree using the red, green, and blue color values as the key.

- find(r,g,b) Find an existing node, or the closest approximation, using the red, green, and blue color values as the search key.

- reduce(n) Reduce the size of the OctTree so that there are n or fewer leaf nodes.

Here is how an OctTree is used to divide the color cube:

- The root of the OctTree represents the entire cube.

- The second level of the `OctTree` represents a single vertical and horizontal slice that evenly divides the cube into 8 pieces.

- The next level of the tree divides each of the 8 sub-cubes into 8 additional cubes for a total of 64 cubes. Notice that the cube represented by the parent node totally contains all of the sub-cubes represented by the children. As we follow any path down the tree we are staying within the boundary of the parent, but getting progressively more specific about the portion of the cube.

- The eighth level of the tree represents the full resolution of 16.7 million colors in our color cube.

Now that you know how we can represent the color cube using an `OctTree`, you may be thinking that the `OctTree` is just another way to divide up the color cube into even parts. You are correct. However, because the `OctTree` is hierarchical we can take advantage of the hierarchy to use large cubes to represent unused portions of the color cube and smaller cubes to represent the popular colors. Here is an overview of how we will use an `OctTree` to do a better job of selecting a subset of the colors in an image:

1. For each pixel in the image:

    (a) Search for the color of this pixel in the `OctTree`. The color will be a leaf node at the eighth level.

    (b) If the color is not found create a new leaf node at the eighth level (and possibly some internal nodes above the leaf).

    (c) If the color is already present in the tree increment the counter in the leaf node to keep track of how many pixels are this color.

2. Repeat until the number of leaf nodes is less than or equal to the target number of colors.

    (a) Find the deepest leaf node with the smallest number of uses.

    (b) Merge the leaf node and all of its siblings together to form a new leaf node.

3. The remaining leaf nodes form the color set for this image.

4. To map an original color to its quantized value simply search down the tree until you get to a leaf node. Return the color values stored in the leaf.

The ideas outlined above are encoded as a Python function to read, quantize, and display an image in the function `buildAndDisplay()` in Listing 7.25.

```python
def buildAndDisplay():
    im = Image.open('bubbles.jpg')
    w,h = im.size
    ot = OctTree()
    for row in range(0,h):
        for col in range(0,w):
            r,g,b = im.getpixel((col,row))
            ot.insert(r,g,b)

    ot.reduce(256)   # reduce to 256 colors

    for row in range(0,h):
        for col in range(0,w):
            r,g,b = im.getpixel((col,row))
            nr,ng,nb = ot.find(r,g,b)
            im.putpixel((col,row),(nr,ng,nb))
# replace pixel with new quantized values

    im.show()
```

Listing 7.25: Build and Display a Quantized Image Using an `OctTree`

The build and display function follows the basic parts just described. First, the loops in lines 5–8 read each pixel and add it to the `OctTree`. The insertion of a pixel into the OctTree is done on line 8. Reduction of the number of leaf nodes is done by the `reduce` method on line 10. The updating of the image is done by searching for a color, using `find`, in the reduced `OctTree` on line 15.

We are using the Python image library for just four simple functions. Opening a pre-existing image file (`Image.open`), reading a pixel (`getpixel`), writing a pixel (`putpixel`), and displaying the result to the screen (`show`).

Now let's look at the `OctTree` class and the key methods. One of the first things to mention about the `OctTree` class is that there are really two classes. The `OctTree` class is used by the `buildAndDisplay` function. Notice that there is just one instance of the `OctTree` class used by `buildAndDisplay`. The second class is `otNode` which is defined inside the the `OctTree` class. A class that is defined inside another class is called an inner-class. The reason that we define `otNode` inside `OctTree` is because each node of an `OctTree` needs to have access to some information that is stored in an instance the `OctTree` class. Another reason for making `otNode` an inner class is that there is no reason for any code outside of the `OctTree` class to use it. The way that an `OctTree` is implemented is really a private detail of the `OctTree` that nobody else needs to know about. This is a good software engineering practice known as "information hiding."

All of the functions used in `buildAndDisplay` are defined in the `OctTree` class. The code for the `OctTree` class is spread across listings 7.26–7.30. First notice that the constructor for an `OctTree` initializes the root node to none. Then it sets up three important attributes that all the nodes of an `OctTree` may need to access. Those attributes are: `maxLevel`, `numLeaves`, and `leafList`. The `maxLevel` attribute limits the total depth of the tree. Notice that in our implementation we have initialized `maxLevel` to five. This is a small optimization that simply allows us to ignore the two least significant bits of color information. It keeps the overall size of the tree much smaller and doesn't hurt the quality of the final image at all. The `numLeaves` and `leafList` attributes allow us to keep track of the number of leaf nodes and allow us direct access to the leaves without traversing all the way down the tree. We will see why this is important shortly.

The `insert` and `find` methods behave exactly like their cousins in chapter 5. They each check to see if a root node exists, and then call the corresponding method in the root node. Notice that `insert` and `find` both use the red, green, and blue components to identify a node in the tree.

The `reduce` method is defined on line 17 of Listing 7.26. This method simply loops until the number of leaves in the leaf list is less than the total number of colors we want to have in the final image (defined by the parameter `maxCubes`). `reduce` makes use of a helper function `findMinCube` to find the node in the `OctTree` with the smallest reference count. Once the node with the smallest reference count is found, that node is merged into a single node with all of its siblings (see line 20). The `findMinCube` method is implemented using the `leafList` and a simple find minimum loop pattern, When the number of leaf nodes is large, and it could be as large is 16.7 million, this approach is not very efficient. In one of the exercises you are asked to modify the `OctTree` and improve the efficiency of `findMinCube`.

Now let's look at the class definition for the nodes in an `OctTree`. The constructor for the `otNode` class has three optional parameters. The parameters allow the `OctTree` functions methods to construct new nodes under a variety of circumstances. As we did with binary search trees, we will keep track of the parent of a node explicitly. The level of the node simply indicates its depth in the tree. The most interesting of these three parameters

```
 1    class OctTree:
 2    def __init__(self):
 3        self.root = None
 4        self.maxLevel = 5
 5        self.numLeaves = 0
 6        self.leafList = []
 7
 8    def insert(self,r,g,b):
 9        if not self.root:
10            self.root = self.otNode(outer=self)
11        self.root.insert(r,g,b,0,self)
12
13    def find(self,r,g,b):
14        if self.root:
15            return self.root.find(r,g,b,0)
16
17    def reduce(self,maxCubes):
18        while len(self.leafList) > maxCubes:
19            smallest = self.findMinCube()
20            smallest.parent.merge()
21            self.leafList.append(smallest.parent)
22            self.numLeaves = self.numLeaves + 1
23
24    def findMinCube(self):
25        minCount = sys.maxint
26        maxLev = 0
27        minCube = None
28        for i in self.leafList:
29            if i.count <= minCount and i.level >= maxLev:
30                minCube = i
31                minCount = i.count
32                maxLev = i.level
33        return minCube
```

Listing 7.26: The OctTree Class

is the `outer` parameter, which is a reference to the instance of the `OctTree` class that created this node. `outer` will function like `self` in that it will allow the instances of `otNode` to access attributes of an instance of `OctTree`.

The other attributes that we want to remember about each node in an `OctTree` include the reference `count` and the red, green, and blue components of the color represented by this tree. As you will note in the `insert` function, only a leaf node of the tree will have values for `red`, `green`, `blue`, and `count`. Also note that since each node can have up to eight children we initialize a list of eight references to keep track of them all. Rather than a left and right child as in binary trees, an `OctTree` has 0–7 children.

```
class otNode:
    def __init__(self,parent=None,level=0,outer=None):
        self.red = 0
        self.green = 0
        self.blue = 0
        self.count = 0
        self.parent = parent
        self.level = level
        self.oTree = outer
        self.children = [None]*8
```

Listing 7.27: The otNode Class and Constructor

Now we get into the really interesting parts of the `OctTree` implementation. The Python code for inserting a new node into an `OctTree` is shown in Listing 7.28. The first problem we need to solve is how to figure out where to place a new node in the tree. In a binary search tree we used the rule that a new node with a key less than its parent went in the left subtree, and a new node with a key greater than its parent went in the right subtree. But with eight possible children for each node it is not that simple. In addition, when indexing colors it is not obvious what the key for each node should be. In an `OctTree` we will use the information from the three color components. Figure 7.36 shows how we can use the red, green, and blue color values to compute an index for the position of the new node at each level of the tree. The corresponding Python code for computing the index is on line 18 of Listing 7.28.

The computation of the index combines bits from each of the red, green, and blue color components, starting at the top of the tree with the highest order bits. Figure 7.36 shows the binary representation of the red, green, and blue components of 163, 98, 231. At the root of the tree we start with the most significant bit from each of the three color components, in this case

```
1   def insert(self,r,g,b,level,outer):
2       if level < self.oTree.maxLevel:
3           idx = self.computeIndex(r,g,b,level)
4           if self.children[idx] == None:
5               self.children[idx] = outer.otNode(parent=self,
6                                                  level=level+1,
7                                                  outer=outer)
8           self.children[idx].insert(r,g,b,level+1,outer)
9       else:
10          if self.count == 0:
11              self.oTree.numLeaves = self.oTree.numLeaves + 1
12              self.oTree.leafList.append(self)
13          self.red += r
14          self.green += g
15          self.blue += b
16          self.count = self.count + 1
17
18  def computeIndex(self,r,g,b,level):
19      shift = 8 - level
20      rc = r >> shift-2 & 0x4
21      gc = g >> shift-1 & 0x2
22      bc = b >> shift & 0x1
23      return(rc | gc | bc)
```

Listing 7.28: otNode insert

the three bits are 1, 0, and 1. Putting these bits together we get binary 101 or decimal 5. You can see the binary manipulation of the red, green, and blue numbers in the computeIndex method on line 18 in Listing 7.28.

The operators used in the computeIndex may be unfamiliar to you. The >> operator is the right shift operation. The & is bitwise **and**, and | is logical **or**. The bitwise **or** and bitwise **and** operations work just like the logical operations used in conditionals, except that they work on the individual bits of a number. The shift operation simply moves the bits n places to the right, filling in with zeros on the left and dropping the bits as they go off the right.

Once we have computed the index appropriate for the level of the tree we are at, we traverse down into the subtree. In the example in Figure 7.36 we follow the link at position 5 in the children array. If there is no node at position 5, we create one. We keep traversing down the tree until we get to maxLevel. At maxLevel we stop searching and store the data. Notice that we do not overwrite the data in the leaf node, but rather we add the color components to any existing components and increment the reference counter. This allows us to compute the average of any color below the current node in the color cube. In this way, a leaf node in the `OctTree` may represent a number of similar colors in the color cube.

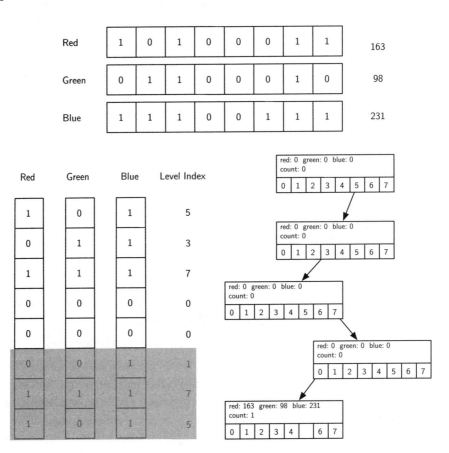

Figure 7.36: Computing an Index to Insert a Node in an OctTree

The `find` method, shown in Listing 7.29, uses the same method of index computation as the `insert` method to traverse the tree in search of a node matching the red, green, and blue components. The `find` method has three exit conditions.

1. We have reached the maximum level of the tree and so we return the average of the color information stored in this leaf node (see line 15).

2. We have found a leaf node at a height less than `maxLevel` (see line 9). This is possible only after the tree has been reduced. See below.

3. We try to follow a path into a non-existant subtree, which is an error.

```
def find(self,r,g,b,level):
    if level < self.oTree.maxLevel:
        idx = self.computeIndex(r,g,b,level)
        if self.children[idx]:
            return self.children[idx].find(r,g,b,level+1)
        elif self.count > 0:
            return ((self.red/self.count,
                        self.green/self.count,
                        self.blue/self.count))
        else:
            print "error: No leaf node for this color"
    else:
        return ((self.red/self.count,
                    self.green/self.count,
                    self.blue/self.count))
```

Listing 7.29: otNode find

The final aspect of the `otNode` class is the `merge` method. The `merge` method allows a parent to subsume all of its children and become a leaf node itself. If you remember back to the structure of the `OctTree` where each parent cube fully encloses all the cubes represented by the children you will see why this makes sense. When we merge a a group of siblings we are effectively taking a weighted average of the colors represented by each of those siblings. Since all the siblings are relatively close to each other in color space, the average is a good representation of all of them. Figure 7.37 illustrates the merge process for some sibling nodes.

Figure 7.37 shows the red, green, and blue components represented by the four leaf nodes whose identifying color values are (101, 122, 167), (100, 122, 183), (123, 108, 163), (126, 113, 166). Remember, the identifying values are different from the total plus count numbers shown in the figure (just divide to get the identifiers). Notice how close they are in the overall color space. The leaf node that gets created from all of these has an id of (112, 115, 168). This is close to the average of the four, but weighted more towards the third color tuple due to the fact that it had a reference count of 12.

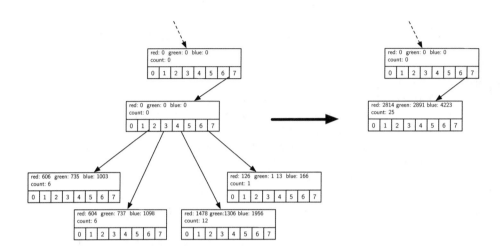

Figure 7.37: Merging 4 Leaf Nodes of an `OctTree`

```
def merge(self):
    for i in self.children:
        if i:
            if i.count > 0:
                self.oTree.leafList.remove(i)
                self.oTree.numLeaves -= 1
            else:
                print "Recursively Merging non-leaf..."
                i.merge()
            self.count += i.count
            self.red += i.red
            self.green += i.green
            self.blue += i.blue
    for i in range(8):
        self.children[i] = None
```

Listing 7.30: otNode Merge

Because the `OctTree` uses only colors that are really present in the image, and faithfully preserves colors that are often used, the final quantized image from the `OctTree` is much higher quality than the simple method we used to start this section. Figure 7.38 shows a comparison of the original image with the quantized image.

(a) Original Image   (b) Image Quantized with `OctTree`

Figure 7.38: Comparison of Original Image with `OctTree` Quantized Image

There are many additional ways to compress images using techniques such as run length encoding, discrete cosine transform, and huffman encoding. Any of these algorithms are within your grasp and we encourage you to look them up and read about them. In addition, quantized images can be improved by using a technique known as **dithering**. Dithering is a process by which different colors are placed near to each other so that the eye blends the colors together, forming a more realistic image. This is an old trick used by newspapers for doing color printing using just three different colors of ink. Again you can research dithering and try to apply it to some images on your own.

7.6 Graphs Revisited: Pattern Matching

Even with the growing interest in computer graphics, processing textual information is still an important area of study. Of particular interest here is the problem of finding patterns, often referred to as **substrings**, that exist in long strings of characters. The task is to perform some type of search that can identify at least the first occurrence of the pattern. We can also consider an extension of the problem that attempts to find all occurrences.

Python includes a built-in substring method called `find` that returns the location of the first occurrence of a pattern in a given string. For example,

```
>>> "ccabababcab".find("ab")
2
>>> "ccabababcab".find("xyz")
-1
```

shows that the substring `"ab"` occurs for the first time starting at index
position 2 in the string `"ccabababcab"`. `find` also returns a -1 if the pattern
does not occur.

7.6.1   Biological Strings

Some of the most exciting work in algorithm development is currently taking
place in the domain of bioinformatics; in particular, finding ways to manage
and process large quantities of biological data. Much of this data takes
the form of coded genetic material stored in the chromosomes of individual
organisms. Deoxyribonucleic acid, more commonly known as DNA, is a very
simple organic molecule that provides the blueprint for protein synthesis.

DNA is basically a long sequence consisting of four chemical bases: ade-
nine(A), thymine(T), guanine(G), and cytosine(C). These four symbols are
often referred to as the "genetic alphabet" and we represent a piece of DNA
as a string or sequence of these base symbols. For example, the **DNA string**
ATCGTAGAGTCAGTAGAGACTADTGGTACGA might code a very small
part of a DNA strand. It turns out that within these long strings, perhaps
thousands and thousands of base symbols long, small pieces exist that provide extensive information as to the meaning of this genetic code. We can see
then that having methods for searching out these pieces is a very important
tool for the bioinformatics researcher.

Our problem then reduces to the following ideas. Given a string of
symbols from the underlying alphabet A, T, G, and C, develop an algorithm
that will allow us to locate a particular pattern within that string. We will
often refer to the DNA string as the "text." If the pattern does not exist,
we would like to know that as well. Further, since these strings are typically
quite long, we need to be sure that the algorithm is efficient.

7.6.2   Simple Comparison

Our first approach is likely the solution that comes immediately to your
mind for solving the DNA string pattern-matching problem. We will simply
try all possibilities for matching the pattern to the text. Figure 7.39 shows
how the algorithm will work. We will start out comparing the pattern from
left to right with the text, starting at the first character in both. If there

is a match, then we proceed to check the second character. Whenever a mismatch occurs, we simply slide the pattern one position to the right and start over.

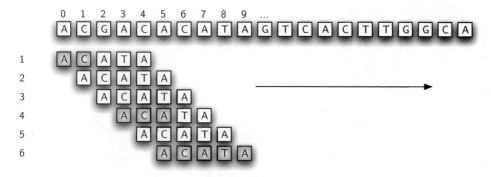

Figure 7.39: A Simple Pattern-Matching Algorithm

In this example, we have found a match on the sixth attempt, starting at position 5. The shaded characters denote the partial matches that occurred as we moved the pattern. Listing 7.31 shows the Python implementation for this method. It takes the pattern and the text as parameters. If there is a pattern match, it returns the position of the starting text character. Otherwise, it returns -1 to signal that the search failed.

The variables i and j serve as indices into the text and pattern respectively. The two boolean variables are used to control for the two conditions that cause the matcher to terminate. stop is set to True if we run out of text characters to check. match is set to True if the entire pattern has matched a sequence of text characters.

Line 7 checks for a match between the current text character and the current pattern character. If the match occurs, both indices are incremented. If the match fails, we move on to the next text character but reset the pattern back to the beginning (line 12). Line 14 checks to see if every character in the pattern has been processed. If so, a match has been found. If not, we need to check to see if there are more characters left in the text (line 17).

If we assume that the length of the text is n characters and the length of the pattern is m characters, then it is easy to see that the complexity of this approach is $O(nm)$. For each of the n characters we may have to compare against almost all m of the pattern characters. This is not so bad if the size of n and m are small. However, if we are considering thousands, or perhaps millions, of characters in our text, and in addition a large pattern, it will be necessary to look for a better approach.

```
1  def simpleMatcher(pattern, text):
2      i=0
3      j=0
4      match = False
5      stop = False
6      while not match and not stop:
7          if text[i] == pattern[j]:
8              i=i+1
9              j=j+1
10         else:
11             i=i+1
12             j=0
13
14         if j == len(pattern):
15             match = True
16         else:
17             if i == len(text):
18                 stop = True
19
20     if match:
21         return i-j
22     else:
23         return -1
```

Listing 7.31: A Simple Pattern Matcher

7.6.3 Using Graphs: Finite State Automata

It is possible to create a $O(n)$ pattern-matcher if we are willing to do some preprocessing with the pattern. One approach is to build what is known as a **deterministic finite automaton**, or **DFA**, that represents the pattern as a graph. Each vertex of the **DFA graph** is a state, keeping track of the amount of the pattern that has been seen so far. Each edge of the graph represents a transition that takes place after processing a character from the text.

Figure 7.40 shows a DFA for the example pattern from the last section (ACATA). The first vertex (state 0) is known as the "start state" (or "initial state") and denotes that we have not seen any matching pattern characters so far. Clearly, before processing the first text character, this is the situation.

The DFA works in a very simple way. We keep track of our current state, setting it to 0 when we start. We read the next character from the text. Depending on the character, we follow the appropriate transition to

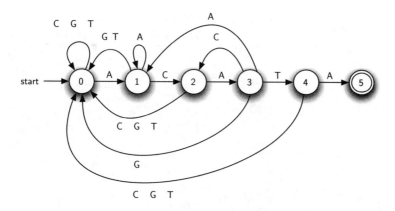

Figure 7.40: A Deterministic Finite Automaton

the next state, which in turn becomes the new current state. By definition, each state has one and only one transition for each character in the alphabet. This means that for our DNA alphabet we know that each state has four possible transitions to a next state. Note that in the figure we have labeled some edges (transitions) with multiple alphabet symbols to denote more than one transition to the same state.

We continue to follow transitions until a termination event occurs. If we enter state 5, known as the "final state" (the two concentric circles denote the final state in the DFA graph), we can stop and report success. The DFA graph has discovered an occurrence of the pattern. You might note that there are no transitions out of the final state, meaning that we must stop at that point. The location of the pattern can be computed from the location of the current character and the size of the pattern. On the other hand, if we run out of text characters and the current state is somewhere else in the DFA, known as a "nonfinal" state, we know that the pattern did not occur.

Figure 7.41 shows a step-by-step trace of the example DFA as it works through the text string ACGACACATA looking for the substring ACATA. The next state computed by the DFA always becomes the current state in the subsequent step. Since there is one and only one next state for every current state–current character combination, the processing through the DFA graph is easy to follow.

Since every character from the text is used once as input to the DFA graph, the complexity of this approach is $O(n)$. However, we need to take into account the preprocessing step that builds the DFA. There are many well-known algorithms for producing a DFA graph from a pattern. Unfortu-

Step	Current State	Current Text Symbol	Next State
1	0	A	1
2	1	C	2
3	2	G	0
4	0	A	1
5	1	C	2
6	2	A	3
7	3	C	2
8	2	A	3
9	3	T	4
10	4	A	5 final

Figure 7.41: A Trace of the DFA Pattern-Matcher

nately, all of them are quite complex mostly due to the fact that each state (vertex) must have a transition (edge) accounting for each alphabet symbol. The question arises as to whether there might be a similar pattern-matcher that employs a more streamlined set of edges.

7.6.4 Using Graphs: Knuth-Morris-Pratt

Recall the simple pattern-matcher presented earlier. Every possible substring of the text was tested against the pattern. In many cases this proved to be a waste of time since the actual starting point for the match was farther down the text string. A possible solution to this inefficiency would be to slide the pattern more than one text character if a mismatch occurs. Figure 7.42 shows this strategy using the rule that we slide the pattern over to the point where the previous mismatch happened.

In step 1, we find that the first two positions match. Since the mismatch occurs in the third character (the shaded character), we slide the entire pattern over and begin our next match at that point. In step 2, we fail immediately so there is no choice but to slide over to the next position. Now, the first three positions match. However, there is a problem. When the mismatch occurs, our algorithm says to slide over to that point. Unfortunately, this is too far and we miss the actual starting point for the pattern in the text string (position 5).

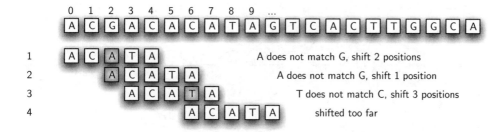

Figure 7.42: Simple Pattern-Matcher with Longer Shifts

The reason this solution failed is that we did not take advantage of information about the content of the pattern and the text that had been seen in a previous attempted match. Note that in step three, the last two characters of the text string that occur at the time of the mismatch (positions 5 and 6) actually match the first two characters of the pattern. We say that a two-character prefix of the pattern matches a two-character suffix of the text string processed up to that point. This is valuable information. Had we been tracking the amount of overlap between prefixes and suffixes, we could have simply slid the pattern two characters, which would have put us in the right place to start step 4.

This observation leads to a pattern matcher known as **Knuth-Morris-Pratt** (or **KMP**), named for the computer scientists who first presented it. The idea is to build a graph representation that will provide information as to the amount of "slide" that will be necessary when a mismatch occurs. The **KMP graph** will again consist of states and transitions (vertices and edges). However, unlike the DFA graph from the previous section, there will be only two transitions leaving each state.

Figure 7.43 shows the complete KMP graph for the example pattern. First, there are two special states. The initial state, marked "get," is responsible for reading the next character from the input text. The subsequent transition, marked with an asterisk, is always taken. Note that the start transition enters this initial state, which means that we initially get the first character from the text and transition immediately to the next state (state 1). The final state (state 6), this time labeled with an "F," again means success and represents a termination point for the graph.

Each remaining vertex is responsible for checking a particular character of the pattern against the current text character. For example, the vertex labeled "C?" asks whether the current text character is C. If so, then the edge labeled "Y" is used. This means "yes," there was a match. In addition, the

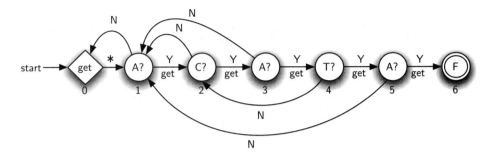

Figure 7.43: An Example KMP Graph

next character is read. In general, whenever a state is successful in matching the character it is responsible for, the next character is read from the text.

The remaining transitions, those labeled "N," denote that a mismatch occurred. In this case, as was explained above, we need to know how many positions to slide the pattern. In essence, we want to keep the current text character and simply move back to a previous point in the pattern. To compute this, we use a simple algorithm (see Listing 7.32) that basically checks the pattern against itself, looking for overlap between a prefix and a suffix. If such an overlap is found, its length tells us how far back to place the mismatch link in the KMP graph. It is important to note that new text characters are not processed when a mismatch link is used.

Here is the example pattern as it is being processed by the `mismatchLinks` method.

```
>>> mismatchLinks("ACATA")
{1: 0, 2: 1, 3: 1, 4: 2, 5: 1}
>>>
```

The value returned by the method is a dictionary containing key-value pairs where the key is the current vertex (state) and the value is its destination vertex for the mismatch link. It can be seen that each state, from 1 to 5, corresponding to each character in the pattern, has a transition back to a previous state in the KMP graph.

As we noted earlier, the mismatch links can be computed by sliding the pattern past itself looking for the longest matching prefix and suffix. The method begins by augmenting the pattern so that the indices on the characters match the vertex labels in the KMP graph. Since the initial state is state 0, we have used the "0" symbol as a placeholder. Now the characters

```
1  def mismatchLinks(pattern):
2      augPattern = "0"+pattern
3      links = {}
4      links[1] = 0
5      for k in range(2,len(augPattern)):
6          s = links[k-1]
7          stop = False
8          while s>=1 and not stop:
9              if augPattern[s] == augPattern[k-1]:
10                 stop = True
11             else:
12                 s = links[s]
13         links[k] = s+1
14     return links
```

Listing 7.32: A Simple Pattern Matcher

1 to m in the augmented pattern correspond directly with the states 1 to m in the graph.

Line 5 creates the first dictionary entry, which is always a transition from vertex 1 back to the initial state where a new character is automatically read from the text string. The iteration that follows simply checks larger and larger pieces of the pattern, looking for prefix and suffix overlap. If such an overlap occurs, the length of the overlap can be used to set the next link.

Figure 7.44 shows the KMP graph as it is being used to locate the example pattern in the text string ACGACACATA. Again, notice that the current character changes only when a match link has been used. In the case of a mismatch, as in steps 4 and 5, the current character remains the same. It is not until step 6, when we have transitioned all the way back to state 0, that we get the next character and return to state 1.

Steps 10 and 11 show the importance of the proper mismatch link. In step 10 the current character, C, does not match the symbol that state 4 needs to match. The result is a mismatch link. However, since we have seen a partial match at that point, the mismatch link reverts back to state 2 where there is a correct match. This eventually leads to a successful pattern match.

As with the DFA graph from the previous section, KMP pattern-matching is $O(n)$ since we process each character of the text string. However, the KMP graph is much easier to construct and requires much less storage as there are only two transitions from every vertex.

Step	Current State	Current Text Symbol	Next State	
1	0	A	1	automatic transition
2	1	A	2	state 1 match, get next
3	2	C	3	state 2 match, get next
4	3	G	1	mismatch
5	1	G	0	mismatch
6	0	A	1	automatic transition
7	1	A	2	
8	2	C	3	
9	3	A	4	
10	4	C	2	mismatch
11	2	C	3	state 2 match
12	3	A	4	
13	4	T	5	
14	5	A	F	success

Figure 7.44: A Trace of the KMP Pattern-Matcher

7.7   Summary

- Lists are collections of items where each item holds a relative position.

- A linked list implementation maintains logical order without requiring physical storage requirements.

- Modification to the head of the linked list is a special case.

- Maps (dictionaries) are associative memory organization structures.

- Skip lists are linked lists that provide expected $O(\log(n))$ searches.

- An OctTree provides an efficient way to reduce the number of colors used to represent an image.

- Text-based pattern-matching is a very common problem in many application areas.

- Simple pattern-matching is inefficient.

- DFA graphs are easy to use but complex to build.

- KMP graphs are easy to use and easy to build.

7.8   Key Terms

Data field	Deterministic finite automaton (DFA)
DFA graph	Dictionary
Dithering	DNA String
Dynamic Programming	Greedy Method
Head	KMP graph
Knuth-Morris-Pratt (KMP)	Level
Linked list	Linked list travesal
List	Map
Node	OctTree
Pixel	Quantization
Skip list	Substring
Tower	

7.9   Discussion Questions

1. What is the result of carrying out both steps of the linked list **add** method in reverse order? What kind of reference results? What types of problems may result?

2. Explain how the linked list **remove** method works when the item to be removed is in the last node.

3. Explain how the **remove** method works when the item is in the *only* node in the linked list.

4. Compare the search algorithm for linked lists with the sequential search algorithm from Chapter 4. What are the similarities?

5. Where do skip lists get their name?

6. Compare the notion of a perfectly balanced binary search tree and a skip list. Can you draw pictures to describe these notions?

7. What would it mean if all towers in a skip list were one level high?

8. Given a set of 20 keys, is it possible that one of the towers could have a height of 20?

9. Run the `OctTree` quantization program on an image of your choice. Try some different settings for the maximum depth of the tree as well as the final number of colors.

10. Explain why the indices for an `OctTree` node are calculated starting with the most significant bit and going to the least significant bit.

11. Draw the nodes in an `OctTree`, down to level 5, after inserting the following two colors: (174, 145, 229) and (92,145,85).

12. Draw a DFA graph for the pattern ATC.

13. Compute the mismatch links for the pattern ATC.

14. Create a KMP graph for the pattern ATCCAT.

15. Using the dynamic programming algorithm for making change, find the smallest number of coins that you can use to make 33 cents in change. In addition to the usual coins assume that you have an 8 cent coin.

7.10 Programming Exercises

1. To implement the `length` method, we counted the number of nodes in the list. An alternative strategy would be to store the number of nodes in the list as an additional piece of data in the head of the list. Modify the `UnorderedList` class to include this information and rewrite the `length` method.

2. Implement the `remove` method so that it works correctly in the case where the item is not in the list.

3. Implement the `length` method recursively.

4. Modify the list classes to allow duplicates. Which methods will be impacted by this change?

5. Implement the `__repr__` method in the UnorderedList class. What would be a good string representation for a list?

6. Implement the `__repr__` method so that lists are displayed the Python way (with square brackets).

7. Implement a stack using linked lists.

8. Implement a queue using linked lists.

9. Implement a deque using linked lists.

10. Implement the `delete` method for a skip list. You can assume that the key is present.

11. Implement methods for skip list that will allow the map to perform the following operations:

    - `hasKey()` will return a boolean result as to whether a key is present in the map

    - `keys()` will return a list of keys in the map

    - `values()` will return a list of values in the map

12. Implement the `__getItem__` and `__setItem__` methods for skip lists.

13. Modify the `OctTree` class to improve the performance of the `reduce` method by using a more efficient data structure for keeping track of the leaf nodes.

14. Add two methods to the `OctTree` class, one to write a quantized image to a disk file and one to read a file of the same format you wrote.

15. Some versions of `OctTree` quantization look at the total count for all the children of a node and use that information to decide which nodes to reduce. Modify the `OctTree` implementation to use this method of node selection for reducing the tree.

16. Implement a version of the simple pattern-matcher that will locate *all* occurrences of the pattern in the text.

17. Modify the graph implementation from Chapter 6 so that it can be used to represent KMP graphs. Using the `mismatchLinks` method, write a method that will take a pattern and create the complete KMP graph. With the graph complete, write a program that will run an arbitrary text against the KMP graph and return whether a match exists.

Bibliography

(1998). The sierpinski gasket and the towers of hanoi, http://www.cut-the-knot.org/triangle/hanoi.shtml.

Adleman, L., Rivest, R. L., and Shamir, A. (1978). A method for obtaining digital signature and public-key cryptosystems. *Communications of the ACM*.

Bellman, R. (1952). On the theory of dynamic programming. *Proceedings of the National Academy of Science*, 38(8):716–719.

Breinholt, G. and Schierz, C. (1998). Algorithm 781: generating hilbert's space-filling curve by recursion. *ACM Trans. Math. Softw.*, 24(2):184–189.

Cormen, Leiserson, Rivest, and Rol (1992). *Algorithms*. McGraw Hill Book Company.

Dale, N. B. and Lilly, S. C. (1995). *Pascal Plus Data Structures, Algorithms and Advanced Programming*. Houghton Mifflin Co., Boston, MA, USA.

Dijkstra, E. (1959). A note on two problems in connection with graphs. *Numerische Math*, 1:269–271.

Gordon, V. S. and Slocum, T. J. (2004). The knight's tour-evolutionary vs. depth-first search. In *Congress on Evolutionary Computation*.

Horowitz, E. and Sahni, S. (1990). *Fundamentals of Data Structures in Pascal*. W. H. Freeman & Co., New York, NY, USA.

Hu, T. C. and Shing, M. T. (1981). Computation of matrix chain products: Part i, part ii. Technical report, Stanford University, Stanford, CA, USA.

Jackson, C. L. and Tanimoto, S. L. (1980). Octtrees and their use in representing three-dimansional objects. *Computer Graphics and Image Processing*, 14(3):249–270.

Jones, N. and Pevzner, P. (2004). *An Introduction to Bioinformatics Algorithms*. MIT Press, Cambridge, MA, USA.

Knuth, D. E. (1998). *The art of computer programming, volume 3: (2nd ed.) sorting and searching*. Addison Wesley Longman Publishing Co., Inc., Redwood City, CA, USA.

Linz, P. (2001). *An Introduction to Formal Languages and Automata*. Jones and Bartlett Publishers, Inc., USA.

Lutz, M. and Ascher, D. (2004). *Learning Python*. O'Reilly, 2 edition.

Masek, W. J. and Paterson, M. (1980). A Faster Algorithm Computing String Edit Distances. *J. Comput. Syst. Sci.*, 20(1):18–31.

Meagher, D. (1982). Geometric modelling using octtree encoding. *Computer Graphics and Image Processing*, 19(2):129–147.

Pugh, W. (1990). Skip lists: a probabilistic alternative to balanced trees. *Commun. ACM*, 33(6):668–676.

Weiss, M. A. (2001). *Data Structures and Problem Solving Using Java*. Addison-Wesley Longman Publishing Co., Inc., Boston, MA, USA.

Yedidyah Langsam, M. A. and Tenenbaum, A. (2003). *Data Structures Using Java*. Pearson Prentice Hall, Upper Saddle River, NJ, USA.

Zelle, J. (2004). *Python Programming: An Introduction to Computer Science*. Franklin Beedle and Associates.

Appendix A Graphics Packages for Python

There are several great graphics packages that are either included, in the box with Python or are freely available for download. Here a some you may want to check out.

VPython Visual python is an easy to use 3D python extension, widely used by Physics teachers and others.

graphics.py Provided with John Zelle's *Python Programming: An Introduction to Computer Science.*

tkinter The Tk toolkit is one of the most widely used graphical widget sets around. With tkinter you can build user interfaces with nice buttons and other widgets.

turtle graphics There are several freely available turtle graphics packages available on the Internet. These packages are especially fun to use for some recursive graphics.

wxPython The wxWindows package is another cross-platform windowing environment. Graphics programs written in wxPython will run on any machine that has this package installed.

PyOpenGL If you are familiar with OpenGL this package gives you the full power.

Index

Operations

351

E

edge, 187, 238
encapsulation, 5
equality
    deep equality, 33
    shallow equality, 33
Euclid's Algorithm, 31
Euclid's algorithm, 118
exchange, 160
exponential, 135

F

FIFO, 75
final state, 337
first-in first-out, 75
flooding, 274
folding, 150
for statement, 21
fraction, 26
front, 75
fully parenthesized, 65
fully parenthesized expression, 100
function, 25, 100

G

gap, 167
graphs, 237
greatest common divisor, 31
greedy method, 298

H

HAS-A, 42
hash function, 148, 149
hash table, 147
hashing, 147
head, 283
heap order property, 226
height, 188

hexadecimal, 63, 103
hierarchical, 197
HTML, 185
huffman encoding, 333

I

identifier, 9
image, 318
immutable, 17
implementation-independence, 6
infix, 65
information hiding, 5, 326
inheritance, 34
inheritance hierarchy, 34
inner-class, 325
inorder, 204
insertion sort, 163
integer division, 104
interface, 3
Internet, 318
intractable, 7
IS-A, 34, 283
iteration, 19
iterative, 100
iterative sum, 100

J–K

Josephus problem, 79
key, 115, 187
KMP graph, 339
knights tour, 253
Knuth-Morris-Pratt, 339

L

leaf node, 187, 202, 325
leaf nodes, 199
left child, 190
level, 187, 309